MEZZE

Delicious Middle Eastern, Turkish & Greek Recipes

DEDICATION

To my father, for making Arabia his life; to my mother, for her enjoyment of its foods; to both, for giving me the opportunity to live in that 'fabled land'.

And in memory of Keith.

MEZZE

Delicious Middle Eastern, Turkish & Greek Recipes

ROSAMOND MAN

Garnet PUBLISHING

This edition © 1995 Garnet Publishing Ltd.
Original text © 1986 Rosamond Man
Revised text © 1995 Rosamond Man
Food photographs copyright © 1995 Terry Chambers

Revised Edition
Some of the material in this book was first published as *The Complete Meze Table*, Ebury Press, 1986.

The right of Rosamond Man to be identified as author of this work has been asserted by her in accordance with the Copyright, Designs and Patents Act, 1988.

ISBN 1 85964 049 4

British Library Cataloguing-in-Publication Data
A catalogue record for this book is available from the British Library.

Design: Mark Slader
Jacket Design: Mark Slader and David Rose
House Editor: Anna Watson
Food Stylist: Maria Kelly
Home Economist: Sue Maggs
Art Director: David Rose
Typesetting: Samantha Abley
Production: Sarah Golden
Reproduction: CCTS, London
Printed in the Lebanon

The photographs on pages 15, 16, 36, 71, 79, 97 and 100 are reproduced courtesy of the Moroccan National Tourist Office, with grateful thanks to Josiane D'Unienville.
The photograph on page 43 is reproduced courtesy of the Turkish Embassy Information Counsellor's Office, with grateful thanks to Nurcan Demirciva.
The photograph on page 68 is reproduced courtesy of the National Tourist Organisation of Greece, with grateful thanks to Karen Pierce.

Published by Garnet Publishing Ltd,
8 Southern Court, South Street,
Reading RG1 4QS, UK.

CONTENTS

ACKNOWLEDGEMENTS

To acknowledge everyone who has had a helping hand in the preparation of this book would fill many pages, but to all of them I give grateful thanks. Especially to those who suggested recipes for which there was, alas, no room on the table, with assurances that I, at least, enjoyed them. To the cooks of my childhood must go an immense appreciation for giving me such insight into the exotic world of the Arab kitchen.

To all the embassies of the different countries, many thanks for their patient answers to often seemingly trivial queries, and I am particularly indebted to Mrs Halet Coruk, Miss Renan Taşçıoğlu, and Miss Defne Akyol, erstwhile of the Turkish Embassy, for their help on many of the finer points of that country's cuisine, language and history.

To the School of Oriental and African Studies many thanks for the wealth of information from that wonderful library, and to the Islamic Culture Board, gratitude for permission to quote from Professor Arberry's incredibly informative and erudite studies: also to Penguin for permission to quote from N. J. Dawood's enchanting translation of *Tales of 1001 Nights*.

To my two original editors, Veronica Sperling and Caroline Schuck, go thanks for making the book a reality in the first place. And now, a particular thank you must be extended to Garnet Publishing for producing this expanded and revised edition, enabling me to restore much of what was lost due to space constrictions in the original.

Re-testing many of those recipes in Sri Lanka, where I now live, I was reminded once again how glorious is the Middle Eastern kitchen and also how innovative is man, for many of the ingredients we have here are the same – and yet their treatment and end result are quite different, albeit deliciously so.

I was also reminded of the first testings and tastings, the recollection of childhood memories when tracking down a particular dish, trying to recall, or place, a particular flavour. And once again, I give a very special thank you to the person who accompanied me on those, often very odd, gastronomic jaunts – my late husband, Keith. Even though he is not here to read this, his friends, many of whom shared in our Arabian feasts, will know how sorely his enthusiasm and pertinent comments were missed in this kitchen.

To anyone who wishes to delve further into the huge cuisine of the area, I can only direct them whole-heartedly to the book which first stirred me to recreate these tastes of my childhood, Claudia Roden's wonderfully extensive *Book of Middle Eastern Food*, and now her enlarged *A New Book of Middle Eastern Food*.

Kandy, Sri Lanka
1995

INTRODUCTION

When to banquet we are eager
Well the table floweth o'er,
And the ready cook doth fill it
With the choicest foods in store:
Forth it comes with goodly burden,
Garnished by his precious lore.

MAHMUD IBN AL-HUSAIN AL-KUSHAJIM[1]

The Middle Eastern kitchen has a vast range, both culinary and geographic. You may meet your first taste of it in Greece and Turkey, then continue on a huge gastronomic tour right round the Mediterranean to Morocco at the western edge of North Africa. You will be treading a historic path, for throughout time the peoples of the area have swept down one upon another, bringing with them varied cultural influences, leaving some behind on retreat, and taking others home as part of the booty of war. Nowhere is this more apparent than in the realm of food. Ingredients, their preparation and their combinations may vary to a greater or lesser degree from country to country, but nearly always there will be a feel of another nation, a whisper of an ancient civilization, testifying to this constant ebb and flow of ideas.

The ancient Persians spread their influence first, *c.* 500–400 BC, but then Alexander the Great engulfed the whole region, founding Alexandria on the way,

Previous page: Grilled Squid (p. 62).

then pushing the boundaries of his empire right across to India. Remarkable man that he was, on his death in 323 BC there lacked a strong successor and the empire fell to pieces while the boots of Rome started to march. The Hellenic civilisation, however, lingered on for centuries, its gradual retreat bringing with it much culinary thought from India, most of which seems to have been deposited in Persia, where the Indian influence is still strong in the kitchen of today.

Meanwhile, Rome captured, fought and lost the Middle East – perhaps because she took more than she ever gave – and Persia rose again in the third century AD. For the next 400 years it was the era of the brilliant Sassanid kings and they spread their tentacles through Syria and Palestine to Egypt. Then came the surge of Islam, sweeping from Damascus in a mighty curve across North Africa to Spain and Sicily. Attacking too in the opposite direction, they conquered Persia and founded Baghdad as their capital in that vanquished land (today, it is the capital of Iraq). Here grew the dazzling court – absorbing all that was great and glorious from the Persian heyday – of the Caliphs of Baghdad. For a while they reigned supreme and this was the era of *The Thousand and One Nights*, of great banquets and of court festivities which gave birth to the fabulous myths and folklore of ancient Arabia. Then the Mongols flew in (and out) and by the fifteenth century the Ottomans were on the move. Constantinople conquered, their empire flooded in all directions – up to the Balkans (where many dishes today still bear Turkish names), down to the Fertile Crescent, from whence they were only dislodged by the Arab uprising of 1916–17. They had time to weld their extravagantly luxuriant touches into the cuisine, then it just remained for the French to add a dash of sophistication, the Greeks and the Italians a cosmopolitan streak. Throughout the many tidal waves of history, the Arab identity has stayed firm, but taking from the invaders those aspects and ideas which have suited their personality – and their kitchen.

Mezze is perhaps the most famous feature of the Middle Eastern kitchen. Its name – apparently gleaned from the Genoese spice traders by their Arab contemporaries from *mezzano*, the Italian word for middle – was quickly swallowed into the many languages of the area, to re-emerge in a variety of forms. *Mezedes* or *mezethakia* in Greece, *mezeler* in Turkey (usually abbreviated to *meze*), *al mezah* or *al maza* or *mezze* in the Arabic-speaking countries.

Whatever the word, what is not in dispute is the essence of the food and its versatility. Despite its original derivation, unlike mezzanine (another derivative) the meaning has now changed and literally would be translated as 'a morsel, a titbit or mouthful'. Such delicious morsels make their appearance at every café, in every house, on many a street corner. They can be anything from a small nibble of toasted pumpkin, marrow or melon seeds to a whole array of salads, pulse dishes, eggs in a multitude of forms, dips with a myriad of spices, vegetables – stuffed and unstuffed, tiny *kebabs*, mounds of olives – minute and gleaming black or enormous and pale green, speckled with crushed coriander seeds and finely chopped garlic – a mass of colour, tastes and textures but all chosen to complement and offset each other. Even apparent main courses can be served as a *mezze* provided they are a replica in miniature. *Mezze* are eaten for breakfast, on the way to work, as a mid-

morning snack, for lunch, tea or as the *hors-d'œuvre* course to a meal. Anywhere, any time in fact.

Eating, and the sharing of food, with guests and strangers is a matter of honour – and a ritual – in the Middle East, and the *mezze* table may often provide a stranger with his first taste of this enormous cuisine. For even a simple drink of iced water (simple to us, very precious to the Arab) or a cup of coffee, small and dark, will never be offered without an accompanying titbit of some sort, while many a formal dinner may well begin with a crowded *mezze* table – from the simplicity of fine matchstick strips of cucumber luxuriantly floating in iced water to enormous stuffed aubergines, gleaming in olive oil. Not a few innocent travellers have been caught unawares, when, deliciously replete on a multitude of *mezze*, they are graciously moved to another room for the dinner 'proper' to begin.

Even in the East however, *mezze* are often served as buffet party food and for this they are ideal. Since invited guests may often bring another (uninvited) guest with them – indeed in Iraq it is almost assumed this will be so, such a guest affectionately called your 'slipper' (*qabqah*) and receiving no less warm a welcome than you – the *mezze* table is a sensible way of coping with what could otherwise be a hostess's nightmare. The variety of dishes at such a feast will always be enormous, their ingredients and spicings differing slightly from country to country and family to family, but few of these spices are unknown to us in the West. It is their usage, rather than their existence, that gives this gorgeous food its particularly Middle Eastern flavour.

And it is this food that I remember so vividly from my childhood, wonderful breakfasts of newly baked pittas stuffed with tiny black olives, misshapen tomatoes, sweet onions and heavy green olive oil. Lunches of long, thin *kibbeh* – minced lamb pounded and seasoned with pungent spices; mounds of fresh herbs mixed into chilled yogurt (hardly ever eaten for breakfast in the Middle East, although its cheeses are). Exciting excursions into the mysterious *attarine* (spice street) of the *souk* (market) with, perhaps, the thrill of being allowed to buy a little twist of *dukkah* (mixed spices) to nibble on the way home. I spent much time in the kitchens of our homes in various countries and, watching the cooks lavish such attention and care on their food, one could not help but be imbued with a feeling of a very ancient, and much treasured, tradition.

Combined with the open and almost overwhelmingly generous hospitality that is so much a part of the Middle East, I can think of no more perfect introduction to that exotic, now sadly troubled, but extraordinarily magical part of the world, than al-Kushajim's poem.

1. Tenth-century poet, astrologer and advisor on food at the Court of Saif al-Daula. Authored an extraordinary thesis on the etiquette of the table, Adab al-nadim, *lived AD 915–967/ 303–356 Islamic calendar.*

NAMES

I have given as close as possible phonetic translations for all the dishes. But, as Lawrence of Arabia wrote to his editor on *The Seven Pillars of Wisdom*, 'Arabic names won't go into English, exactly, for their consonants are not the same as ours, and their vowels, like ours, vary from district to district. There are some 'scientific systems' of transliteration, helpful to people who know enough Arabic not to need helping, but a washout for the world.' Later, on the inconsistency of the spelling of Arabic names, one name having been spelt in six different ways, 'Good egg. I call this really ingenious.' I have tried, with the help of my late father, a classical Arabic scholar with, too, a phenomenal knowledge of many dialects, not to be so ingenious. Rather, hopefully, to help those who may be trying to eat in the area to perhaps ask for, or recognise, some of the delicious food they may be offered.

QUANTITIES AND COOKING TIMES

The one aspect common to all Middle Eastern recipes is their vagueness. It is over this that I have spent more hours and careful calculations, to try and arrive at a reasonable Western equivalent, than anything else. '2 round cigarette tins, 4 hazelnut knobs, a handful (small), and 1–2 pinches, mixed with . . . the size of a hen egg, cooked on a good fire while rolling the pastry, and it will be ready. Will feed a family.' And yet, it is not so very illogical. The round cigarette tins in question held 50 cigarettes (the flat ones, 25) and after much juggling with cigarettes and containers I finally discovered it to be roughly 225 ml (17 tbsp): much easier to use the tin, especially when they were always available. As a child I was often asked to lend my hand and pick up as much as I could of the parsley or coriander, so that wasn't too difficult. In England my neighbour's daughter had little hands, and they were willing – equal to 60–75 ml (4–5 tbsp). The rest was subject to much experimentation. The average Arab family not only included several children, but aunts, uncles, mothers and sisters-in-law, cousins, distant visiting relatives and also untold friends who might have been invited by any of the family, but who also might just turn up. The door is never closed. And an Arab would never dream of greeting an unheralded visitor with the words 'we were just sitting down to dinner' without an invitation to join them. So quantities are loose and infinitely expandable, and, so too, the cooking time. If the pot has to stay on the stove for five more minutes, because the conversation is animated, so be it. Apart from the little fried pastries, which must not overdo, most dishes will happily simmer for a moment or two longer, and if something must come off the stove this instant, it can be piled on its serving dish and put on the table. Very rarely is food served boiling hot, and often the flavours are enhanced by a slight cooling. So, the Middle Eastern kitchen is very relaxed: if you haven't a particular ingredient, another can usually be substituted. A dish can often be gently poached on top of the cooker as easily as in the oven, or vice versa. And if you think a little more food is needed, there are always olives, pickles, cheeses waiting in their olive oil, extra pittas, another salad quickly made – a veritable storecupboard of standbys. It is a welcoming and hospitable kitchen and the *mezze* table, in particular, is ever-flexible. The quantities I have given are for serving one *mezze* as a starter, so a number may be expanded proportionately. Although I warn you when a particular taste is found that suits one person's buds, even these quantities may be unreliable. I entertained a three-year-old recently who declared himself very content with the bowl of pumpkin seeds. It was meant for six.

NIBBLES

Dukkah

Thereon impose a regimented line
Of almonds and of walnuts, flavoured fine;
With cheese and olives prick the points thereon,
And add the vowels of mint and tarragon.[1]

IBN AL-RUMI[2]

Everywhere you go in the Middle East, be it the bustling streets of Cairo or Istanbul, the old *souks* (markets) of Baghdad or Damascus, or for a leisurely stroll along the seafront in Alexandria, there will be scores of street vendors tempting you with a myriad tastes and smells. Among the most popular will be those stalls selling ready-to-eat snacks and nibbles – for the people of the Middle East have no inhibitions about munching on 'a little something' between meals. And when you see what is on offer, the temptations are irresistible.

Pyramids of olives, all shapes and sizes, in a rainbow of muted colours from palest green to shining violet and the blackest of blacks. Trays of seeds – from pumpkins, sunflowers and melons – dried in the sun, then roasted and spiced with garlic and salt. Mounds of gleaming golden beans – dried then fried – and salted chick peas. Small rounds of creamy yogurt cheese, floating in huge bowls of heavy green olive oil, waiting to be scooped out, drained and rolled in fresh herbs and spices.

Favourite of all, for me at any rate, were the little twisted paper cones filled with *dukkah* or *do'a* (the

Previous page (l–r): Yogurt Cheese in Oil (p. 22), Sesame and Coriander Mix (p. 17), Hazelnut, Mint and Coriander Mix (p. 17), Salted Chick Peas (p. 16) and Grilled Feta (p. 22).

Egyptian name – where I first met them; *za'atar* elsewhere), wonderful mixtures of crushed roasted seeds, nuts and herbs. The aroma of garlic, coriander, sesame seed, fresh thyme, mint, wild marjoram and sweet cinnamon filled the air and I used to take huge deep breaths, turning from one vendor to another until I felt quite dizzy, pleading that I would only feel better if I could have something to eat! There would follow a blissful 10 minutes of happy juggling with two or three tiny packets, firmly clutched in one hand, while the other held a still hot, newly baked pitta – to be dipped into the bowl of olive oil high up on the vendor's stand, and then into that little twist of paper, savouring each mix one by one, always leaving a morsel of my favourite (which daily changed) until the last mouthful.

Nostalgia plays a great part in one's love of certain foods and almost more than anything else, these mixes take me back to my childhood days. I make them often and also serve them as a starter to a meal. Unusual and simple to prepare, they are a great inducer of conviviality as people try them, quickly finding the blends they like the best. They taste just as good eaten under the shade of the damson tree in an English country garden as they ever did in those hot Cairo streets. And most of the herbs needed can easily be grown in the garden, though many, surprisingly are easier in

Europe than in the tropical climes I am faced with. I struggle with thyme and marjoram – treasuring the puny results while dill (weed and seed) I gratefully receive as gifts from England. There, of course, I couldn't pluck my own cinnamon, cardamom or cumin. Nor chillies. But most of the others flourished happily enough, a few hibernating in the winter. So plant your herbs nearby, crush a few leaves while you nibble and let the heady scents take you East.

1. A reference to Arabic calligraphy, the points being the distinguishing signs for various letters of the alphabet which would otherwise appear the same; the vowels in Arabic script being represented by small lines and dots, added after the main line of script has been written.
2. Famous Arab poet, murdered approximately AD 896/283 Islamic calendar.

© Philippe Ploquin

Cinnamon and pot-pourri on sale at a Moroccan spice market.

SALTED CHICK PEAS

Humus bil Milh

There always seemed to be a huge pot of gently simmering chick peas on the stove in our Baghdad kitchen. Once cooked, they would be spread out on metal trays – burning hot from standing in the sun – and sprinkled with salt. By next day they had shrunk considerably and were gloriously crunchy. A similar effect can be achieved in cooler climes by lightly frying the chick peas, then drying them out in a very low oven. For garlic lovers, I also scatter over a finely chopped garlic clove with the salt before putting the peas in the oven.

Serves 6–8
225 g (8 oz) chick peas, soaked overnight or
    2 x 400 g (14 oz) cans chick peas, drained
60–75 ml (4–5 tbsp) olive oil
Maldon or coarse sea salt
1–2 garlic cloves, finely chopped (optional)

If using dried chick peas, first skim off any skins which have floated to the top of the bowl, then drain the peas and rinse in fresh cold water. Bring them to the boil in a large saucepan, well covered with water, and then simmer gently for about 1 hour until they are cooked. They may need a bit longer depending on age but you can easily tell when they are done as they will be soft to the bite. It's virtually impossible to over-cook these peas in any case.

Drain thoroughly and pat lightly dry. If using canned peas, rinse in cold water, then dry. Heat 60 ml (4 tbsp) of the oil in a large frying pan, then add enough chick peas to completely cover the base of the pan and fry for 4–5 minutes, turning the peas around to brown all over – chopsticks are the ideal tool for this.

Cook the remaining chick peas the same way, adding the extra oil if you need it, then spread them out on a baking tray and sprinkle generously with salt, and the garlic, if using. Dry in the oven at 140°C–150°C (275°F–300°F), mark 1–2, for 15–20 minutes, until browned and slightly shrunken.

Good warm or cold – they get nuttier on cooling. Will keep for a couple of days in an airtight tin.

ROASTED PUMPKIN SEEDS

Buzur Qara Mishwi

Very popular in Lebanon, this can also be made using sunflower or melon seeds. If taking the seeds from home grown produce, wash them well and scrape off all the fibres, then dry thoroughly before cooking. In England, I used to put them in the airing cupboard for 2–3 days but you could put them in the oven, at

Fresh dates being brought to market.

© Philippe Ploquin

the lowest possible setting, overnight. In hotter climates, the seeds are usually sun-dried, although in tropical monsoons oven-drying is the only way. Even then, they should be eaten within 24 hours: the intense humidity is all too conducive to mould.

Serves 6

225 g (8 oz) pumpkin, sunflower or melon seeds, skinned
2 large garlic cloves, skinned and finely chopped
Maldon or coarse sea salt

Heat the oven to 200°C (400°F), mark 6. Spread the seeds out on a baking tray, then dry roast them for 12–15 minutes until darker in colour but not too browned. Pour into a bowl, scatter over the garlic and a generous pinch of salt, mixing everything thoroughly. Cover and leave to cool – the longer the better, as this allows the garlic to permeate the seeds. Overnight is ideal, but they can be eaten almost immediately if you wish.

SPICE MIXTURES

Dukkah/Do'a/Za'atar

The general name for the mixtures – endless in variety – of nuts, seeds, herbs and spices, sold in little paper twists, to be nibbled at or eaten with pitta or sesame bread rings dipped into olive oil. The mixture is always a dry one with the nuts lightly crushed or very finely chopped rather than completely pulverised, so if using a blender or spice grinder just whizz it very briefly. The secret is to release the flavour but not the oils, or the mix turns into a paste and will then go rancid if not eaten immediately.

Each family has their own recipe and favoured combinations, so experiment until you find the ones you like the best. Here are a few of my favourites.

SESAME AND CORIANDER MIX

Simsim wa Kuzbari

Serves 6–8

175 g (6 oz) sesame seeds
50 g (2 oz) coriander seeds
50 g (2 oz) hazelnuts
Maldon or coarse sea salt
coarsely ground black pepper

Grill the sesame seeds under a medium heat for a minute or two, turning constantly and watching they don't burn. Put aside, then grill the coriander seeds and hazelnuts, separately, again constantly turning them. Crush the coriander seeds first, either in a blender or spice grinder, then tip into a bowl. Briefly grind the hazelnuts, just to coarsely break up, then add to the coriander. Lastly grind the sesame seeds; a few seconds is usually adequate or the oils will start to run. Mix everything together, and sprinkle generously with salt and freshly ground black pepper. You can make this in much larger quantities if you like, as it keeps excellently in screw-topped jars – provided, of course, the nuts, particularly the sesame, have not been over-ground.

HAZELNUT, MINT AND CORIANDER MIX

Lauz, Na'na wa Kuzbari

I sometimes use fresh mint instead of the dried – double the quantities – to give a sweeter more herby flavour. Eau-de-Cologne mint is particularly good.

Serves 6–8

225 g (8 oz) hazelnuts
50 g (2 oz) coriander seeds
45 ml (3 tbsp) dried or 90 ml (6 tbsp) very finely chopped fresh mint
Maldon or sea salt

Grill the hazelnuts and coriander seeds separately, until browned but not burnt, then grind briefly. Mix with the mint and a good pinch of salt.

CUMIN, CINNAMON AND CHICK PEA MIX

Kamun, Qirfa wa Humus

Either use home-salted chick peas (page 16) – in which case leave them, covered with a cloth, for a few hours after drying out in the oven. Or you can buy precooked, salted and dried chick peas from many Greek or Cypriot delicatessens. These are much tinier than the home-made version, round, and white in colour.

Serves 4–6

60 ml (4 tbsp) cumin seeds
5 cm (2 inch) cinnamon stick
275 g (10 oz) Salted Chick Peas (page 16)

Dry fry the cumin seeds, stirring constantly until aromatic, then transfer to the spice grinder. Grill the cinnamon stick for a few minutes until lightly bronzed, then break into three or four pieces. Grind the cumin first, pour into a bowl, then grind the cinnamon until very finely broken up and add to the cumin. Lastly grind the chick peas and mix well in.

CUMIN, MINT AND SALT MIX

Kamun, Na'na Wa Milh

Sometimes the very poor could not even afford the nut *dukkahs* and would make do with very simple herb mixtures. This, though humble in content, is sophisticated in flavour.

Serves 4

25 g (1 oz) cumin seeds
15 g (½ oz) dried mint
Maldon or coarse sea salt

Dry fry the cumin seeds for a few minutes, until the aroma comes out, then grind briefly. Mix with the mint and season generously with salt. A classic accompaniment to hard-boiled eggs and delicious, too, sprinkled on cottage or cream cheese.

THYME AND PEPPER MIX

Mannaeish Za'atar

A combination much favoured in the Lebanon where wild thyme bushes cover the hillsides. I like to make this, and the following recipes, in small quantities so the full impact of the fresh herbs can be appreciated. Any leftover I pop into a jar and use for spicing other dishes.

Serves 4–6

good handful of fresh thyme sprigs
2½–5 ml (½–1 tsp) coarsely ground black pepper

Chop the thyme sprigs into two or three pieces, discarding any thick woody bits of stem, then grind briefly. Mix with the pepper – start with a little at a time to see how much you like. I like lots. Excellent with newly baked wholemeal bread and olive oil.

SESAME AND THYME MIX

Simsim wa Za'atar

A favourite breakfast, made by my young nanny, born and bred in Palestine. She said it was 'more ancient than possible' (we communicated in a highly personal mix of English, French and kitchen Arabic) and she called it Hyssop and Sesame. What she in fact picked was wild thyme – according to her, not quite what they had had when she was a child but the nearest in flavour. Years later I discovered that the hyssop so favoured in ancient Palestine and the Bible was not the plant we know in Europe today. What the Biblical hyssop was, no one knows for sure: perhaps savory, which certainly grows abundantly in Syria and what was the former Palestine. That plant's flavour, however, is more pungent and lacking the sweetness that I remember of this mix. Strangely, when I made it first in England, I used hyssop (*Hyssopus officinalis*) – absent-mindedly thinking of the name she gave it – and the taste of those roof-top breakfasts was instantly, and vividly, recalled. Hyssop is, of course, a member of the thyme family – but with a hint of mint, though I can't remember mint being added. No matter, whichever you use, an excellent mix. Particularly for livening up winter salads when fresh herbs may be rather thin on the ground. If you want to grow hyssop – and it's very easy (and almost impossible to buy), give it good drainage and a sunny position. But don't let it be too generous with its flowers else it will seed itself to death.

Serves 4–6
100 g (4 oz) sesame seeds
60 ml (4 tbsp) thyme or hyssop leaves, stripped
    from the stalks
Maldon or coarse sea salt
freshly ground black pepper

Grill the sesame seeds, watching they don't burn, then lightly crush or very briefly whizz in a grinder. Tip into a bowl, then quickly grind the leaves. Mix together with salt and lots of black pepper.

PERSIAN FRESH HERB MIX

Ushb Taza

In Persia, fresh herbs are an essential component of almost every meal and large bowls of assorted herbs nearly always form part of the *mezze* table. Many are endowed with magical qualities – particularly if women eat them with cheese and bread. This is believed to help keep their husband's affections and deter him from looking for a new – and younger – wife.

Serves 4–6
1 handful each of all, or at least three, of the
    following:
fresh basil
fresh coriander leaves
fresh parsley
fresh mint
fresh dillweed
fresh tarragon
spring onions
fresh chives

Wash and shake dry the herbs, trimming the roots of the spring onions and cutting off all but 5–7½ cm (2–3 inches) of the green tops (keep these for another dish or for flavouring soups and stocks). Chop the herbs, not too finely, and arrange in a large shallow bowl, keeping the piles separate. Though not strictly traditional, I like to sprinkle lightly with salt and freshly ground black pepper and have a pile of walnuts and sultanas in the middle. A lovely post-Christmas treat, and a good use for any leftover nuts and dried fruit. The fresh herbs – at that time of year – are the treat.

CORIANDER AND GARLIC MIX

Ta'klia

Strictly speaking, this is a spicing combination, much loved all over the Middle East but particularly in Egypt where it is an essential 'finish' to many of the dishes. The two ingredients are fried in a little oil just before the meat, chick peas or vegetables are ready to be served, then strewn on top. Interestingly, 'tempering' is a common process also in Sri Lanka – though usually it is onion, garlic and mustard seed that is used. Introduced by the Portuguese – who undoubtedly learnt it from the Moors. For me, *ta'klia* also makes a good *dukkah* – especially with some chopped fresh herbs added. Marjoram seems to have a particular affinity.

Serves 4
50 g (2 oz) coriander seeds
3–4 large garlic cloves, skinned and finely
  chopped
Maldon or sea salt (optional)

Dry fry the coriander seeds for 4–5 minutes, turning frequently. Then add the garlic and fry for another minute or so – watch it doesn't burn, you just want to bring out its flavour and lightly dry it. Blend the two together in a spice grinder, then season with a little salt, unless using as a spicing mix. If you want to add fresh herbs, chop them very finely, then mix at the last minute into the coriander.

CORIANDER AND CHILLI MIX

T'atbil

Another spicing mixture, this time from Tunisia where chilli is a favoured addition to many dishes.

Serves 3–4
50 g (2 oz) coriander seeds
6 garlic cloves, skinned and finely chopped
25 g (1 oz) caraway seeds
1–2 dried red chillies, seeded and coarsely
  chopped
Maldon or sea salt (optional)

Dry fry the coriander seeds until the aroma develops, add the garlic and fry for another minute, constantly stirring so it doesn't burn. Tip into the spice grinder and blend briefly. Fry the caraway seeds and red chilli (use two, if you like things hot) then grind briefly. Mix everything together and season lightly with salt, unless you are using the mix for spicing.

CORIANDER SPICED CRACKED OLIVES

Coriander'li Zeytin

Huge pale green olives are marinated in oil with coriander, garlic and rigani to make this Cypriot favourite.

Makes 2 × 450 g (1 lb) jars
450 g (1 lb) large green olives
45 ml (3 tbsp) coriander seeds
2–3 garlic cloves, skinned and finely chopped
30 ml (2 tbsp) rigani or dried oregano
about 300 ml (½ pint) olive oil

Cut a cross at the top and bottom of each olive, cutting right through to the stone. Grind the coriander seeds in a spice grinder, then pack the olives into jars, sprinkling a little coriander seed, some garlic and rigani over each layer. Leave a good 2½ cm (1 inch) at the top of the jar and then fill with olive oil. Cover tightly and leave to marinate for at least 2–3 weeks to let the flavours permeate. I was sometimes the lucky recipient of huge 5 kg (11 lb) jars of olives from generous Turkish friends and then made this in vast quantity. Still delicious (though wrinkled) a year later – and the oil heavenly for cooking. A dimly recalled dream now – we have coriander aplenty in Sri Lanka but lack the cool to ripen our local olives.

FRIED DRIED BEANS

Ful Jaf Muhammar

Traditionally, these are deep fried after the soaking stage but unless you can be absolutely sure of the freshness of the beans, I find it more satisfactory to part cook them first. Then they're nicely crunchy rather than bullet-like!

Serves 6–8
225 g (8 oz) dried broad beans, soaked overnight
Maldon or coarse sea salt
corn oil, for frying
15 ml (1 tbsp) cumin seeds

Remove any floating skins from the top of the bowl, rinse the beans in fresh cold water, then bring to the boil in a large pan, covering the beans well with water. Simmer for about 25–40 minutes until the beans are soft but still with a definite bite. Drain and pat dry as much as possible with kitchen paper, then sprinkle fairly generously with salt.

Heat the oil in a large pan (about one-third full) with a frying basket if you have one, until the oil is at 180°C, 350°F – a cube of stale bread will brown in one minute. Lift out the basket, scatter a layer of beans on the bottom and gently lower into the oil. Wear a kitchen glove or wrap a towel round your hand and stand well back while doing this – just in case the fat spatters. Cook for 4–5 minutes until the beans are quite a deep gold. Drain and cook the rest the same way. Pile into a large bowl and sprinkle with the cumin seed and more salt if you wish.

BROAD BEAN PATTIES

Falafel or Ta'amia

Almost the national dish of Egypt, where they are eaten for breakfast, lunch, supper – and at any time of the day. The Christian Copts claim the dish originated with them and during Lent, which they strictly observe, enormous quantities are cooked every day – not just for themselves but to be given to friends too. An ideal candidate for the freezer – cook from frozen giving 3–4 minutes longer.

Makes 40–48 patties
450g (1 lb) dried broad beans, soaked overnight
2 medium onions, skinned and finely chopped
3–4 large garlic cloves, skinned and crushed
small bunch of parsley, finely chopped
small handful of fresh dillweed, very finely
   chopped
Maldon or sea salt
15 ml (1 tbsp) coriander seeds, lightly crushed
cayenne pepper
cumin seeds
corn oil, for frying
To serve lemon wedges

Drain and rinse the beans, skinning them if very large. Either put them and the onions through a mincer – the fine blade, twice – or, much easier, put everything except the cumin seeds into a food processor and whizz until pounded to a thick pasty consistency. Form into small balls about the size of a walnut, flatten slightly, then dip each side into the cumin seeds, pressing the patties in between the palms of your hands to make sure the seeds stick. Leave, covered, for 30 minutes.

Heat the oil in a large pan until it's almost smoking, then lower in a few *falafel* at a time and cook for about 6–7 minutes until deeply golden. Drain well and serve with *Salata Tahina* (page 26), *Pitta* (page 146) and lemon wedges.

YOGURT CHEESE IN OIL

Labneh

Huge jars of small round cheeses, gleaming in olive oil and magnified through the glass of the jar, sit on every café counter and line the shelves in shop windows. Rolled in fresh herbs or paprika, they make a favourite Arab breakfast.

Makes about 16–20 small cheeses
10 ml (2 tsp) salt
2.3 litres (4 pints) natural yogurt
fresh mint, finely chopped
fresh marjoram, finely chopped
fresh tarragon, finely chopped
paprika
olive oil

Line a colander or two large sieves with scalded muslin or cheese cloth and stand over a large bowl (or two bowls). Whisk the salt into the yogurt, then pour into the colander. If you have a suitably placed hook, tie the four corners of the cloth together and suspend over the colander and bowl – this is not absolutely necessary but it helps the draining process. Leave to drain overnight. By morning, you will have a soft creamy curd. Drink or discard the whey and form the curd into small rounds. Lightly wet the palms of your hands between every 2–3 balls to prevent the curd sticking. Place on a perforated dish or basket (I use small fruit baskets) and leave in the refrigerator for at least a day. After 24 hours, you will have a soft mild cheese, ready for immediate eating. Taste for salt, add if needed, then roll in the herbs or paprika. If you want to keep them, leave to dry out in the refrigerator for another 2–4 days, depending on how creamy you want the end result. Then pack into a kilner jar, cover with oil and store in the larder. When you want them, simply lift out of the oil and sprinkle with the desired herbs. They keep for months – gaining pungency with age. Lovely presents.

GRILLED FETA

Izgara Beyaz Peynir

A particularly delicious *mezze* and much loved in Turkey where it used to be served in small squares of very thinly battened silver. You can also wrap the cubes of cheese in tiny fresh vine leaves – fiddly, but worth the effort as the flavour is gorgeous. This is the (ancient) Middle Eastern equivalent of that darling of 'nouvelle cuisine' – grilled goat's cheeses. Feta, of course, is also a goat's cheese . . .

In Egypt and Iraq, the cheese was quickly fried in a little very hot oil, and in Baghdad sprinkled with lime juice. Matured Cheddar makes an excellent substitute though the flavour will not be so pungent. Feta, Hallumi or Kasseri are all naturally more salt.

Makes about 16–20 cubes
450 g (1 lb) Feta cheese, Cypriot Hallumi or
    Kasseri
lemon juice
paprika (optional)

If the cheese is very moist, let it dry out for a few hours – but not more or it will crumble too easily. Cut into small cubes and either arrange on a grill grid or, better still, a barbecuing double grill as this makes the turning so much easier. Put under a hot grill for a few minutes until the cheese just starts to melt, turning over after 1–2 minutes. Serve immediately sprinkled with lemon juice, paprika if liked, and accompanied by hot pittas.

DIPS AND SAUCES

Salsa

Accept, I beg, this tray of wicker made
With serried cups symmetrically laid;
Whate'er yon red and yellow bowls contain
The man of taste will surely not disdain.

ABDULLAH IBN AL-MU'TAZZ DIWAN[1]

On any *mezze* table, there will be a multitude of small bowls full of soft, puréed mixtures – begging to be dipped into. Almost translucent aubergine, deep pink taramasalata, creamy ground almonds, flaming red chillies, stony-coloured tahina, the bright green of fresh herbs and glowing orange sauces – all will be artfully arranged on the table to best show off their colours and the textures of the foods they are to accompany. For many are not only eaten as dips, with bread, but are also there to complement meats, fish, salads and mounds of soft, fluffy rice.

Garlic, bread, potatoes, olive oil, eggs, lemon juice, tomatoes and nuts of all sorts are transformed in a variety of ways to produce each country's specialities. Egg and lemon is a favourite in Greece, so too the thick, wonderfully garlicky *Skorthaliá* (page 25). Garlic appears in many guises throughout the region – in a thin olive oil sauce and in a rich mayonnaise in Turkey; with tahina all over the Middle East; with hazelnuts in Iraq; with almonds in Syria, Egypt and Persia. Walnuts or delicate pine nuts dominate the sauces in Turkey while masses of fresh herbs are used in the Lebanon.

Yogurt knows no boundaries and a bowl of chilled, freshly made yogurt will appear on almost every table at almost every meal. Heavily laced with

mint it makes a cooling salad. Cucumber is added in Turkey, or sometimes a touch of tomato paste – to faintly tinge it pink. Paprika is also favoured here, usually mixed with olive oil and dribbled over in a decorative pattern – a much loved garnish for many dips, especially the earthy-tasting *Humus bi Tahina* (page 24).

Chillies make their appearance in Iraq, the Yemen and North Africa – it seems the hotter the climate, the hotter the sauce. The Yemen, with its sizzling high temperatures – you can literally fry an egg on a flat stone in the sun – has a sauce to match. An old recipe I have calls for two 'tinfuls' of dried red chillies – roughly 20 chillies – to two large tomatoes!

Perfection in the art of sauce-making must, though, go to Persia. Here fruits and meats are slowly simmered, enticingly seasoned with subtle spices – often rose-water too – and then served with their wonderful crusty rice, *Chelo* (page 140). Whatever else is on the Persian table, a dish of *chelo*, with a sauce, will invariably be there as well – a tribute to centuries' experimenting in the kitchen.

1. Collected Poems *(Cairo, 1891). The poet/king was tragically murdered after an all-too-brief reign of 24 hours in* AD *908/296 Islamic calendar.*

CHICK PEA PURÉE WITH SESAME SEED PASTE

Humus bi Tahina

One of the most popular and well known Middle Eastern dishes – and rightly so, with its deliciously nutty, earthy flavour. Widely available now in cans, or from delicatessens – mostly, I suspect, also out of a can. But perfectly passable if extra tahina, olive oil and lemon juice (lots) are added. An excellent store-cupboard standby – though I still prefer the rougher, nuttier-tasting home-made version.

Serves 3–4
150 g (5 oz) dried chick peas, soaked overnight, or
    400 g (14 oz) can chick peas
juice of 3 large lemons
125–150 ml (4–5 fl oz) tahina paste
3 large garlic cloves, skinned and crushed
Maldon or sea salt
pinch of cayenne pepper
To garnish 25 ml (1½ tbsp) olive oil
5 ml (1 tsp) paprika
30 ml (2 tbsp) finely chopped parsley

If using dried chick peas, skim off any floating skins and debris, then rinse well. Place in a large saucepan, cover with water and boil for about 1 hour until quite soft. Drain and reserve a few chick peas for the garnish. Canned chick peas simply need to be drained, then cooked in fresh water for 15 minutes.

Either put the peas through a mincer and then mash to a paste or put in a food processor with the lemon juice and 30–45 ml (2–3 tbsp) of the cooking water and whizz until puréed. Add the tahina (use the lesser amount with canned chick peas, adding more if necessary), garlic cloves, a large pinch of salt and a small one of cayenne and whizz again. Check to see if it needs more salt, and maybe a little water if very thick, then turn the purée into a bowl. If you are making the dip by hand, add the ingredients to the minced and mashed chick peas, a little at a time, whisking well between each addition – the purée

should be quite creamy (although inevitably not as smooth as the canned) by the time you have finished.

Throughout time, this has had the traditional decoration of olive oil, mixed with paprika, drizzled over the surface of the cream. Parsley is then sprinkled on top, and the whole chick peas formed into a pattern – often a star. In Persia, pomegranate seeds may be added too, while in the Lebanon *sumac* is often preferred to the paprika.

SMOKED COD'S ROE PURÉE

Taramasalata

Taramá is the dried, salt, pressed and lightly smoked roe of the grey mullet. Since, even in its native habitat – Greece and Turkey – this has always been expensive, smoked cod's roe is often used instead. This produces the rosy pink cream so familiar now in the West, although some shop versions are such a pale pink they must be blushing with shame at their lack of the vital ingredient. If you should ever see a taramasalata glowing with a burnt-orange colour, don't pass it by – for this will be made with the genuine mullet roe.

Serves 6
125 g (4 oz) smoked cod's roe
2 slices white bread, crusts removed
2 garlic cloves, skinned and crushed
½ small onion, skinned and grated
juice of 1–2 lemons
large pinch of paprika
90–120 ml (6–8 tbsp) olive oil
To garnish black olives

Skin the roe and either pound thoroughly to a paste or cut up coarsely and put in a food processor. Soak the bread in cold water for 5 minutes, then squeeze dry and crumble. Either beat into the paste or add to the processor.

If making by hand, now add the garlic, grated onion and half the lemon juice and whisk thoroughly, then stir in the paprika. Then add the olive oil, 15 ml (1 tbsp) at a time and alternating with 15 ml (1 tbsp) of cold water to every 30 ml (2 tbsp) of oil, whisking very well between each addition. Stop adding oil when the cream has the texture and glossiness of a thick mayonnaise.

To make in a food processor, simply add all the ingredients except the olives to the roe and bread, and whizz till you have a rich creamy texture. Add some cold water in proportion to the oil used and blend again.

Put the purée in a dish, smooth the top and garnish with the black olives. Eat with *Pitta* (page 146), or hot thin toast.

GARLIC AND BREADCRUMB SAUCE

Skorthaliá

The simplest version of this gloriously garlicky Greek sauce is made with breadcrumbs, garlic, olive oil and lemon juice. It's a pungent and gutsy sauce – good with fried fish and strongly flavoured vegetables. For blander foods, I personally prefer the more refined version, given below, in which ground almonds are substituted for half the breadcrumbs. Both are ideal in very hot weather since they will not curdle or separate like mayonnaise, but I have another recipe which does include egg yolks making it very similar to the French *aïoli*. Be warned though, it curdles extremely easily.

Serves 4–6
3–4 slices white bread, crusts removed
4–6 large garlic cloves, skinned
salt
50 g (2 oz) ground almonds
about 150 ml (¼ pint) olive oil
juice of 1 large lemon

Break up the bread, grind to crumbs in a grinder or food processor. Put into a bowl, cover with water and soak for a few minutes. Crush the garlic in a mortar with the salt until completely pulpy, then transfer to a large bowl.

Squeeze the breadcrumbs dry and mix with the garlic pulp, then mix in the almonds, stirring well. Add the olive oil, a drop at a time to begin with, then in a drizzle, and beat until the mixture is very thick. Gradually add the lemon juice, still beating hard, until the mixture resembles mayonnaise. Taste for sharpness adding more lemon if necessary, or oil if you find it too sharp – the garlic has quite a tang. Serve with fish or vegetables. If you want to make it more of a pouring sauce, thin down with cold water. And should you wish to make the ultra-refined version using egg yolks, add them first to the garlic, then beat in the oil as if making mayonnaise before mixing in the breadcrumbs and almonds. Thin at the end with lemon juice or white wine vinegar.

GARLIC SAUCE

Tarator Sade

This is a rich, and again garlicky, sauce from Turkey where it is used especially with fish and plain boiled potatoes. Good too with cold meat.

Serves 3–4
8 garlic cloves, skinned
Maldon or sea salt
45–60 ml (3–4 tbsp) olive oil
lemon juice
pinch of paprika

Crush the garlic in a pestle and mortar with about 2½ ml (½ tsp) of salt, pounding until really mushy. Very slowly add 15 ml (1 tbsp) oil, beating all the time, then gradually add up to another 45 ml (3 tbsp) oil, constantly beating until it resembles a very thick mayonnaise. Season to taste with lemon juice – in Turkey they like it fairly sharp. I prefer a mellower flavour, so use your own judgement. Add more salt if need be, then beat in the paprika.

TAHINA CREAM DIP

Salata Tahina

The sesame seed paste called tahina must be one of the most loved – and versatile – ingredients in the Arab kitchen. Not only is it added to a multitude of other things, it is also, classically, served as a dip or accompaniment to most cold, and many hot, dishes. Although the basic ingredients for this are hardly varied throughout the Middle East, the proportions are very much a matter of personal taste.

Serves 6
2–4 garlic cloves, skinned and coarsely chopped
Maldon or sea salt
juice of 2–3 large lemons
150 ml (¼ pint) tahina paste
1–5 ml (¼–1 tsp) cumin seeds
15–75 ml (1–5 tbsp) finely chopped parsley

Crush the garlic together with the salt in a mortar with a pestle, then gradually beat in about half the lemon juice. Stir the tahina paste in the jar to mix in the oil which always rises to the top when the jar is standing, then measure out the desired quantity into a large bowl. Whisk in the garlic and lemon mixture, then add 45–60 ml (3–4 tbsp) of cold water and beat vigorously into the paste.

Grind the cumin seeds in a spice grinder, then add a little at a time, until you are satisfied with the taste. Add more lemon juice, and more water if necessary to achieve a thick-cream consistency. At this stage, it is very much what you like which determines how much you add. Sprinkle with the desired quantity of parsley and serve with *Pitta* (page 146).

ALMOND DIP

Nouggada

One of the most glorious sights – and smells – comes with the flowering of the almond trees, often as early as January or February. A profusion of sparkling white blossom with its sweet, far-reaching scent, heralds a good crop in the autumn. Widely grown in Greece, Turkey and Persia, the sweet nuts are much used all over the Middle East, particularly in this, one of the most delicate of sauces. Also, imaginatively served as a salad in Syria, with cold fish, poultry or their beloved *Kibbeh* (page 91). Excellent.

Serves 4–6
225 g (8 oz) ground almonds
2–3 garlic cloves, skinned and crushed
pinch of caster sugar
juice of 2 lemons
75–105 ml (5–7 tbsp) olive oil
Maldon or sea salt
freshly ground black or white pepper
60 ml (4 tbsp) finely chopped parsley
To garnish paprika

Mix the almonds with the garlic and a pinch of sugar. Stir in the lemon juice, then gradually whisk in the oil. Taste after 75 ml (5 tbsp) and add more if necessary. Season with salt and black or white pepper or a bit of both, then sprinkle on the parsley. Dribble over a little more oil, then decorate with a pinch or two of paprika.

TAHINA WITH ALMONDS

Tahina Ma'Lauz

Here, earthy tahina is combined with almonds to give a gutsier but still subtle dip. A favourite in Baghdad.

Serves 6–8
1 garlic clove
Maldon or sea salt
juice of 2–3 lemons
150 ml (¼ pint) tahina paste
1½–2½ ml (¼–½ tsp) caster sugar
90 ml (6 tbsp) ground almonds
To garnish flaked almonds
few sprigs fresh mint

Crush the garlic with the salt, then beat in the juice of 2 lemons. Either whisk into the tahina or blend together in a processor, then add the sugar – start with a little as the sweetness of the almonds can vary considerably. Mix in the nuts and then add just enough cold water to make a thick creamy paste. Check to see if you need more lemon juice, sugar and possibly salt. Arrange in a bowl with a few flaked almonds scattered on top and garnish with the mint sprigs. Superb, if unorthodox, with baked potatoes.

TAHINA WITH WALNUT SAUCE

Teradot

Another nut-and-tahina combination, this time from Turkey. Traditionally served with fried mussels or cold baked fish but also on occasion with vegetables, in which case mint is often substituted for the parsley – and paprika added.

Serves 3–4
175 g (6 oz) walnuts
juice of 2–3 lemons
75–90 ml (5–6 tbsp) tahina paste
3 garlic cloves, skinned and crushed
salt
45–60 ml (3–4 tbsp) finely chopped fresh dillweed or
     parsley

Grind the walnuts in a spice grinder until they reach the gritty stage – take care not to over-grind, you don't want a powder. Tip into a blender, add the juice of 2 lemons, 75 ml (5 tbsp) tahina, the garlic and a good pinch of salt and blend thoroughly. If mixing by hand, whisk in a large bowl until well amalgamated. Season to taste with lemon juice and tahina. Tip into a bowl. Mix in the dill or parsley, leaving a little to scatter over the top.

WALNUT SAUCE

Taratur

Walnuts are often used on their own for sauces or dips in Turkey, so prolifically do they grow. Again often served with fish and, classically, *Circassian chicken* (page 109).

Serves 4–6
175 g (6 oz) walnuts
juice of 1–2 lemons
45–60 ml (3–4 tbsp) olive oil
Maldon or sea salt
To garnish finely chopped parsley

Grind the walnuts in a spice grinder until fairly finely chopped but not powdery. Tip into a bowl then beat in about two-thirds of the lemon juice and 45 ml (3 tbsp) olive oil. Season lightly with salt, then check to see if more lemon or oil is needed, adding it accordingly. Thin with a little water to a thick pouring consistency, then pour into a bowl (or over the fish) and sprinkle with parsley.

PINE NUT SAUCE

Cousbareyah

The tiny pink-cream kernels that lie in the folds of the large cones of the Mediterranean Stone Pine (*Pinus pinea*) have long been a delicacy of the Mediterranean kitchen. Wildly expensive outside their growing areas but abundant in the Middle East, where they are used with an extravagant hand. This sauce, found in Lebanon, Syria and Egypt, is particularly popular with baked fish, usually served whole and often spectacularly decorated with huge radishes, olives, lemons or limes, fried pine nuts and tiny pickled cucumbers. Our cook in Damascus, passionate about his tiny patch of roof garden, also used to strew on rose petals.

Serves 6–8
175 g (6 oz) pine nuts
2 slices of white bread, crusts removed
Maldon or sea salt
1 large garlic clove, skinned and crushed
juice of 1–2 lemons or 2–3 limes
60–90 ml (4–6 tbsp) fish, veal or chicken stock

Grind the pine nuts in a spice grinder until powdery. (Our cook used to very lightly fry the nuts in a little olive oil before pounding them. It gives a nuttier taste but is not strictly traditional). Soak the bread in cold water for 5 minutes, then squeeze out all the moisture.

Put in a blender with the nuts, salt, garlic and half the lemon juice and purée. Add a little stock (you can use water if stock is unavailable or you want to stay vegetarian) and blend again. Check to see if you need more lemon or lime juice, adding if necessary, and then add just enough stock or water to make a paste about the consistency of barely beaten double cream. If you want to pour the sauce over, say, a boned fish or chicken pieces, make it a little thinner. Otherwise serve in bowls.

TURKISH PINE NUT SAUCE

Tarator Camfistgı Sosu

In Turkey, they make a very thick pine nut sauce, akin to a mayonnaise, to serve with fish, chicken and other cold meats. Heavenly as a dip for crudités.

Serves 4–6
125 g (4 oz) pine nuts, plus a few to garnish
2 large garlic cloves, crushed
Maldon or sea salt
finely ground white pepper
30–45 ml (2–3 tbsp) olive oil
15–30 ml (1–2 tbsp) lemon juice

Grind the pine nuts in a spice grinder until powdery, then put in a blender with the garlic, salt and a pinch of white pepper. Add 15 ml (1 tbsp) oil and the same of lemon juice, and blend to a thick purée. With the machine still running, gradually add more oil, a little at a time, until the mixture resembles a mayonnaise. Taste to see if more lemon is needed, and add. Serve in a small bowl, strewn with a few whole pine nuts.

HAZELNUT SAUCE

Taratur Fendukh

In Iraq hazels are the nut favoured for the sauces served with chicken and boiled lamb. I also thin it down considerably sometimes with chicken stock to make a delicious soup.

Serves 6–8
225 g (8 oz) hazelnuts
2 slices of white bread, crusts removed
2 large garlic cloves, skinned and crushed
juice of 1 lemon
Maldon or sea salt
about 120 ml (8 tbsp) chicken stock
15 ml (1 tbsp) paprika

Grind the nuts quite finely. Soak the bread in cold water and then squeeze dry. Put the nuts, bread, garlic, lemon, salt and 90 ml (6 tbsp) stock into the blender and blend into a thick purée. Add more stock until you have a thick but just pourable sauce, then mix in the paprika. If you want to serve this with hot chicken then warm the stock first. When making as a soup, I add a handful of finely chopped mint or whatever fresh herb is available.

EGG AND LEMON SAUCE

Avgolemono

The classic Greek sauce for almost anything – fish, chicken, meatballs. The Turks are fond of it too – particularly for minced lamb meatballs. The one 'must' is that the stock should match the dish the sauce is being served with. The only exception is when serving with lamb – here water is usually substituted, as a lamb stock would be overpowering.

Serves 3–4
3 egg yolks
juice of 1–1½ lemons
150 ml (¼ pint) fish, chicken or vegetable stock
salt
freshly ground black pepper

Beat the egg yolks until frothy, add the lemon juice – the greater amount for a really tangy flavour – and whisk again. Then slowly add the stock, or water, constantly beating. Season lightly with salt and pepper then either put over a saucepan of simmering water, or put on a very gentle heat, and stir until thick. Do not let the mixture boil or it will curdle, but if you are careful you can dispense with the double boiler. If at all in doubt, use it. Delicious with fish, meats, vegetables, stirred into soups or with rice.

HERB SAUCE

Salkha

A wonderfully herby green vinaigrette from the Lebanon. Traditionally, the herbs were pounded with large pestles and mortars or between flat round stones but I make it in large quantities using a blender – a matter of minutes – and keep it in a cool, dark place. If you want to make a smaller amount, reduce by half, chop the herbs fairly finely and give a quick whizz in a spice grinder or blender just to lightly crush and release the oils. Then it's an easy matter to whisk them by hand into the dressing.

Makes a generous 600 ml (1 pint)
about 350 ml (12 fl oz) olive oil
Maldon or sea salt
5 ml (1 tsp) dry mustard powder
generous pinch of cayenne pepper
1½ ml (¼ tsp) allspice berries
about 150 ml (¼ pint) red wine vinegar
15 ml (1 tbsp) chopped tarragon
15 ml (1 tbsp) chopped marjoram
15 ml (1 tbsp) snipped chives
15 ml (1 tbsp) snipped spring onion tops
15 ml (1 tbsp) chopped parsley
15 ml (1 tbsp) chopped chervil
5 ml (1 tsp) caster sugar

Put the olive oil in the blender with a generous 5 ml (1 tsp) of salt and the mustard powder and whizz briefly. Add the cayenne pepper. Quickly grind the allspice berries in a spice grinder and add them to the blender. With the machine running, gradually add the vinegar, a little at first, then in a constant dribble. Put in the herbs and sugar and blend until emulsified. Taste to see if more oil, vinegar or salt is needed and adjust accordingly, then store in a screw-topped jar for up to one month. If you know you are going to want to keep it, add slightly less oil than you will finally need and cover the dressing with a thin film of oil. Considerably improved, in any case, if made the day before using, as the flavours then have time to meld.

CUMIN AND FRESH CORIANDER SAUCE

Salsa Kamun wa Kuzbari Taza

We used to make this in Baghdad where coriander grew prolifically. (It will flourish in England too, though vanishing for the winter since it is an annual: but it self seeds all over the place. 200 years ago, the Sussex downs were a noted gathering place for the herb.) This is a marriage between two powerful personalities so needs a strong-tasting partner: mutton or well-hung beef are ideal. So is raw cauliflower.

Makes about 150 ml (¼ pint)
1 small bunch fresh coriander leaves
15–45 ml (1–3 tbsp) cumin seeds
Maldon or sea salt
good pinch of ground cinnamon
about 120 ml (8 tbsp) olive oil
30–45 ml (2–3 tbsp) red or white wine vinegar
pinch of sugar

Chop the coriander leaves fairly finely, discarding the stalks. Grind the cumin in a spice grinder, then put in a blender with the coriander, about 1½ ml (¼ tsp) salt, the cinnamon and half the oil. Blend, and with the machine running, gradually add the remaining oil. Then, again gradually, add up to 30 ml (2 tbsp) vinegar, and a good pinch of sugar. Taste to see if you want more oil or vinegar, then pour into a bowl and leave for at least 2 hours to let the flavours amalgamate.

HOT CHILLI SAUCE

Harissa

I have a Tunisian friend who can eat a whole bowl of this – admittedly a small bowl – neat! For less fiery mortals, the quantity below, which is about the least you can decently serve, will be quite adequate for people to dip into. Any left over can be stored in a small screw-topped jar – cover the paste with a little more olive oil to preserve.

Serves 4–6
24 red chillies, seeded if wished (I do, some don't)
2–3 garlic cloves, skinned and crushed
30–45 ml (2–3 tbsp) caraway seeds (optional)
Maldon or sea salt
olive oil

Chop the chillies, then grind in a spice grinder until powdery. Add the garlic and caraway seeds (plain *Harissa* is made without caraway but I think it vastly improves the flavour) and a goodly amount of salt – start with a generous 2½ ml (½ tsp), and blend again. Taste by dipping in a piece of bread or raw vegetable to see if it needs more salt, then either tip into a small jar and just cover with olive oil until you want to use it: or, if using straight away, mix in a little oil to make a thick paste and serve in a small bowl.

APRICOT SAUCE

Salsa Mishmish

One of my most treasured memories of Damascus was walking through the orchards and picking up just-fallen apricots, still warm from the sun, soft, juicy and incredibly perfumed. (The unwritten law was that you never picked them off the tree – to this day, a law I find difficult to break.) Since apricots will not keep well, many found their way into the cooking pot, particularly for this sauce which greatly enhanced our rather stringy chickens. It is undoubtedly Persian in origin and I have not met it elsewhere in the Middle East, but in Persia it is usually served with lamb – indeed the two are cooked together.

Serves 6–8
45 ml (3 tbsp) olive oil
2 onions, skinned and finely chopped
225 g (8 oz) apricots, stoned or 125 g (4 oz) dried
   apricots, soaked overnight if necessary
3 cloves

5 cm (2 inch) piece cinnamon stick
2½ cm (1 inch) piece root ginger, peeled and
　　coarsely chopped
300 ml (½ pint) chicken stock
juice of 1 lemon

Heat the oil in a large pan, add the onions and fry gently for 10–15 minutes until golden and very soft. Add the apricots – with a few cracked stones if you wish – and turn them around until gleaming and starting to go soft. Grind the cloves and the cinnamon in a spice grinder, then add the ginger and grind again. Add to the pan, then pour in the chicken stock. Simmer very gently, covered, for about 45 minutes until the mixture is very mushy – add a little more stock or water if it becomes too dry. When very thick and soft, remove and discard the stones if they were added, then either pound with a wooden spoon until pulpy or quickly whizz in the blender – this makes a much creamier, smoother sauce. Add lemon juice to taste and serve with chicken or lamb.

ORANGE SAUCE

Khoresh Portagal

My favourite of the famous Persian fruit and meat sauces which are traditionally served on their crusty-topped steamed rice, *Chelo* (page 140). Perfected and refined through hundreds of years, they are the pinnacle of the Persian kitchen with their subtle blends of delicate spices, fresh herbs, meats, fruit, vegetables and nuts. They are very much a seasonal dish, changing daily according to what is on display in the markets. There must be thousands of recipes for each family has their own variation, their favourite seasonings, the combinations they particularly delight in, and a *khoresh* of one sort or another will appear on the table at least once, if not twice, a day – every day. No two will ever be quite the same but the secret of perfection never changes – a very long, and gentle, simmering to achieve that delicate harmony and balance of flavours.

Serves 4–6
60 ml (4 tbsp) olive oil
900 g (2 lb) lean lamb, cubed, or chicken or duck
　　weighed off the bone, then cut into small pieces
5 ml (1 tsp) paprika
5 ml (1 tsp) cinnamon
salt and freshly ground black pepper
freshly grated nutmeg
25 g (1 oz) unsalted butter
1 large onion, skinned and finely sliced
juice of 1 small lemon
5 oranges
75 g (3 oz) sugar
75 ml (3 fl oz) cider vinegar

Heat the oil in a large saucepan, add the meat and seal on all sides, then sprinkle on the paprika, cinnamon, salt and pepper (not too much pepper – the seasonings should be subtle not overpowering) and a good grating of nutmeg. Cover the meat with water, but only just, then simmer very gently with the pan covered, for 25–40 minutes until tender. Lamb will take longer than chicken or duck, and you may need to top up the water.

Meanwhile, melt the butter in another pan, add the onion and fry slowly until golden – but not quite brown – and soft. Stir in the lemon juice then reserve, off the heat. Once the onion is cooking, peel the oranges over a bowl to catch any juice that drips, and taking care to remove all the pith. Divide the segments, then make a tiny nick in each one to take out the pips.

Put the oranges in another small pan, sprinkle over the sugar, then pour on the vinegar. Let stew gently for about 15 minutes, stirring occasionally.

Place the onion over the meat, then pile the oranges on top and pour over the liquid remaining in their pan. Cover and simmer – extremely gently – for another 30–45 minutes, until the meat is meltingly tender. Serve with *Chelo* (page 140).

AUBERGINE PURÉE

Patlıcan Püre

Commonly called 'poor man's caviar' due to its delicate and subtle flavour, this is hugely popular all over the Middle East. Ordering it once in a Turkish restaurant in London, we were presented with a dish incredibly pale in colour: I thought we had been given puréed onions. Their secret they wouldn't divulge but a Turkish friend told me she immediately puts the skinned aubergines into a large bowl of acidulated water. Then, when they're all skinned, you can squeeze out the juices and chop the flesh. This certainly produces a paler than usual sauce – though still not so delicately cream in colour. The flavour however was very fine.

Serves 4–6
2–3 large aubergines
45–60 ml (3–4 tbsp) olive oil
2 garlic cloves, skinned and crushed
½ small onion, grated (optional)
juice of 1–2 lemons, extra if soaking after skinning
salt
45 ml (3 tbsp) finely chopped parsley

Grill the aubergines, whole and unpeeled, under a very hot grill or char over the flame of a gas cooker, until the skins are quite black and blistering. (If the aubergines are huge and you are grilling them, start with a medium heat, then turn it up after 6–7 minutes, or the flesh will not have time to soften right through). The whole process takes about 20 minutes – when they feel soft and spongy, they are ready. Run the aubergines under the cold tap and peel off the skin, being careful to remove all traces of charred skin. Then slit in half lengthways with a sharp knife, and very gently squeeze each half to be rid of the bitter juices. Put to soak in a bowl of water with juice of 1 lemon if wished, as you cut each half. When all are skinned, squeeze again to drain.

Chop up the flesh roughly then put into a blender and whizz briefly. Add a little oil and whizz again,

then, with the machine still running, gradually add up to 45 ml (3 tbsp) oil. If the mixture is quite shiny at this stage, then add the garlic, onion, juice of 1 lemon and a generous sprinkling of salt and whizz again. Taste to see if it needs more oil, lemon or salt, then pour into a bowl. Mix in 15 ml (1 tbsp) chopped parsley. Just before serving dribble over a little more oil – a few drops, no more – and sprinkle on the remaining parsley.

AUBERGINE AND YOGURT PURÉE

Yogurtlu Patlıcan Püresi

In ancient Baghdad, according to the thirteenth century manuscript of Al-Baghdadi, they enjoyed this dish with fried meat balls. It is still served as such, but I remember having it as a dip with hot pitta. Also very good with raw vegetables.

Serves 6–8
3 medium aubergines
60 ml (4 tbsp) olive oil
175–225 ml (6–8 fl oz) thick yogurt
juice of 2–3 limes
2 garlic cloves, crushed
5 ml (1 tsp) cumin seeds, well crushed
1¼ ml (¼ tsp) ground cinnamon
salt
finely chopped parsley

Grill or char the aubergines over a flame until the skin is blackened and blistering. Peel off the skin and all charred bits under a cold tap, then squeeze the aubergines gently until all the juices have run out.

Chop the flesh and put into a blender, then whizz to a purée. Add the oil, a little at a time, then blend in 175 ml (6 fl oz) yogurt, the lime juice, garlic, cumin and cinnamon. Season fairly generously with salt, then taste to see if it needs more yogurt, adding if necessary. Pile into a serving bowl, sprinkle with lots of chopped parsley and chill.

AUBERGINE AND TAHINA PURÉE

Mutabbul

Another Turkish variation on the same theme. Said to have been invented by the ladies of the Sultan's harem – to win his favours.

Serves 6–8
2–3 large aubergines
3–4 garlic cloves, skinned and crushed
75–100 ml (3–4 fl oz) tahina paste
juice of 1 large lemon
large pinch of paprika
salt
To garnish 30 ml (2 tbsp) finely chopped mint or
    15 ml (1 tbsp) dried mint
olive oil

Grill the aubergines – under a medium heat first, then a high heat after about 7 minutes, until well blackened and soft, about 20–25 minutes. Remove the skin while holding the aubergine under a cold tap, then gently squeeze to get rid of the juices.

Blend the flesh in a food processor, then add the garlic and 75 ml (3 fl oz) tahina and blend again. Add the lemon juice, paprika and salt to taste, then whizz until very smooth. Taste to see if you want to add some more tahina, otherwise pour into a bowl and sprinkle over the mint. Just before serving, pour about 5 ml (1 tsp) oil over the surface. Serve with *Pitta* (page 146) or sesame bread.

YOGURT

Laban

Laban in Arabic, meaning 'soured milk' and called 'Persian milk' by al-Baghdadi, yogurt (as it's known to the Turks), and the making of yogurt, has been a part of everyday life in the Middle East for thousands of years. Originally, no doubt, a clever way of

'preserving' fresh milk (*halib*) which stays fresh with difficulty in those hot, humid climes, yogurt is now vital to the Arab kitchen. A bowl of chilled yogurt will always be on the table, spiced or plain, in cooling salads, lovely sharp cheeses, tenderising marinades, softening spicy stews, refreshing drinks. Yogurt is used every day and in every way – the perfect anti-dote to fiery temperatures, both meteorological and culinary. It is also child's play to make and, since I have used it in quantity throughout this book, and all too often the supermarket shelf is bare of natural yogurt leaving a myriad fruity flavours uselessly staring at one, I give the recipe here. You do not even need the thermos flask, although I find it easier and utterly foolproof. But a large bowl wrapped in a couple of towels will do, provided you give it a warm home for the 'making' period: an airing cupboard or the top of a solid fuel stove overnight are both ideal. Friends in Sri Lanka, with neither airing cupboard nor solid fuel stoves, ingeniously place the bowl in the rigifoam boxes used here as cooler boxes, beside an open jar filled with boiling water. Equally effective. We, of course, are lucky enough to have buffalo curd – thick and creamy, and not dissimilar to the goat-milk yogurt I so loved in Damascus. Whatever the method, don't forget, first time around you will need a 'starter'.

Makes about 1 litre (1¾ pints)
1.1 litres (2 pints) milk
15–30 ml (1–2 tbsp) natural yogurt

Bring the milk to the boil, then turn off the heat and leave until you can hold your little finger, well dipped in, for a slow count to 15. If you want to use a thermometer, the temperature should be 41°–43°C (106°–109°F) so, by the time you have finished your count, your finger should be well pleased to come out. If the milk is too cool (or too hot), the yogurt will not thicken.

Beat the starter – this can be any plain commercial yogurt provided it has not been pasteurised – and spoon into a large thermos flask. If you use the lesser

Following page (l–r): Herb Sauce (p. 29), Aubergine Purée (p. 32), Hot Chilli Sauce (p. 30), Taramasalata (p. 24) and Chick Pea Purée (p. 24).

amount of starter the yogurt will not be quite so thick. It's still fine for salads, marinades, or drinks but for making cheese (and my ritual breakfast bowl, with a little honey) I prefer the slightly thicker texture that 30 ml (2 tbsp) give. When the milk is ready, strain it into a jug and pour a little into the thermos. Whisk (chopsticks are the perfect length) then gradually pour in the rest of the milk, whisking all the time. You will feel it almost imperceptibly thickening while you stir. Screw on the top and leave for 8–12 hours. I used to put the flask by a night storage heater in the winter, but left it on the kitchen table once by mistake. The yogurt was still perfect. When you open the thermos, you will see a slight layer of watery liquid on the top. Unless you want to make cheese immediately, or need really thick yogurt, simply pour the whole lot into a large bowl, whisk and chill.

Otherwise pour through a fine sieve, dropping the thick yogurt in the sieve into a second bowl every now and again as you pour. The thin yogurt can be drunk, after chilling, and the thick used as the starter for cheese. (It will of course need a further draining, see page 22.) The Arabs by the way do not discard the skin from the top of the milk. Mixed with a little sugar, it is considered a great delicacy, and in our household in Baghdad, the cook's mother – very ancient and disgustingly healthy – always used to be called out for her morning 'tipple', which she slurped down with great enthusiasm. Chilled, the yogurt will keep for about a week, although I confess it never stays around that long with me, and it is really at its best within 3–4 days. Just remember to keep back a couple of spoonfuls from the first batch to make the next. A simple and satisfying daily ritual.

An orchard of almond trees in the Atlas mountains of Morocco.

© Françoise Peuriot

STUFFED PASTRIES AND LEAVES

Sanbusak, böreği wa dolmades

If thou wouldst know what food gives most delight,
Best let me tell, for none hath subtler sight. . . .
Then, as thou wilt, in pastry wrap it round,
And fasten well the edges, firm and sound.

ISHAQ IBN IBRAHIM OF MOSUL[1]

These are the glory of the *mezze* table. In no other food is the Arab attitude of time, care, love and leisurely attention so visibly displayed. Tiny parcels, of soft dough, crisp golden pastry, brittle, paper-thin *fila*, darkly green vine leaves – all are filled with meat, chicken, cheese, eggs, fish, rice, onions, pine nuts, spinach, almonds, and sweet seasonings, to give a delectable mouthful – gone in an instant. There is an ancient Syrian proverb about the woman who worked for three days, the results to disappear before her eyes:- What had she been doing? *Börek, sanbusak, briouats, lahma bi ajeen, bstilla, briks, dolmadés* – their names read like a Middle Eastern roll of honour. The shapes are varied, in size as well as outline – triangles, squares, coils, tiny flower pots, long slim fingers, envelopes, half-moons, truly enormous pies; each country, and family, clinging to their favoured design, and fillings. All have in common time and care lavished upon them: making the pastry, rolling it out – sometimes stretched onion-skin thin, cutting into tiny pieces, then grinding the spices, cooking the filling. Then lastly the stuffing, a hundred teaspoons or more neatly wrapped and arranged on trays, ready for the final frying or baking, an impressive centrepiece for the table.

The pastries are age-old; the poem describes in detail their making, which has hardly changed to this day. The leaves – vine, cabbage or spinach – and vegetables so loved for stuffing, courgettes, aubergines, tomatoes, onions, are a reminder of the Ottoman court. Endless banquets, and perhaps satiation, required a novelty, a tantalising enticement, a *bonne bouche* to whet the appetite. A wonderful combination of supremely sophisticated simplicity; all that is required of the cook is patience, and time. The results are elegantly satisfying, and always well received. No *mezze* table should be without them.

1. Died AD 851/236 Islamic calendar.

Following page (l–r): Cold Stuffed Vine Leaves (p. 48), Arab Pizzas (p. 41), Cigarette Börek (top, p. 44), Turkish Stuffed Pastries (bottom, p. 42), Greek Spinach and Cheese Pies (p. 47), and Coiled Börek (p. 44).

CHEESE PASTRIES

Sanbusak – I

At the end of our walk through the apricot orchards, if I had been very good, we would wander to the edge of the *souk* where a street vendor sold these wonderful little half-moon shaped pastries gleaming gold and warm from recent frying. They were filled either with a melting, salty cheese mixture or spicy minced meat stuffing sweetened with pine nuts, and I still go through the same agonies today in deciding which to eat first, which to keep for the last. For once one was bitten into, it was too more-ish not to go on.

The recipe for these has hardly changed from ages past; the dough in every country is rendered: '1 coffee cup of oil, 1 coffee cup of melted butter, 1 coffee cup of warm water, 1 teaspoon of salt. Add as much flour as it takes.'[1] The recipe my mother has from our cook in Damascus actually says '1 round tin full of oil, etc. etc.' referring to the cigarette tins he used as a measure – but then he did make enormous quantities of the things! Interestingly the method of decoration does not seem to have changed much either. I can remember thinking how ingenious 'my' street vendor was in marking his pattern on the half-moons with a nail. Then when I came upon Professor Arberry's treatise, I found the poem by Ibn Ibrahim, and in it quite clear instructions: 'Then with the rolling-pin let it [the dough] be spread and with the nails its edges docketed.' It is this sense of early sophistication, and the continuity with the past, that I find so fascinating about Arab cookery.

1. Professor A J Arberry, 'A Baghdad Cookery Book', Islamic Culture No 13, January and April 1939, from which all the poems are quoted; and also much reference made to his translation of the manual, discovered in Istanbul in the 1930s, written in 1226 by Muhammad ibn al-Hasan ibn Muhammad ibn al-Karim al Katib al-Baghdadi (normally known as al-Baghdadi). Who he was is a mystery – but he obviously knew his subject intimately and his book throws much light on the dishes of the court of Baghdad, many of which were previously unknown.

Makes 15–18 pastries
For the pastry
50 g (2 oz) unsalted butter
50 ml (2 fl oz) olive oil
2½ ml (½ tsp) Maldon or sea salt
about 225 g (8 oz) flour
30–45 ml (2–3 tbsp) sesame seeds
1 egg, beaten (optional)
olive oil, for deep frying (optional)
For the filling
225 g (8 oz) Feta or Hallumi cheese
1 egg, separated
30 ml (2 tbsp) finely chopped fresh mint or 15 ml (1 tbsp) dried
freshly ground white pepper

Put the butter into a small heavy pan and melt gently, taking care not to let it bubble, then mix in the oil and 50 ml (2 fl oz) of warm water and take off the heat. I'm afraid I may shock the traditionalists next because I use a food processor to mix the dough. It is much quicker, less messy and I, at any rate, get better results. For the dough has to be soft, very well mixed – yet handled as little as possible. So, if you do mix by hand, use a very large bowl and bear that in mind. Pour the warm butter and oil mixture into the food processor, add the salt and whizz for a second. Then pour a little flour in and whizz again. Gradually add up to 225 g (8 oz) flour, whizzing constantly towards the end. The dough should be very soft – almost like a soft pastry, and leave the sides of the bowl clean. Take it out and put on a lightly floured surface. If it feels too greasy, lightly and gently work in a spoonful or so more flour. Break into four equal-sized pieces, then roll each one, on a floured surface, quite thin and cut out rounds roughly 7½ cm (3 inches) in diameter. Now, if you are going to fry the pastries, which I think is marginally more melt-in-the-mouth, but undoubtedly more calorific and harder work, but it's the way I remember them, spread the sesame seeds over a large flat surface and dip the bottom of the rounds in the seeds, very lightly pressing them down so the seeds stick on. If you're going to bake them, wait.

Make the filling by crumbling or grating the cheese – Feta may need to be mashed a little with a fork, then mix with the egg yolk, mint and a generous seasoning of white pepper. The mixture should be soft but not sloppy, if it is very thick though – and this will depend a bit on the cheese – mix in 5 ml (1 tsp) or so of the egg white until it is not quite at the 'dropping' stage. Put 5 ml (1 tsp) of filling on each pastry round, slightly off centre, and fold over the pastry to make a semi-circle – don't press the filling down too much, it shouldn't reach the sides or it can burst during the cooking. Seal the edges firmly and indent with a fork or nail, if you wish (I have a special 'baking' nail for this – it makes one feel somewhat historic, idiotic really . . .). If baking, put the pastries on an ungreased and unfloured baking tray – they won't stick. Brush with the beaten egg, and then sprinkle with sesame seeds. Bake at 180°C (350°F), mark 4, for 30–40 minutes until they are delicately golden and lift up easily from the tray. For frying, heat a good 5 cm (2 inches) oil in a deep pan. Cook the *sanbusak* – a few at a time – in hot but not smoking oil for 3–5 minutes until golden brown and crisp. Drain well. Either way, enjoy them.

MEAT FILLED PASTRIES

Sanbusak – II

Equally popular in Syria, Lebanon and Egypt is this meat filling. My Damascus pastries were filled with pine nuts, but in Lebanon I also had a version which included poached brains mashed with the minced meat to give a softly creamy texture, slightly moister than the plain meat variety. There is also a recipe which calls only for brains, which I confess I've never had. However, since *briouats* with brains are delicious (page 45), I should think it is very good – you would probably need about 350 g (¾ lb) brains, maybe a bit less. Wash them, taking off the outer membranes, then poach with a dash of vinegar for about 10 minutes, before mashing with chopped herbs, salt and pepper. If you want to include brains in the filling below, one set is enough and traditionally, they would replace the pine nuts. But pine nuts are my weakness.

Makes 15–18 pastries
sanbusak pastry (page 40)

For the filling
15 ml (1 tbsp) olive oil
1 medium onion, skinned and very finely chopped
2½ ml (½ tsp) ground cinnamon
1½ ml (¼ tsp) ground ginger
freshly ground allspice
pinch of caster sugar
225 g (8 oz) lamb, minced
30 ml (2 tbsp) pine nuts
Maldon or sea salt
freshly ground white pepper
juice of ½ lemon

Prepare the pastry and cut out as in the previous recipe, but omit the sesame seeds if using pine nuts for the filling: their flavour is too delicate to cope with the sesame.

To make the filling: coat the bottom of a frying pan with the oil, add the onion and cook, very gently, for about 10 minutes until quite soft. Sprinkle over the cinnamon, ground ginger, a fair bit of freshly ground allspice and the sugar and stir for another 2 minutes. Add the meat and cook until coloured, 4–5 minutes, then stir in the pine nuts and fry until they become pink-brown. Season with salt and freshly ground white pepper, then stir in the lemon juice and 30 ml (2 tbsp) water to moisten. The mixture shouldn't be too wet; on the other hand if it's too dry, it will crumble. Simmer for another 3–4 minutes until the meat is juicy but not liquid. Cool for 10 minutes before stuffing the pastries, then either fry or bake, as wished.

ARAB PIZZA

Lahma bi Ajeen

Also called *lahmajoun* (pronounced the same in Turkish but spelt *lahmacun* – the 'c' without a cedilla sounded hard, as 'j'), this is the Arab answer to the pizza – in miniature, and cooked very quickly so that the base is still white and soft, perfect for folding over to eat easily, and instantly. They can also be warmed up in a moderate oven for a few minutes, which is ideal for parties. (I put them on a baking tray and cover them in foil, to keep them supple.) For me, they are a nostalgic reminder of lunches eaten on the edge of my tiny hexagonal swimming pool. Feet dangling in the cool water, I would watch the cook pounding away with the pestle and mortar, the smell of spices wafting across the courtyard to mingle with the yeasty aroma of my little pizzas.

Makes about 20 pizzas

225 g (8 oz) plain flour
2½ ml (½ tsp) Maldon or sea salt
5 ml (1 tsp) Easy Blend yeast (see page 158)
15 ml (1 tbsp) olive oil, plus extra for greasing

For the filling

15 ml (1 tbsp) olive oil
1 large onion, skinned and chopped
450 g (1 lb) lean lamb or beef, minced
1 large beef steak tomato, blanched and skinned,
    or 2 canned plum tomatoes
15 ml (1 tbsp) cumin seeds, ground
pinch of caster sugar
freshly ground allspice
Maldon or sea salt
freshly ground white or black pepper
30–45 ml (2–3 tbsp) finely chopped coriander
    leaves or parsley
15 ml (1 tbsp) tomato purée
juice of ½ lemon
25 g (1 oz) pine nuts (optional)

Sift the flour into a large bowl or food processor. Sprinkle on the salt and the yeast and mix. Dribble the oil over the flour, then gradually add 150 ml (¼ pint) warm water, constantly mixing or with the machine running, until a soft dough is formed. Knead hard for 10–15 minutes or whizz the machine for 3–4 minutes until the dough is very elastic and leaves the bowl clean. (Even though I do use a food processor for this, I still in fact then knead for 1–2 minutes by hand – lightly flour your hands first – it makes the dough very light and supple.) Brush a clean bowl with oil, then turn the ball of dough in it so it's thoroughly coated – this prevents the upper surface from drying out. Cover with a cloth and leave in a warm place for 1½–2 hours for the dough to rise.

Heat the oil and cook the onion for 5–6 minutes until soft but not coloured. Drain thoroughly, then put in a large bowl. Add the meat. Chop the tomato, discarding the seeds and excess juice (this also applies if using canned tomatoes), then add with the cumin seeds, sugar, allspice, salt, pepper and coriander leaves. Mix the tomato purée with the lemon juice and stir in. I now also add pine nuts – traditionally either tomatoes or pine nuts are used but I happen to like both. Mix everything together very well. Don't worry if the mixture seems a bit dry – you do not want too much liquid or you'll have soggy pizzas.

Knock back the risen dough a few times, then divide the mixture into four pieces, and each of these into 5–6 lumps. Roll into a small ball, then flatten between your hands and gently pull out to make a circle roughly 10 cm (4 inches) in diameter. Or you can using a rolling pin – roll quite thin, but I quite enjoy doing this by hand. There is a mild challenge to see how thin, and evenly sized, one can make them! Arrange on a lightly oiled baking tray, then spread a little filling all over each circle. Go right to the edges, not only to keep the pizzas soft but to make them look enticing – a blob of filling, surrounded by acres of pastry, is anything but. Bake for 7–10 minutes in the oven at 210°C (425°F), mark 7 – the bases should be soft but cooked through. Serve hot or warm with lots of salad.

TURKISH STUFFED PASTRIES

Börek

In Turkey, little stuffed pastries are called *börek*. They come in many shapes from fat squares or triangles for a family lunch to long slim fingers or 'cigarettes' for a more formal party. The fillings are varied, and so is the pastry. It can be a shortcrust, with or without eggs (I have even seen a plain flour and water dough in some recipes). More rarely it can be a pizza dough, similar to the one used for the previous recipe. Lighter are those made with a flaky or puff pastry, while most delicious of all, to my mind, are those using the paper thin sheets of *fila* pastry (*phyllo* to the Greeks, *yufka* to the Turks, *brik* to the Tunisians and *ouarka* to the Moroccans). How a simple mixture of flour and water can be transformed merely by kneading, flattening and stretching – you can almost see through it – is something that never ceases to amaze me. Thankfully, though, there are the experts, and *fila* is quite widely available, in packets of 12 or 24 sheets, usually 30 x 50 cm (12 x 20 inches) in size although this does vary considerably. Rolled and sealed in polythene they will keep in the refrigerator for 6–7 days (I have kept it longer but it was a bit brittle). But it freezes well, and almost for ever. Gentle, completely thorough defrosting is essential however; otherwise it will just break when you use it. I tend to buy 450 g (1 lb) packets – 20–24 sheets – then divide that up into parcels of 5–6, immediately rerolling and sealing in polythene before freezing. Provided you always make sure it's quite pliable before starting, and keep sheets not actually being filled covered with a damp cloth, it is easiness itself to work with. The result is so light, without the extra richness of puff pastry, that I think it justifies the minimal effort involved. Having said all that, I do also use flaky or puff pastry sometimes, and very good it is too. Again, I tend to take a shortcut here, especially as I often used to make *börek* in the summer, when hot weather can cause havoc with pastry-making. But a good commercial brand, rolled out, then dotted with a little butter over two-thirds of

the rectangle, folded into three and chilled before a final rolling out, produces excellent results. As a rule 450 g (1 lb) of pastry will make about 30–36 *böreks*, depending on size and shape.

Since living in Sri Lanka – where *fila* is not available – I have discovered that Chinese spring-roll pastry leaves are equally suitable. Just use fewer layers, otherwise treat the same.

Makes 18–20 börek

450 g (1 lb) fresh spinach or 225 g (8 oz) frozen
25 g (1 oz) unsalted butter
100 g (4 oz) Feta cheese
30 ml (2 tbsp) walnuts, chopped finely
1 small egg, beaten
freshly ground allspice
freshly ground black pepper
225 g (8 oz) *fila* pastry
oil, for brushing and frying

If using fresh spinach, wash, trim and finely chop it. Otherwise defrost the frozen spinach, then stew gently with the butter and 30 ml (2 tbsp) water until tender. Crumble the cheese and add to the pan with the walnuts. As the cheese starts to melt, stir in the

The Topkapı Palace, Istanbul.

beaten egg and cook for another 2–3 minutes. Season with allspice and black pepper, you won't need salt as the cheese provides enough, and leave to cool while you organise the pastry.

Have a damp, not soaking wet, clean cloth to hand. Take out one sheet of *fila*, roll up the rest, and cover lightly with the cloth. Cut the *fila* into long strips roughly 7½ cm (3 inches) wide, and lightly brush each strip with a little oil. If your *fila* is the standard size of 30 x 50 cm (12 x 20 inches) you will need one strip per *börek*. If, however, you find – as I have on occasion, and certainly with the spring roll pastry – that it is approximately 35 cm (14 inches) square, then I think you need two. (Either way, the weight given should make 18–20 *börek*.) So, if necessary, lie one strip on top of another. Then put a good 5 ml (1 tsp) filling at one end, about 2½ cm (1 inch) from the short side and slightly off centre (I work from left to right, so would place it nearer the top edge). Then lift the bottom corner up to meet the long top edge, making a triangle. You then lift the whole triangle to the right – you now have a straight edge on the left. Take the top left hand corner and fold this over to meet the long bottom edge. Again lift the complete triangle and fold over to the right, and so on, until you come to the end of the strip. Either tuck in the leftover *fila*, or just fold over and press it lightly down, brushing with a tiny bit more oil, if necessary, to make it stick. (This is much more complicated to describe than do – try it first with a long strip of paper!)

You can now either fry or bake the pastries, on a greased baking tray, at 190°C (375°F), mark 5, for about 20–30 minutes until they are lightly golden on top. Keep checking as ovens vary so much. I prefer to fry mine, unless I am making enormous quantities when obviously the oven is easier. Heat a good 2½ cm (1 inch) oil in a large deep pan until not quite smoking hot (a piece of broken *fila* will sizzle and colour in about 30 seconds), then add a few *börek* at a time, and fry, turning once, until golden all over. Lift out quickly – they brown in an instant, and drain well. You can, if you like, keep them warm in a very low oven while finishing the rest but I find that if you do about 4 at a time, the first are still warm by the end, so hot are they when they come out of the pan.

'CIGARETTE' BÖREK

Sigara Böreği

These are *börek* rolled up in the shape of a small cigar. Traditionally a cheese filling, similar to the one for *Sanbusek* (page 40) is used. You will need to cut the *fila* into rectangles 10 cm (4 inches) wide by 30–35 cm (12–14 inches) long, using 1 sheet per cigar. Spread 5 ml (1 tsp) filling in a long thin line about 1 cm (½ inch) away from the shorter edge, roll over a couple of times, then fold over the long sides to enclose the stuffing, and continue rolling as if making a cigar. You will probably get more cigarettes than triangles out of the same *fila*, up to 24, so increase the quantities of filling slightly. Any leftovers are cook's perks!

COILED BÖREK

Burma Böreği

There is another shape often used for spinach fillings, which never fails to impress. But it absolutely has to be made with very pliable *fila* – I don't even use very slowly defrosted pastry as it can prove unreliable. So, when you have very fresh *fila*, make these lovely coils. Roll a long, long cigar, using half a large sheet of *fila* and spreading your filling – a good 15 ml (1 tbsp) or more in a long, thin line down the longest side of the sheet. Then, very carefully coil the cigar round and round itself, making a spiral. These have to be baked otherwise they unroll, and should be packed tightly on the greased sheet. Once cooked, the danger is over. Start checking their colour after 15 minutes. Many people omit the cheese from this filling, substituting a finely chopped onion, and adding a few more nuts (pine nuts are nice) and some sultanas. In this case, don't forget also to add some salt. Again, 225 g (8 oz) *fila* will make about 18 coils.

MOROCCAN FILA PASTRIES

Briouats

The slight variation in the name betrays the influence of the French in Morocco, but the little *fila* parcels are just as popular here as elsewhere in the Middle East. Squares, cigars and triangles are the shapes used – with a wonderful variety of fillings. The Moroccan imagination is given full rein here, for the stuffings are not only savoury but sweet too. A particularly glorious one is made from a ground almond and beaten egg paste, the *briouats* being dipped in boiling honey once fried, then left to cool. Even savouries are often given a sweet touch, parcels filled with a minced meat filling, or rice simmered in milk and butter with almonds, being lightly dusted – after cooking – with icing sugar and ground cinnamon. Surprisingly good. The most delicious *briouats* though, to my mind, are those filled with poached, fried brains (egged and floured first) and – best of all – those with *merguez*, the tiny but bitingly hot sausages. I have substituted *chorizo* (the hotter variety) quite successfully for these, cutting the sausage into four lengthways (to make a small 'cigarette') and sprinkling the pastry – before rolling – with finely chopped parsley – and sometimes a little cayenne pepper for extra spice. Excellent.

TUNISIAN STUFFED PASTRIES

Briks à l'Oeuf

Be gentlemanly when you serve this Tunisian speciality – and warn your guests! For the innocent-looking *fila* envelope contains not only a delicious tuna and onion mixture – but a whole egg slipped on top just before the parcel is folded. I was caught unawares – once, and luckily on the beach near Carthage, so the disaster wasn't too terrible. But I had wondered why everyone was sitting with their heads thrown back – like baby birds in a nest – before taking their first mouthful. The eating technique is soon acquired though, but I must admit the preparation terrified me for ages. Then I took the plunge, and it was really quite simple. For days we ate *briks* – with every conceivable filling. Wonderful.

Serves 6
peanut oil
1 large onion, skinned and finely chopped
175 g (6 oz) canned tuna fish, drained and mashed
small bunch parsley, finely chopped
juice of ½–1 lemon
Maldon or sea salt
freshly ground black pepper
pinch of cayenne pepper (optional)
6 sheets *fila* pastry
6 eggs

Sweat the onion in 15 ml (1 tbsp) oil for about 10 minutes until softened but not too coloured. Drain and mix into the fish, then add the parsley, half the lemon juice and season with salt, pepper and cayenne, if using. Taste and add more lemon if necessary.

Brush one sheet of the *fila* with a little oil, cut in half and place one half on top of the other. Spread some of the filling about 7½ cm (3 inches) from one of the shorter ends of the *fila* strip. I make a slight hollow with the back of a spoon so the egg doesn't float about too much, then break the egg on top of the filling. Carefully, fold over the end of the *fila* to cover, then gently fold in the right and left edges to seal the sides, and quickly bring the long edge back (over the filling) and then roll completely up. Fill the remainder in the same way.

Fill a large deep pan with a good 5 cm (2 inches) oil and heat gently. The oil should be hot but not smoking. Carefully lower 2–3 *briks* into the pan and cook gently until golden, turning over once; about 2–3 minutes each side should be sufficient to lightly set the eggs without burning the *fila*. Drain well on absorbent kitchen paper and serve hot. Have paper napkins to hand.

MOROCCAN PIGEON PIE

Bstilla

From the small and impressive to the impressively large. Said to have been brought back from southern Spain by the conquering Moors, this magnificent dish, commonly called 'food of the Gods', is served on very special occasions. Pronounced *pastela* or *pastilla*, it is usually huge, being baked in a dish or *'tbsil'* enormous in its dimensions. The recipe I have calls for forty pigeons, forty eggs, five pounds of butter and nearly four pounds of almonds! What it does not tell me is the quantity of servings.

Although the Middle Eastern pigeon is much milder in taste than its European counterpart, the often suggested alternative – chicken – although very good, lacks, I feel, the impetus the dish should have. After many experiments, I have compromised and now use a small chicken and three or four pigeons, the latter enriching both the stock and the flavour of the dish. Traditionally served as a starter to a festive meal, I like it as the finale to the *mezze* table. Spectacular – and worth every minute of the effort, which is considerable. I usually prepare it the day before a party, then keep it, covered with a damp cloth, in the refrigerator. Take out 1 hour before baking to bring to room temperature.

Serves 8–12
1 chicken, about 1½ kg (3¼ lb) in weight
4 wood pigeons
225 g (8 oz) butter
3 large onions, minced or grated
bunch of fresh parsley, finely chopped
5 ml (1 tsp) ground cinnamon
2 mace blades, crumbled finely
2½ ml (½ tsp) freshly ground black pepper
Maldon or sea salt
2–3 saffron strands, crushed
7 large eggs
18–20 sheets *fila* pastry
30 ml (2 tbsp) oil
150 g (5 oz) blanched almonds, flaked or finely chopped

15 ml (1 tbsp) caster sugar
For the glaze
1 large egg yolk, beaten
15 ml (1 tbsp) icing sugar
15 ml (1 tbsp) ground cinnamon

Wash the chicken and the pigeons inside and out, then arrange in a large flameproof casserole, in one layer. Cut 50 g (2 oz) butter into small pieces and dot around the birds, then put in the onions, parsley, half the cinnamon, the mace, the pepper and a little salt. Bring a scant 600 ml (1 pint) water to the boil and pour over the saffron strands in a jug, stirring them until the colour starts to run, then pour over the chicken and pigeons. Simmer very gently for 2–2½ hours until the flesh on the birds is practically falling off the bones; only add a little water if the pan is becoming too dry (you want about 150 ml (¼ pint) liquid at the finish).

Take the birds out, skin the chicken and chop all its flesh into small pieces, then cut the breasts off the pigeons and cut into long, thin diagonal slices. (The leg meat will be enough for a small dish of potted pigeon.) If there was too much liquid in the pan, gently simmer it down while chopping the meat, otherwise just take the pan off the heat. Then return it to the stove, beat the eggs in a bowl and whisk into the pan. Stir constantly until thickened, rather like a custard, then taste for seasoning and add more salt and pepper if necessary. The final result should be smooth, creamy and almost setting – but not scrambled.

Melt the remaining butter in a small saucepan, then brush a baking dish, about 30 cm (12 inches) square with a little of the butter. Working with the *fila* one sheet at a time, lay it in the dish so that the edges overlap the tin edges (if your *fila*, for some reason, is smaller than the tin, overlap 2 sheets for this bottom layer). Brush with melted butter – lightly – then lay on 5 more sheets of *fila*, brushing each one before putting on the next.

Heat the oil in a small frying pan, add the almonds and sauté for 2 minutes until lightly golden. Remove with a slotted spoon and scatter over the top sheet of *fila*. Sprinkle the sugar over the almonds, then the remaining cinnamon. Spread about two-thirds of the creamy egg mixture evenly over the *fila*, then cover with another 6 sheets of pastry, again brushing with melted butter between each layer.

Arrange the chopped chicken flesh on the *fila*, then spread the pigeon strips on top of the chicken and cover with the rest of the egg mixture. Finally cover with the remaining *fila*, each sheet naturally brushed with butter. Tuck the overhanging edges underneath the top sheets, then slip the overlap from the top sheets underneath the whole pie. Glaze the top with beaten egg, then scatter on the icing sugar mixed with the cinnamon. (In Morocco, they often add the sugar – in far greater quantities – to the simmering birds, but this tends to be too sweet for most Western tastes).

Bake in the oven at 170°C (325°F), mark 3, for 45 minutes, then raise the heat to 200°C (400°F), mark 6, and bake for a further 15–20 minutes until the top is crisp and golden-brown. Score the top into diamond shapes and serve hot. A wonderful one-course supper, with a green leaf and herb salad. And a good red wine.

GREEK SPINACH AND CHEESE PIES

Spanakopittá and Tyrópittá

While not so stunning as the Moroccan pie, nonetheless these two Greek dishes are extremely good. And useful if time is short – or you don't want to make individual *börek*. *Spanakopittá* is traditionally made with spinach and Feta cheese, while *Tyrópittá* has a cheese and egg filling. For 12 sheets of *fila*, you'll need about 1.1 kg (2½ lb) spinach plus 175 g (6 oz) Feta, while for the cheese stuffing 500 g (1¼ lb) Feta, and 3 large eggs should be sufficient. Nutmeg and cinnamon are the preferred spices for the former, finely chopped fresh herbs for the latter. Bake at 190°C (375°F), mark 5, for 40–45 minutes and then at 220°C (450°F), mark 8, for 5–6 minutes to brown. Both these pies can, of course, be made in small triangular versions – *trigoná spanakópittés* and *trigoná tyrópittés* respectively in Greek. Bake at 190°C (375°F), mark 5, for 20–30 minutes.

STUFFED VINE LEAVES (HOT)

Dolma

Named after the Turkish verb 'to stuff', these enticing rolls, smoky in flavour from the grapevine leaves, appear on tables throughout the Middle East. In winter, spinach and cabbage leaves are often used instead, while an elegant variation in Cyprus uses the beautifully marbled leaves of the tiny wild cyclamen. This was taboo in my house, since I spent my life encouraging the little creatures to increase – their minute flowers, purest white and brilliant pink, being one of the jewels of the winter garden. But it's a delightful notion – if fiddly, for I doubt that their largest leaves would hold even a teaspoon of stuffing. However, I am lucky enough to have access to a fresh vine, and all through the dry season wonderful flat, fat packages arrive through the letter box – leaves, large and small, tenderly packed in tissue paper by a thoughtful friend. A good wash, a quick blanching and they're ready for the freezer – carefully stored quite flat so they don't crumble once frozen; even more than with *fila* pastry is a gentle defrosting necessary since they are very brittle. Packets of leaves in brine are now widely available if you haven't a vine to raid and these keep well in the refrigerator, although once opened you should use them within a couple of days or they will dry out. *Dolma* are served hot and cold, usually stuffed with meat for the former, rice in the latter. Both can be cooked, then frozen, so it's worth making quite a large quantity at one time: open-freeze, then pack in dozens so you can take out a few at a time.

Makes 30–36 dolma
40–45 large vine leaves
125 g (4 oz) long grain rice
225 g (8 oz) lamb, minced
1 medium onion, skinned and grated or minced
1 large tomato, blanched, skinned and chopped
small bunch parsley, finely chopped
15 ml (1 tbsp) dried mint
5 ml (1 tsp) ground cinnamon

2–6 garlic cloves, skinned
Maldon or sea salt
freshly ground black pepper
juice of 1–2 lemons
30–45 ml (2–3 tbsp) tomato purée

Packeted vine leaves need soaking in boiling water for 30 minutes, then draining and soaking in fresh cold water for another 5 minutes. Fresh leaves should be blanched in a large pan of boiling water – 3–5 minutes will usually be sufficient to make them go limp, then drain and rinse in cold water.

Wash the rice by pouring boiling water over it, leave for 5 minutes, then rinse well in cold water and drain thoroughly. Mix in a large bowl with the lamb, onion, tomato, herbs and spices, then season with salt and pepper.

To stuff the leaves, lay them on a flat surface, veins facing up. Snip off the stalks then put about 5 ml (1 tsp) filling in the middle of the leaf, slightly nearer to the stalk end than the tip. Fold up the bottom edge of the leaf, then fold over the left and right sides to cover the filling, and continue rolling up to the tip. Put on a plate, tip underneath so it doesn't unroll again – it also helps to slightly squeeze each roll before stacking. Allow a few extra leaves in case of tears, but once you've done a few, you'll slip into the technique easily.

Line a large heavy saucepan with a layer of leaves, then arrange the rolls tightly side by side – you will probably have to make two layers but try not to have loose rolls on top. Cut some of the garlic into fine slivers and crush the rest. Tuck the slivers in between the rolls here and there, then mix the crushed garlic with the lemon juice and tomato purée. Stir in about 150 ml (¼ pint) warm water and pour over the *dolma*, then lay a plate on top of them – inside the pan – to stop them moving around in the cooking. Cover the pan and simmer very gently for 1½–2 hours (fresh leaves will need the longer time), checking every 30 minutes or so and adding a little water as and when necessary. Pile on a serving dish, with any liquid left in the pan poured over. Traditionally served hot but leftovers are excellent cold.

STUFFED VINE LEAVES (COLD)

Yalanci Dolma

Nicknamed 'liar' *dolma* since their stuffing contains no meat, these are glorious, with a spiced rice filling, cooked and cooled in a mixture of oil and lemon juice, to give a delicate contrast between the sweet and the tangy. In Persia, a couple of ounces of raisins are usually added, and in Iraq we often used hazelnuts.

Makes about 36 dolmas
45 large vine leaves
225 g (8 oz) long grain rice
1 large onion, skinned and finely chopped
50 g (2 oz) pine nuts or walnuts, finely chopped
1–2 large tomatoes, blanched, skinned and chopped
45–60 ml (3–4 tbsp) finely chopped parsley
30 ml (2 tbsp) dried mint or dillweed
freshly ground allspice
5 ml (1 tsp) ground cinnamon
Maldon or sea salt
freshly ground black pepper
3 large garlic cloves, skinned and finely chopped
175 ml (6 fl oz) olive oil
juice of 2 lemons
pinch of caster sugar

Wash and blanch fresh leaves in boiling water for a few minutes until soft, or soak packeted leaves in boiling water for 30 minutes, then drain and soak in cold water for another 5 minutes. Trim off the stalks and lay the leaves on a flat work surface, vein sides up.

Wash the rice in boiling water, then rinse in cold, and drain thoroughly. Mix with the onion, nuts, tomatoes, herbs and spices then season – fairly highly – with salt and pepper. Stuff the leaves, rolling firmly but not too tightly to allow room for the rice to expand. Put a layer of leaves at the bottom of a large pan, and arrange the rolls in layers, side by side.

Sprinkle over the chopped garlic, then mix the oil, lemon juice, sugar and about 150 ml (¼ pint) warm water and pour over the *dolma*. Tuck a small plate on top of the parcels, then cover the pan and simmer gently for 1½–2 hours until the leaves are quite tender. Add a little water from time to time as the liquid is absorbed. Cool, covered, in the pan, then pile on a serving plate. These are often beautifully arranged in Turkey, in ever diminishing circles, with a slice of lemon tucked in between each *dolma*.

SMALL FISH IN VINE LEAVES

Samak Fi Waraqa An Nabat

Another popular use for vine leaves, particularly in Turkey and Greece. Any small fish, red mullet, sardines or even fresh anchovies, can be cooked in this way, giving them a lovely, smoky flavour.

Serves 6

12 fresh or frozen sardines, or 6 small red mullet
juice of 2 lemons
12–18 large vine leaves
olive oil
3 sprigs fresh thyme, leaves stripped from the
     stalks (optional) or 5 ml (1 tsp) rigani (optional)
3 large garlic cloves, finely chopped
Maldon or sea salt
freshly ground black pepper

Wash the sardines, nicking out their innards if you wish by slipping a small thin knife through the gills (I leave them whole, but some people find the flavour rather strong). If using mullet, have them cleaned but leave the livers in, as these are a delicacy. Rinse the fish, pat dry, then put in a dish and squeeze over the lemon juice. Leave for 30–40 minutes.

Soak the vine leaves in boiling water for 30 minutes if they are packeted, then drain and soak in cold water. Fresh leaves should be boiled for a few minutes until limp, then drained and rinsed in cold water. Snip off the stalks.

Put the vine leaves, vein-sides up, on a flat surface and brush each one liberally with oil. You may need 2 leaves per fish if they are large, in which case overlap the leaves, stalk ends opposite – the oil will keep them together. Sprinkle each leaf with a little thyme or rigani, a few pieces of garlic and a little salt and pepper, then put a fish across the middle of the leaves. Scatter with the rest of the herbs and garlic, then roll up – heads and tails may protrude slightly from either end, this doesn't matter. Brush the parcels with the lemon juice left in the dish, and some more oil. Cook under a hot grill for 4–6 minutes each side, brushing with more oil as you turn, or if they appear to be getting too crisp. Serve hot, with lemon wedges.

FISH

Samak

Here pungent garlic greets the eager sight
And whets with savour sharp the appetite,
While olives turn to shadowed night the day,
And salted fish in slices rims the tray.

ABDULLAH IBN AL-MU'TAZZ DIWAN[1]

Cocktail parties were a source of endless fascination for me as a child. Firstly, of course, there was the aura of mystery that hung over them, since I was obviously far too young to attend – and the forbidden is always fascinating. Secondly, there were the preparations, which always started the day before. In these I was allowed to partake. And here, I met my first fish in the Middle East. Strangely, although Iraq has two great, romantically historic rivers, the Euphrates and the Tigris, fish is not a favourite food – apart from *Masgouf*, the freshly smoked trout eaten with a hot, spicy sauce (page 59). What is popular though, and has been all over the Middle East since early times, is salt fish. The salting was then a necessity, in order to preserve the fish for a long time and over long distances: now it is loved and eaten for its own deliciousness. Whether our cook was consciously bringing to life al-Mu'tazz' poem, I doubt. Nonetheless, round silver platters of violet olives surrounded by the thinnest slivers of pale salt cod we did prepare. The mountain of olives was his domain; to me, fell the task of the surrounding sea. Paper-fine slices of soaked salt cod were poached in milk, and garlic, of course, then cooled. I now had to arrange them in overlapping circles around the edges of the dishes.

Then, with a quick flick of the tip of a knife, the exposed end of each slice was curled over to produce a pool of white wave crests, in the centre of which he would painstakingly build his dark tower. Oddly enough, I had completely forgotten this ritual until researching this book when I came across that poem – then it came suddenly flooding back. The pride in my beautiful 'seas', the holding of breath as he piled the olives higher and higher, and the rather wicked thoughts I occasionally had – almost willing them to come tumbling down. But he was far too professional for that.

However, it was not until we went to Beirut and Alexandria for holidays that I realised how much fish is, in fact, eaten in the Middle East. The Mediterranean abounds in wonderful varieties, and all are popular. None more so than the brightly coloured red mullet, *Sultan Ibrahim* to the Arabs, *barbounia* to the Turks and Greeks. Prepared in a multitude of ways, charcoal grilled, deep fried, wrapped in vine leaves, marinated, with various sauces, herbs and spices, or simply with garlic and lemon, you will, somehow, meet it in almost every country. Also abundant are the bigger grey mullet, a sea bream called *murgan* or *arous*, sea bass (*loukoz*), sole – quaintly named Moses' fish (*samak Moussa*), shad – considered a great delicacy in Morocco, mackerel (*uskumru*) – beautifully stuffed in Turkey, sardines – boned and stuffed in Tunisia, swordfish – popular on skewers (*alla shish*), huge fresh tuna – baked in Morocco, tiny fresh anchovies – soused in Turkey (*hamsi bugulamsi*). Not to mention the more familiar cod, turbot, haddock, and a wonderful monster of a fish (unknown to us, but adored by the Syrians) called *sollar*, which is so repulsive that the poor creature is instantly beheaded on capture. In spite, or perhaps because, of this plethora of choice, most Middle Eastern recipes – and menus – merely state 'fish' (*samak*, *balik*, or *psari* depending where you are) and local cooks will use whatever is to hand on the particular day they are cooking. Nonetheless, certain species lend themselves to certain dishes more readily than others. So, when substituting, you should pay attention not just to size but also to flavour and especially oiliness.

Within that small constraint, the world is your oyster. They, incidentally, were said to have been discovered by the Greeks but the ancients' enthusiasm for them is not shared by their descendants today. Turks on the other hand have always appreciated the delectable mollusc. Evliya Chelebi, writing in the sixteenth century of the incredible palace built by the Sultan Ibrahim on the seashore at Tersane, warned that 'people who eat oysters without wine will find them a powerful aphrodisiac.' Myths don't change . . .

Mussels also find favour in Turkey, as does shellfish – prawns, shrimps, and sweet succulent lobsters from the waters of the Bosphorus. That other strange family of sea creatures – the cephalopods – is most commended in Greece. Before the advent of package holidays to those enchanted isles, hardly a squid was to be seen on the fishmonger's slab. Now *kalamari* is a familiar dish, not just deep fried as a *mezze*, but stewed in red wine, and dramatically stuffed. This last appears occasionally on Lebanese and Egyptian menus too, but elsewhere is not much found.

1. Collected Poems (Cairo, 1891). Died AD 908/296 Islamic calendar.

GRILLED SWORDFISH STEAKS

Kilic Baligi Izgarasi

This elegant fish, so-named after its long, sword-like snout, is popular all over Turkey – in a variety of guises. For the *mezze* table, I cut the steaks into small pieces, after cooking, but you could also chop them beforehand and thread them on small skewers to make another Turkish favourite. Any firm, sweet, white fish may be substituted.

Serves 6
1 kg (2¼ lb) swordfish, in one piece
1 medium onion, skinned and grated, then
    squeezed to extract the juice
juice of 1 large lemon
15 ml (1 tbsp) olive oil
2 garlic cloves, skinned and crushed
15 ml (1 tbsp) coriander seeds, crushed
pinch of cayenne pepper
Maldon or sea salt
For the dressing
30 ml (2 tbsp) olive oil
30–45 ml (2–3 tbsp) lemon juice
30 ml (2 tbsp) finely chopped parsley
pinch of ground cinnamon

Skin the fish – it is quite thick and pulls off easily, then cut into 6 thick steaks, and put these in a large, shallow dish. Mix together the onion and lemon juices, olive oil, garlic, coriander seeds and cayenne pepper, and pour over the fish. Leave to marinate for at least 3–4 hours, 5–6 if possible.

Just before cooking, sprinkle the fish with salt, then grill under a high heat for 4–6 minutes on each side until done right through. Cut the steaks into bite-sized pieces, arrange on a large dish, then mix the dressing ingredients together and pour over while the fish is still hot. Delicious served immediately but also good once cooled.

RED MULLET WITH GARLIC

Sultan Ibrahim bi Tom

Crunchy, gleaming red mullet aromatic with garlic were a Beirut holiday treat. When I discovered a street stall in Cairo selling the same dish, using only the smallest fish, I was overjoyed. Room for this – and something else!

Serves 6
6 small or medium red mullet (see below)
90 ml (6 tbsp) finely chopped parsley
4 garlic cloves
Maldon or sea salt
freshly ground black pepper
45 ml (3 tbsp) plain flour
olive oil, for deep frying
To serve chopped parsley
lemon wedges

Have the mullet cleaned but leave the livers in – these are a great delicacy and contribute greatly to the wonderful smoky flavour. Mix the parsley with two of the garlic cloves, well crushed, then stuff about 15 ml (1 tbsp) of this into each fish. I find it easy to push it through the gills using a chopstick. Crush the remaining garlic with a good pinch or two of salt and a generous grinding of black pepper, then rub all over the skin of the fish.

Lightly sprinkle on both sides with flour, then heat a deep-fat fryer with a good 5 cm (2 inches) olive oil until beginning to smoke. Cook the fish in the deep-fat fryer, not more than two at a time and then only if small, for 4–5 minutes until thoroughly crisp. Drain well, sprinkle with a little more parsley and serve with lemon wedges.

GRILLED RED MULLET

Barbounia sti-skara

Simplicity itself, from Greece. Here the mullet are grilled, with frequent bastings of oil and lemon juice, then served sprinkled with parsley and chopped garlic, on a bed of thick, fresh tomato sauce. In other countries, the mullet may be fried, as in the previous recipe, or grilled, then served with a mayonnaise, tahina or walnut sauce. All are good – the difficulty is choosing.

Serves 6
6 small or medium red mullet, cleaned but livers left in
Maldon or sea salt
freshly ground black pepper
90 ml (6 tbsp) olive oil
juice of 1 lemon
For the sauce
3 large beef steak tomatoes
pinch of sugar
salt
15 ml (1 tbsp) olive oil
To garnish 2 garlic cloves, skinned and finely chopped
30–45 ml (2–3 tbsp) finely chopped parsley

Rub the fish on both sides with salt and plenty of black pepper, then leave for 15 minutes. Meanwhile, make the sauce: blanch the tomatoes, skin them and chop coarsely. Put in a pan, with a pinch of sugar and salt, then pour over the oil mixed with 45 ml (3 tbsp) water. Stew gently until soft but still holding their shape, about 5–7 minutes, then take off the heat.

Just before cooking the fish, whisk together the oil and lemon juice then brush a little over each fish. Grill for about 5 minutes on each side, under a high heat, and basting frequently with the rest of the oil and lemon, until nicely crisp. Reheat the sauce, if necessary, but do not let it boil. Arrange the fish on a platter with a little of the tomato sauce beside each one, then sprinkle with the chopped garlic and parsley. Good hot, scrumptious cold.

FISH WITH CUMIN

Kammounial Samak

In Egypt and the Lebanon, cumin is often used to flavour fish – a surprisingly good marriage. I first had this dish in London, cooked by a Jordanian brought up in Alexandria and Tripoli – and there are influences from all three countries in her recipe.

Serves 4–6
450 g (1 lb) fish heads and trimmings
1 small onion, skinned but left whole
1 bay leaf
6 black peppercorns
15 ml (1 tbsp) white wine vinegar or lemon juice
2–3 sprigs fresh parsley
900 g (2 lb) sea bass, grey mullet or any firm white fish
Maldon or sea salt
freshly ground black pepper
60–90 ml (4–6 tbsp) olive oil
2 large onions, skinned and finely chopped
1–2 garlic cloves, skinned and crushed
5 ml (1 tsp) cumin seeds, lightly crushed
7–8 sprigs fresh coriander leaves, finely chopped
juice of 1 lemon
cayenne pepper

Put the fish heads and trimmings into a large pan with the onion, bay leaf, peppercorns, vinegar and parsley. Add about 600 ml (1 pint) cold water, bring to the boil, skim and simmer gently for about 25 minutes. Strain, then return the stock to the pan and reduce by rapid boiling to a generous 300 ml (½ pint).

Meanwhile, cut the fish into long, thickish strips, sprinkle with salt and pepper and leave for 30 minutes.

Heat 60 ml (4 tbsp) oil in a large frying pan, add the onions, garlic and cumin seeds and sauté gently for 10 minutes, until the onions are softened and the garlic and cumin begin to give out their aromas. Stir in the coriander leaves and cook for another 5 minutes, then remove with a slotted spoon and spread over the bottom of an ovenproof dish. Add the remaining oil to the pan, giving it 1–2 minutes to get

hot, then fry the fish for about 4–5 minutes until golden all over. Drain and arrange on top of the onion mixture. Pour over the reserved fish stock, and cook in the oven, at 180ºC (350ºF), mark 4, for 10 minutes. Sprinkle with lemon juice and a good pinch of cayenne pepper and let it completely cool, in the dish, before serving. Nice with a rice salad, and particularly good with sesame seed bread.

FISH STICKS

Blehat Samak

Popular all over the Middle East – only the spices varying with the country. The Turks also have a delicious hot version, *balik koftesi* (fish balls), in which the mixture, once shaped, is lightly rolled in flour then fried in hot oil. No sauce, just lots of lemon wedges and a sprinkling of parsley and cinnamon – very good.

Serves 4–6
450g (1 lb) fish heads and trimmings
1 small onion, skinned but left whole
few celery leaves
6 white peppercorns
2½ ml (½ tsp) turmeric
900 g (2 lb) sea bream, bass, haddock, cod or halibut, skinned and filleted
3 slices white bread, crusts removed
1 medium onion, skinned and grated or minced
2–3 garlic cloves, skinned and crushed
Maldon or sea salt
freshly ground black pepper
45–60 ml (3–4 tbsp) finely chopped parsley or coriander leaves
5 ml (1 tsp) cumin seeds
5 ml (1 tsp) allspice or coriander seeds
1 large egg
plain flour
corn oil or other light oil, for deep frying
juice of 1 lemon or 2 limes
To garnish chopped parsley

Put the fish heads and trimmings into a large pan with the onion, celery leaves, peppercorns and turmeric. Add about 1 litre (1¼ pints) cold water, bring to the boil, then simmer gently for about 25 minutes. Strain and reserve.

Put the fish through a mincer or whizz in a food processor. Soak the bread in cold water for 5 minutes, then squeeze, and add to the fish and blend. (If making by hand, crumble and mix well with the fish). Then add the onion, garlic, a generous seasoning of salt and black pepper and the parsley or coriander leaves. Grind the cumin seeds with either the allspice or coriander seeds in a spice grinder, beat the egg lightly, then add the spices and egg to the fish and mix thoroughly. Take small lumps of the mixture and roll into small fingers. Sprinkle lightly with a very little flour.

Heat about 2½ cm (1 inch) oil in a large pan until nearly smoking, then add a few rissoles and deep fry, turning occasionally, for 4–5 minutes until golden. Drain. Arrange in a clean pan, preferably wide and shallow, and pour over just enough of the reserved stock to cover the fish sticks. Squeeze in the lemon or lime juice, then bring to the boil quickly, lower the heat and simmer very gently for 15–20 minutes. Transfer the fish to a serving dish, pour over the sauce – which will set to a beautiful yellow jelly – and cool thoroughly. Serve, sprinkled with a little extra chopped parsley.

FISH KEBABS

Samak Kebab

Memory is odd. If I had forgotten my 'cocktail party platters' I can recall, only too clearly, the shame on throwing up a vast plate of spaghetti on the terrace of the gorgeous Hôtel Beau Rivage at Alexandria. What I did not confess at the time was my pre-lunch snack (walking along the sea-front with my grandfather, an ever-willing companion on illicit eating expeditions) of three little sticks of *samak kebab*. They were delicious. But I was rather sad about the spaghetti . . .

Serves 6
900 g (2 lb) sea bass, bream, cod, turbot, or haddock, filleted
juice of 3–4 lemons
3 onions, skinned and grated, then squeezed to extract the juice
10 ml (2 tsp) cumin seeds, ground
2 garlic cloves, skinned and finely chopped
5 ml (1 tsp) paprika
Maldon or sea salt
freshly ground black pepper
about 45 ml (3 tbsp) olive oil
To serve finely chopped parsley
lemon wedges
paprika (optional)

Cut the fish into chunks about 2½ cm (1 inch) square, and put in a large shallow dish. Mix the lemon, onion juices, cumin, garlic and paprika with a good pinch of salt and lots of black pepper, then pour over the fish. Leave for at least 1 hour, turning two or three times.

Thread the fish on skewers, and brush all over with olive oil. Grill, ideally over charcoal, otherwise under a medium heat for 5–6 minutes until golden. Serve on a mound of chopped parsley, with lemon wedges, and an extra dusting of paprika if wished. Also good with king prawns.

FRIED TARAMA BALLS

Taramá Keftedes

Smoked cod's roe is not just reserved for taramasalata in Greece. It also makes its appearance in this delicious and unusual *mezze*. Expensive, but worth it.

Serves 6–8
450 g (1 lb) smoked cod's roe
1 large onion, skinned and coarsely chopped
75–90 ml (5–6 tbsp) fresh white breadcrumbs
30 ml (2 tbsp) lemon juice

2–3 garlic cloves, skinned and crushed
freshly ground black pepper
15 ml (1 tbsp) finely chopped fresh marjoram
60 ml (4 tbsp) finely chopped parsley
2–3 egg whites (keep one in a separate bowl)
60–75 ml (4–5 tbsp) plain flour
olive oil, for deep frying
To serve lemon wedges

Skin the cod's roe, then chop coarsely, and mix with the onion, 75 ml (5 tbsp) breadcrumbs, lemon juice, garlic and herbs. Either put through a mincer or whizz in a food processor, in which case add two of the egg whites. (If mincing, add to the egg whites afterwards.) If the texture is too thin add the remaining breadcrumbs, if too thick, beat in the extra egg white, then chill for 2–3 hours – bear in mind that it will stiffen up with chilling.

Form into small balls or rissoles, keep your hands wet during this process, then roll lightly in flour. Heat a good 2½ cm (1 inch) oil in a pan until nearly smoking, then add the rissoles, not more than 4 or 5 at a time, and fry until crisp and golden. Drain and serve with lemon wedges .

COLD FISH WITH PAPRIKA

Yakhnit Samak Harrak

The Lebanese version of a dish found throughout the Middle East, where cold fish dishes are much appreciated – an appreciation that I think we in the West should learn to share. Apart from the ubiquitous salmon in aspic, we almost completely ignore this delicious and versatile aspect of fish cookery.

Serves 4–6
900 g (2 lb) sea bass, cod or haddock, filleted
Maldon or sea salt
the head and trimmings of the fish
60–75 ml (4–5 tbsp) olive oil
2 large onions, skinned and finely sliced
2–4 garlic cloves, skinned and finely chopped

5 ml (1 tsp) paprika
5 ml (1 tsp) ground cinnamon
1½–2½ ml (¼–½ tsp) cayenne pepper
2½ ml (½ tsp) caraway seeds, lightly crushed
juice of 1– 2 lemons

Rub the fish with salt on both sides, then leave to stand for 1 hour. Make a stock with the fish trimmings and a scant 600 ml (1 pint) cold water, then strain and reserve. Heat the oil in a frying pan, add the fish and fry on both sides until golden, about 5–6 minutes. Remove from the pan, add the onions and fry for 5 minutes until softened, then add the garlic and cook for 10 minutes until coloured. Drain off all the oil, arrange the fish on top of the onions, sprinkle over the spices (use even less cayenne if you don't like things hot) and the juice of 1 lemon, then pour on enough fish stock to come level with the fish. Bring to the boil, then simmer gently for 15–20 minutes. Remove from the heat, sprinkle over more lemon juice if you think it needs it (I like it lemony) and a little salt. Cool to room temperature before serving with hot, soft *Pittas* (page 146).

COLD MACKEREL

Uskumru Papaz Yahnisi

A famous Turkish speciality and a particularly good way of cooking mackerel, its sometimes rather strong taste being softened by the vegetables. Variations use swordfish, cut in thick slices, or whole red mullet.

Serves 6
900 g–1.4 kg (2–3 lb) mackerel (whole fish)
60 ml (4 tbsp) olive oil
2 large onions, skinned and finely sliced
1 green pepper, finely sliced
3–4 garlic cloves, skinned and finely chopped
3 large tomatoes, blanched, skinned and thickly sliced
90 ml (6 tbsp) finely chopped parsley
15–30 ml (1–2 tbsp) tomato purée
pinch of sugar
Maldon or sea salt

freshly ground black pepper
juice of 1–2 lemons
50 g (2 oz) small black olives, stoned

Have the fish cleaned but leave them whole, just making a few scores on either side with a sharp knife. Heat the oil in a large frying pan, then sauté the fish on both sides for about 3–4 minutes until nicely browned and remove from the pan. You will need to do this in batches. Add the onions and cook until softened and lightly coloured – about 10 minutes, then add the green pepper and garlic and fry for a further 5 minutes. Put the tomatoes in the pan, scatter over the parsley, then mix the tomato purée and sugar with about 150 ml (¼ pint) water and pour over. Season with salt and black pepper, bring to a bubble, then simmer for 10–15 minutes. Transfer to a shallow, flameproof dish (I use a roasting pan) unless your frying pan is very large – the fish must be kept in one layer. Smooth the sauce to cover the pan and gently lay the fish on top. Then push down carefully to cover them with the sauce and cook for 10 minutes, spooning over a little sauce after 5 minutes if necessary. Transfer to a serving dish, squeeze over the juice of 1–2 lemons and scatter on the olives. Leave to cool completely, then cut into thick slices.

STUFFED MACKEREL

Uskumru Dolmasi

One of the nicest facets of Middle Eastern cooking is how the simplest of ingredients are transformed into magnificent dishes. This is one of the most spectacular when, for festive occasions, the flesh of the mackerel is squeezed out of the fish, boned, then mixed with a spicy nut and onion stuffing and returned to the fish skins. For less brave souls, I give a somewhat easier version here but I am assured by Turkish friends that the process is not complicated – you merely need confidence. One good tip I received was to skin the fish rather than squeeze out the flesh: cut off the head, rub the fish roughly between your hands, then turn down the top centimetre (½ inch) of skin nearest the head and pull, backwards, on the backbone (which is now visible) ripping it out and pulling off the skin simultaneously. I shall try – one day.

Serves 6
For the stuffing
3 medium onions, skinned and finely chopped
30 ml (2 tbsp) olive oil
75 g (3 oz) chopped walnuts
50 g (2 oz) hazelnuts
25 g (1 oz) pine nuts
50 g (2 oz) sultanas
Maldon or sea salt
freshly ground black pepper
2½ ml (½ tsp) ground allspice
2½ ml (½ tsp) ground cinnamon
10 ml (2 tsp) dried dillweed
60 ml (4 tbsp) finely chopped parsley
For the fish
6 small mackerel, cleaned but left whole
2 large eggs, beaten
40 g (1½ oz) dry, fine white breadcrumbs
90 ml (6 tbsp) olive oil
To serve lemon wedges

First make the stuffing: fry the onions gently in the olive oil until soft and golden. Put the walnuts and hazelnuts into a grinder and grind coarsely – you want a certain amount of grittiness to contrast with the soft flesh of the fish. Add the nuts to the onions, then add the pine nuts, sultanas and a generous seasoning of salt and pepper and cook for a further 5–7 minutes. Stir in the spices and herbs, mixing well.

Wash the mackerel, running cold water through them to remove any blood, then dry. Divide the stuffing mixture into 6, and stuff into each fish. Either secure the openings with cocktail sticks or sew up (I find it easier to cook the fish if they are sewn but *en famille* I confess to using sticks), then dip the fish first in the beaten egg, then in breadcrumbs, coating well.

Heat 30 ml (2 tbsp) olive oil in a large frying pan, add no more than 2 fish at a time (you probably won't be able to anyway) and fry for 4 minutes on each side until crisp. Drain, and cook the rest of the fish in the same way. Can be eaten straight away but I think even better when allowed to cool, cut into thick slices and served with lemon wedges.

BAKED FISH

Balik Pilakisi

Any large fish, such as sea bream, bass, John Dory, halibut, cod or haddock is used for this Turkish dish, which is again served cold. In Greece, where it is called *psari plakí* it is usually served hot (rather, warm – no food is ever served really hot), the potatoes are omitted and about half a teaspoon of rigani is added.

Serves 6
900 g (2 lb) filleted fish, cut into thick slices
1 large lemon
2 medium potatoes, finely sliced
2 large onions, skinned and finely sliced
3–4 garlic cloves, skinned and finely chopped
3 large tomatoes, blanched, skinned and sliced
small bunch of parsley, finely chopped
Maldon or sea salt
freshly ground black pepper
90 ml (6 tbsp) olive oil

Arrange the fish in a large shallow baking dish. Peel the lemon (keep the zest for flavouring stocks and sauces) then cut into thin slices and lay on the fish. Cover with a layer of overlapping sliced potatoes, then strew on the onions. Scatter over the chopped garlic, then arrange the tomatoes on top and sprinkle thickly with the chopped parsley. Season, fairly highly, with salt and freshly ground black pepper, then mix the oil with about 300 ml (½ pint) water. Pour over the dish – the liquid should just reach the tomatoes, so if necessary, add a little more water.

Bake for 45 minutes to 1 hour in the oven at 180°C (350°F), mark 4. When a fork goes through to the bottom of the dish easily – it is ready. Remove and leave to cool to room temperature. For the *mezze* table, I usually cut into diamond shapes, for easy serving. A spoonful or two is particularly good tucked into a warm *Pitta* (page 146).

ROASTED FISH

Samak Maschwi

This is a dish for joyous occasions – always a large gathering. Particularly popular in Syria, Egypt and the Lebanon – and ideal for the centre of the *mezze* table. Smaller fish also are baked in the same way, then dressed with oil, lemon juice and parsley, whisked together.

Serves 8–12
1.8 kg (4 lb) sea bass, bream or grey mullet, cleaned but left whole (see below)
Maldon or sea salt
freshly ground black pepper
60–90 ml (4–6 tbsp) olive oil
1 lettuce, shredded
To garnish black and green olives, stoned
lemons, sliced
parsley sprigs
whole radishes
strips of red and green peppers
sliced pickled cucumbers
fried almonds and/or pine nuts

Traditional recipes for this always instruct you to remove the eyes. If you are squeamish, get your fishmonger to do this for you when he's cleaning it. Rinse the fish, then rub all over with salt and chill for 30 minutes. Bring back to room temperature, then rub with lots of black pepper, and olive oil. Brush a large piece of thick foil with oil, then lay the fish on it, wrap and seal well. Bake in the oven at 180°C (350°F), mark 4. Check after 1 hour – if the fish is firm and opaque yet flakes easily, it's done. Otherwise give it another 10–15 minutes, but take care not to overcook. Carefully transfer to a huge serving dish lined with the shredded lettuce, then garnish decoratively in an eastern pattern, using stars, crescents and criss-cross lines. Olives, lemon slices and parsley sprigs are a must – from the rest, choose two or three or all. Serve cold with bowls of mayonnaise – preferably garlicky, and *Cousbareyah* (page 28).

HOT SPICED BASS

Loukhoz Harrah

In the Lebanon, bass is the favourite fish for large gatherings – again always served whole. This dish, with its fiery sauce of Yemeni origin, I remember having at a picnic in the hills overlooking Beirut. I can still recall being incredulous at the thought of those snow-capped mountains above, while down below the beaches were crowded with tiny figures, sunbathing and swimming – a mere turn of my back separating the two scenes.

Serves 6–8
900 g–1.4 kg (2–3 lb) sea bass, cleaned but left whole
1 medium onion, skinned and grated or minced
4 garlic cloves, skinned and crushed
2½ ml (½ tsp) Maldon or sea salt
15 ml (1 tbsp) paprika
1½ ml (¼ tsp) cayenne pepper
1½ ml (¼ tsp) fenugreek seeds, ground (see p. 155)
2½ ml (½ tsp) cumin seeds, crushed
small bunch fresh parsley, finely chopped
handful fresh coriander or celery leaves, finely chopped
150 ml (¼ pint) olive oil
juice of 2 lemons
To serve lemon juice

Wash the fish, and score two or three times on both sides. Mix the onion and garlic with the seasonings, including parsley and coriander or celery leaves, then whisk in the olive oil and lemon juice until you have a thick pasty sauce. Alternatively, whizz everything together in a blender, then coat the fish thickly, on one side, using half the paste. Grill under a medium heat for 15–20 minutes, brushing with a little more oil if necessary, then turn over, coat the other side with the rest of the paste and cook for another 20–25 minutes – again basting with more oil if need be. When the fish flakes easily and the skin is deeply golden and crisp, it is done. Cut into thick slices, sprinkle with a little more lemon juice and serve hot or cold.

FRIED FISH

Samak Maqlu

In modern day cookery, this title will encompass all kinds of fish, though more often than not red mullet, simply salted for an hour, then floured and fried in oil and served with a tahina or pine nut sauce and lemon wedges, of course. In al-Baghdadi's manual, it is a much more sophisticated affair: the challenge was irresistible. So too, I think, the end result – aromatically spiced and delicately coloured with saffron. After much experimenting, I think sole, or plaice fillets the best fish – although it is good too with trout, the nearest relative to the Iraqi *shabbut*.

Serves 6
12 fillets of sole or plaice
2–3 garlic cloves
Maldon or sea salt
2–3 sprigs thyme, leaves stripped off the stalks
5 ml (1 tsp) coriander seeds
5 ml (1 tsp) cumin seeds
2½ cm (1 inch) piece cinnamon bark
2–3 strands saffron
5 ml (1 tsp) rose-water
5 ml (1 tsp) sesame oil
45 ml (3 tbsp) olive oil
lemon juice

Cut the fillets crossways in two. Skin the garlic and crush with about 2½ ml (½ tsp) salt, then pound with the thyme leaves until they are well crushed. Grind the coriander and cumin seeds with the cinnamon in a spice grinder until fine, then mix with the garlic and thyme. Spread a little mixture over each fillet, then roll up and secure with a cocktail stick. Crumble the saffron, then stir the rose-water into 150 ml (¼ pint) boiling water, adding the saffron, and leave for 5 minutes.

Put the fillets into a frying pan, pour over the saffron water, and simmer gently for 5–10 minutes until the rolls are nicely coloured (turn them quite frequently) and most of the water has been absorbed. Drain and pat dry, discarding any liquid left in the pan.

Mix the sesame oil with the olive oil (al-Baghdadi uses only sesame oil for frying, but with the Chinese sesame oil – the one most readily available – the flavour is too overpowering), heat, then add the fish rolls and fry for 3–4 minutes, again turning all the time, until golden all over. Put on a serving dish, sprinkle with lemon juice and eat hot or cold – I prefer the latter. Cooling seems to enhance the delicacy of the flavours, yet makes them more definite.

FRESH SMOKED FISH WITH CURRIED PEPPER SAUCE

Masgouf

The speciality for which Iraq is famous. As night fell on the shores of the River Tigris, the sparkle of small fires lit up the black sky – a glittering necklace of beacons as far as the eye could see. Cries of triumph echoed up and down the banks as the fish were caught – Tigris Salmon we called it, in fact a type of large trout known as *shabbut* to the Arabs. Split down the belly, held open by thin skewers of thorn bush, they were then hung around the fire, flesh inward to absorb the smoke, skins outward gleaming silver in the moonshine. On the fire beneath, were huge pans of sizzling onion and tomatoes, hotly peppered and aromatically spiced, waiting for the fish to be almost smoked, when they would be laid on the ashes, skin-side down, and spread with the fiery sauce. A few nicks with a knife tip to let the sauce permeate the sweet flesh then, when the skin was charred and blistered, they were ready. And so were we.

It is impossible to reproduce this dish far away from that fabled river. The best approximation I ever achieved was by half-cooking fresh trout over a smoking barbecue then, when the smoke had died down and the coals were glowing, I finished their cooking by grilling them – covered in sauce – on the grid. Good, but tricky to get right – and devilish should the wind suddenly change direction. Furthermore, when I tasted the fish – the penny dropped. For it was remarkably similar to a dish my mother had often cooked in London. Somehow, I had always thought it Turkish, perhaps because she used cod steaks. It was, of course, her adaptation of *Masgouf*: delicious and simplicity itself to make.

Serves 6

6 small trout or 6 cod steaks
30 ml (2 tbsp) coriander seeds
15 ml (1 tbsp) white peppercorns
2½ ml (½ tsp) Maldon or sea salt
6 cardamom pods, husks removed
5 ml (1 tsp) cumin seeds
1½ ml (¼ tsp) fenugreek seeds
2½ cm (1 inch) piece fresh root ginger, peeled and sliced
2½ cm (1 inch) piece cinnamon bark
2–3 large onions, skinned and finely sliced
3 large tomatoes, blanched, skinned and finely sliced
90 ml (6 tbsp) olive oil
juice of 2 lemons
3–4 garlic cloves, skinned and finely chopped
To garnish fresh coriander leaves, finely chopped

If using trout, split them open, clean and wash but leave the heads and tails on. Cod steaks merely need a quick rinse. Put all the spices, except the ginger and cinnamon bark, into a spice grinder and grind until fine, then add the ginger and cinnamon and grind again. Rub the mixture over the fish – on the flesh side only with the trout, both sides for cod, and leave to stand for 30 minutes.

Lightly grease a large baking dish, then arrange the fish side by side. Cover each with a layer of onion, then tomatoes. Mix the oil and lemon juice with about 90 ml (6 tbsp) of water and pour over the fish, then scatter on the garlic. Bake in the oven, at 180°C (350°F), mark 4, for 45 minutes to 1 hour, until the fish is done. Sprinkle with finely chopped coriander leaves and serve hot or cold.

STUFFED SARDINES

Sardinát Muhnnat

In much of the Middle East, fish is endowed with magical omens, particularly so in Tunisia, where it is almost a national symbol, beautifully painted on houses, crockery and materials. The purpose of the fish is protection from the 'evil eye'. Even jewellery is fashioned from the fish. One of the most beautiful bracelets I bought in Tunis consists of fourteen little fish, delicately outlined in pure gold filigree, linked to lie side by side encircling the wrist. Regrettably, I could not afford the exquisite enamelled version, which came in a dazzling array of colours. One day perhaps.

Newly wed couples traditionally walk over a large fish to ensure marital happiness, while in Egypt a new home will be blessed with a first meal of fish – which delighted my grandfather, who moved often and adored fish, in all its forms. Even in far away Persia, not a great fish eating nation (though they have some of the finest caviar in the world) New Year's Eve is nearly always celebrated with a fish dish to purify oneself and bring luck in the year to come.

These stuffed sardines, a Tunisian speciality, always remind me of that beautiful country – and the bracelets I left behind.

Serves 6
12 fresh sardines
15 ml (1 tbsp) olive oil
1 onion, skinned and finely chopped
small bunch of parsley, very finely chopped
15 ml (1 tbsp) cumin seeds, crushed
3–4 garlic cloves, skinned and crushed
1½ ml (¼ tsp) cayenne pepper
Maldon or sea salt
freshly ground black pepper
2 large eggs, beaten
homemade dried finely crushed white bread-
    crumbs, for coating
oil, for deep frying
To serve lemon wedges

Cut off the heads and tails of the sardines, wash and then slip out the backbones. Heat the oil, add the onion and cook, gently, for 10–15 minutes until very soft and lightly golden. Add the parsley, cumin, garlic, cayenne and a good seasoning of salt and black pepper, and fry for another 3–4 minutes, mixing well. Tip into a bowl and moisten with about 15 ml (1 tbsp) of the beaten eggs, then spread a little stuffing down the middle of each sardine. Skewer them together with cocktail sticks, threading in and out to ensure the stuffing doesn't fall out. Dip the fish in the eggs, then roll well in the breadcrumbs, pressing them lightly on with your fingertips.

Heat a good 5 cm (2 inches) oil in a wide, deep pan. When just smoking, add 2 sardines and cook for about 5–6 minutes, turning once, until nicely browned and crisp. Drain, cook the remaining fish, and serve with lemon wedges. Also very good cold.

SOUSED ANCHOVIES

Hamsi Bugulamsi

Anchovies, in any form, I have always adored, so this Turkish dish is a great favourite. Small sardines make an ideal substitute when fresh anchovies are unobtainable (which in England was nearly always) but I did occasionally find a fishmonger who had these wee fish – and then it was not just the pussies who were purring! In Sri Lanka we have anchovies – by the barrel. A different member of the family to the Mediterranean dweller – which matters not a jot, but usually caught when really tiny (like whitebait) which matters a lot. To find three or four-inch fish can be quite a search. Sardines, however, abound. So, too, flying-fish, much neglected here. An excellent substitute. Both anchovies and sardines, as well as red mullet, are also often wrapped in vine leaves and simply grilled. All are good.

Serves 6

1 kg (2¼ lb) fresh anchovies or sardines, about 10 cm (4 inches) in length

120 ml (8 tbsp) olive oil
pinch of Maldon or sea salt
30 ml (2 tbsp) finely chopped fresh dillweed
2½ ml (½ tsp) dried dill seed
45 ml (3 tbsp) finely chopped parsley
freshly ground black pepper (optional)
1½ ml (¼ tsp) ground cinnamon (optional)
juice of 1–1½ lemons

Make a small slit in the belly of each anchovy, then slip a knife in and tweak out the innards (this is a bit fiddly but I think it's worth it – with sardines I don't bother, as I like the rather musky flavour, but many people don't). Wash quickly under cold water, then pat dry. Arrange the fish, side by side, head to tail, preferably in one layer so use a baking tin if you haven't a large enough frying pan. Pour over the oil and a sprinkling of salt (I mean a sprinkling), then add about 300 ml (½ pint) cold water, the dillweed and seed, parsley, pepper and cinnamon, if using (these last seasonings vary from region to region). Cover the pan, bring gently to the boil and simmer for 7–8 minutes. Take off the heat, sprinkle over the juice of 1 lemon, then leave to cool. Check if the sauce needs a little more lemon juice, adding if necessary, then serve with warm, crusty sesame bread – to mop up the juices. Lovely for *mezze* – even better for supper .

SALT FISH IN MILK

Malih bi-Laban

I was delighted to find this recipe in al-Baghdadi, so reminiscent of our 'party platters'. I think, though, that our cook must have eliminated the initial frying since his fish was always milky-white. And yet, when I did that the flavour was not quite right. No matter, the golden cubes (easier than fine slices) are enticing especially with a mound of pale green olives – and they taste perfect. A good introduction to those who are under the impression that they abhor salt fish.

Serves 4–6
700 g (1½ lb) salt cod
olive oil, for deep frying
about 150 ml (¼ pint) milk
2 garlic cloves, skinned and crushed
freshly ground black pepper
2½ ml (½ tsp) coriander seeds
2½ ml (½ tsp) cumin seeds
1 cm (½ inch) piece cinnamon bark
To serve lime wedges (optional)

Soak the cod in cold water for at least 24 hours, changing the water every 2–3 hours. Even better, if you can organise it, is to leave the fish under running water for 12–14 hours. Put into a large pan, well covered with fresh water, and bring to the boil, then simmer for 25–30 minutes. Drain the fish, cool until easy to handle, then skin and bone. Cut into ¾-inch cubes. Heat a good 2½ cm (1 inch) olive oil in a large pan until nearly smoking, then add 6–8 pieces of fish and fry, turning over once or twice, until golden. This will take 2–3 minutes: don't be tempted to put too much fish in at one time or the temperature of the oil will drop and the fish will be soggy. When all the fish has been fried, put in a large shallow pan and just cover with milk. Stir in the garlic and a generous amount of freshly ground black pepper and simmer for about 12–15 minutes until the milk has all but disappeared. Put on a serving dish. Grind the coriander, cumin and cinnamon until very fine, sprinkle over the fish, and leave to cool. I particularly like this with a little fresh lime juice sprinkled over.

SALT COD FRITTERS WITH GARLIC SAUCE

Bakaliaros Skorthaliá

Having rediscovered salt cod, which can be a problem to find in England, therefore when I did, I bought large quantities, I had to experiment with it all ways. These Greek fritters, supremely simple, are also exquisitely more-ish.

Serves 4–6
700 g (1½ lb) salt cod
For the batter
100 g (4 oz) plain flour
good pinch of Maldon or sea salt
15 ml (1 tbsp) olive oil
1 egg white
olive oil, for frying
To serve *Skorthaliá Sauce* (page 25)
lemon wedges
radishes

Soak the salt cod in cold water for 24 hours, changing the water frequently. Or, leave under cold running water for about 12 hours. Then strip off the skin and bone. Cut into large cubes – about 5 cm (2 inches) square.

To make the batter: sift the flour with the salt, pour over the oil and a good 150 ml (¼ pint) tepid water and whisk together thoroughly. Leave to stand for 1 hour at room temperature – do not chill. Just before cooking, whisk again, then beat the egg white until stiff peaks form and fold into the batter. Dip the pieces of fish into the batter while heating enough oil in a large pan to deep fry. When it is nearly smoking, add a few cubes of fish, and fry quickly until golden all over, about 5 minutes. Drain and cook the rest. Serve with *Skorthaliá Sauce* (page 25), lemon wedges and – traditionally – a plate of radishes.

GRILLED SQUID

Kalamari

Squid is one of the prizes of the Mediterranean much unappreciated elsewhere, except in Japan. In Greece, Turkey and Cyprus though they have long realised its excellence, nowhere more so than in this delicious, and simple, *mezze*. Very tiny squid, *kalamarákia*, which I like for this dish, are, in Greece, more usually dipped in batter, deep fried and served with lemon wedges. Octopus, too, make their appearance on the *mezze* table, particularly on the Greek islands and Cyprus, where the sight of fishermen bashing them on the rocks is a familiar one. Mystically, and traditionally, ninety-nine times is the requisite number to render the poor creatures tender. They are then hung in the sun to dry for a day, before being slowly simmered – in their own juices – for two hours in a low oven. Only then are they ready for skinning, chopping into small pieces (tentacles and body – the ink sac having been removed before the bashing) to be cooked over a charcoal fire, served with olive oil and lemon. I quite like the slight chew of the octopus but many do not, so stick to the more tenderer squid to begin with. The smaller you can find them, the better. Incidentally, if you do buy octopus, even frozen it will require a preliminary beating – a rolling pin is most efficacious. And check to see that it has two rows of suckers on each tentacle – those from northern waters have only one, and really can be tough specimens.

Serves 6–8
1.4 kg (3 lb) squid
Maldon or sea salt
freshly ground black pepper
15–30 ml (1–2 tbsp) finely chopped fresh marjoram
90 ml (6 tbsp) olive oil
juice of 1 large lemon
2–3 garlic cloves, skinned and finely chopped

To clean the squid, stretch out the tentacles away from the body, grip them and pull hard. The head and insides of the squid will come cleanly away. Cut off the tentacles just above the head – keeping them, discarding the rest, including the ink sac. Slip the nib-like transparent bone out of the body, then rinse the body in cold running water – inside and out, rubbing off the pale pink thin membrane. Wash the tentacles. You will now have a pale translucent body with two little flaps (perfectly edible) and rose-coloured tentacles ready for cooking. The whole operation only takes 1–2 minutes, so don't be daunted.

Chop the body and tentacles into small rings and arrange on a grill pan with the grid removed. Sprinkle with salt, pepper and marjoram. Mix together the oil, lemon juice and chopped garlic and pour over. Grill, under a high heat, for 15–20 minutes until tender. Baby squid only take about 5 minutes. Then serve, with the pan juices poured over and crusty bread to mop them up.

SQUID STEWED IN WINE

Kalamária Kathista

Another squid favourite, particularly in Cyprus. Either red or white wine may be used – I prefer white for appearances' sake, but red gives a lovely gutsy flavour.

Serves 4–6
1.4 kg (3 lb) squid
60 ml (4 tbsp) olive oil
2–3 large onions, skinned and finely chopped
2–3 large garlic cloves, skinned and crushed
Maldon or sea salt
freshly ground black pepper
2½ cm (1 inch) piece cinnamon bark
pinch of sugar
300 ml (½ pint) dry white, or red, wine
45–60 ml (3–4 tbsp) finely chopped parsley

Clean the squid by pulling on the tentacles, then cut off just above the head, discarding the head and innards. Wash the body inside and out, and pull away the pinkish outer membrane. Rinse the tentacles. Chop everything into small rings.

Heat the olive oil, add the onions and fry gently for about 5 minutes. Add the squid and garlic and cook for a further 10 minutes until the onions are softened. Season, then add the cinnamon bark, sugar and wine. Bring to the boil, lower the heat and half cover the pan. Simmer gently for about 1 hour until the squid is quite tender and most of the liquid has been absorbed. Pile on a serving dish, with the pan juices poured over. Sprinkle on the parsley and cool to room temperature before serving.

DEEP-FRIED MUSSELS

Midye Tavasi

Istanbul, despite its ever-expanding girth, more new streets, more houses, more cars, is still utterly exotic. Nowhere else has quite such sharp contrasts between the old and the new, the silently peaceful and the chaotically noisy. The fish market, glorious as it is, is definitely the latter. The square which forms the wharfside – where the Bosporus comes to greet the Golden Horn – is crammed with people jostling to get near the beflagged fishing boats, themselves jostling to reach the wharf. There was also, the last time I was there, a quite frenetic bus terminus. The fishermen shout out their prices, the bus drivers their destinations: buyers haggle over both. Once bargains are struck, fish, suitcases, baskets and very oddly shaped parcels, appear to move in all directions with alarming speed. Sadly, long gone are the tiny makeshift eating-places where you could buy a few prawns, mussels, fish large or small, to be fried in front of you, eaten then with warm bread and a cool salad. This, one of the specialities, is simple to reproduce though. And excellent. A pint of mussels, incidentally, is equivalent to 450 g (1 lb).

Serves 6–8
For the batter
1 large egg
225 g (8 oz) plain flour

For the mussels
36 large mussels, about 3 pints
Maldon or sea salt
plain flour
olive oil, for deep frying
lemon juice

Make the batter first, by whisking the egg until frothy, then beating in 300 ml (½ pint) water, and gradually sifting in the flour, beating all the time. Leave to stand for 1 hour.

This gives you plenty of time to prepare the mussels. Nowadays, they can often be bought already cleaned, in which case I find a quick rinse in cold water, simply pulling on the little beard which protrudes from each shell, and discarding it, is enough. If they have not already been cleaned, you will have to scrub each one, under cold running water, to remove any barnacles, seaweed and, of course, the beards. Either way, any mussels that do not close quickly when tapped sharply should be thrown away, as should any that are broken or feel inordinately heavy for their size (these will probably be full of mud which will ruin the dish). Once the water is continually clear, with no sand or grit floating in it, the mussels are ready. Put them into a very large saucepan, pour over about 150 ml (¼ pint) of water and sprinkle with salt. Cover the pan and cook over a very high heat for about 5–7 minutes, shaking the pan every now and again. Once the mussels are opened, they can be removed from the pan (do this in batches as they open). Discard any that don't open. Drain the mussels on a clean tea towel and take out of their shells. All this can be done 2–3 hours in advance of the final cooking, but do not refrigerate or they will toughen.

Just before cooking, whisk the batter once more, roll the mussels lightly in the flour, then dip into the batter. Heat the oil in a deep-fat fryer or large sauce-pan, when it just begins to smoke carefully drop in a few mussels, 5–6 at once, no more, and cook for 1 minute, until golden and puffed up. Drain, cook the rest the same way, then serve, sprinkled with lemon juice and accompanied by *Teradot* (page 27) and a cucumber salad.

STUFFED MUSSELS

Midye Dolmasi

Though the picturesque sail-curtained cafés and their grander cousins under the Galata Bridge are now just a romantic memory, compensation can readily be found in the new truly elegant restaurants that have sprung up further out of town, across the bridge away from the old quarter of Istanbul. New they may be, but wonderfully decorated with intricately patterned tiles and fretwork in the style of the old palaces. And, adorned with antique enamel lamps and the carpets for which Turkey is so famous, they are a proud reminder of the glories of the Ottoman Empire. Glorious too are these mussels – plump with a sweet-spiced stuffing. Like many good things in life, they need time, for the preparation is fiddly. But the consolation is that they can be completed several hours ahead of serving.

Serves 6–8
36 large mussels, about 3 pints
30 ml (2 tbsp) olive oil
1 large onion, skinned and grated or minced
50 g (2 oz) pine nuts
2 small tomatoes, blanched, skinned, seeded and finely chopped
50 g (2 oz) currants
45 ml (3 tbsp) finely chopped parsley
5 ml (1 tsp) sugar
5 ml (1 tsp) ground allspice
5 ml (1 tsp) finely chopped fresh dillweed
Maldon or sea salt
freshly ground black pepper
50 g (2 oz) long grain rice
150 ml (¼ pint) fish stock
To serve finely chopped parsley (optional)
lemon wedges

Clean the mussels, scrubbing them if necessary, then pull off the beards and leave them to soak in fresh cold water. Heat the oil, add the onion and sauté for 3–4 minutes until softened. Add the pine nuts, toma-toes, currants, parsley, sugar and spices and cook for another 2 minutes. Then season fairly highly with salt and black pepper, add the rice and stir until all the grains are gleaming. Pour in the stock, or you can use water, bring to the boil, then simmer gently for about 10–15 minutes until the rice is almost cooked and the liquid absorbed. Cool.

Now, for the tricky bit. Put the mussels in a large bowl of cold water, have ready a clean large pan, some cotton and scissors. Using an oyster knife, or a stout, thick-bladed knife, slightly force open each mussel, loosening but not separating the two shells. I find the easiest way to do this, is to pick out a mussel from the bowl that is already slightly open – even inserting the knife blade between the shells before taking out of the water. That way, even if the mussel tries to shut immediately, at least the knife is in! Over the pan, force it open – any juices can then fall into the pan. Put a scant 5 ml (1 tsp) of stuffing into each mussel, then close the shell and tie with string. Arrange in the pan, side by side, making close-fitting layers. Add enough boiling water to just cover the mussels and simmer for about 15 minutes. Remove from the pan, arrange on a serving dish and cool to room temperature. Just before serving, snip the cotton, sprinkle with a little more chopped parsley if wished, and have plenty of lemon wedges. Very, very good.

DEEP-FRIED PRAWNS

Karidesli Tavasi

The huge prawns, so expensive in England (and even the Mediterranean now sadly, with ever-growing pollution) are abundant and cheap in Sri Lanka. Watching the catch coming in, I am reminded of the rush from the wharf on the Bosporus to those 'café-stalls'. In a matter of minutes, the prawns had been shelled, poached in sea water and quickly deep-fried. They tasted shockingly fresh – with a strong tang of the sea. Try to buy large, uncooked prawns – otherwise omit the poaching.

Serves 6
700 g–1 kg (1½–2¼ lb) large uncooked prawns
75 g (3 oz) salt
1 large egg, beaten
Maldon or sea salt
Freshly ground black pepper
plain flour
olive oil, for deep frying
To serve lemon wedges
Tarator Sade (page 25) or *Cousbareyah* (page 28)

Uncooked prawns will usually have been shelled, apart from the small tail piece. If you are buying unshelled ones, buy the larger quantity and shell them yourself: pull off the head, then the legs. This will leave the body shell which easily peels away. Leave the tail piece. De-vein. Bring a large pan of water – about 1 litre (1¼ pints) – to the boil, throw in the salt (this produces the nearest equivalent to sea water – the best method for boiling any shellfish), let it bubble again, then add the prawns and cook for about 4–6 minutes. Test when the tail shells start turning bright red – you don't want the prawns underdone or they'll be slushy; on the other hand overcooking will toughen them. Drain on absorbent kitchen paper.

Dip each prawn in the egg, then season with salt (lightly) and freshly ground black pepper, and coat with flour.

Bring a large pan of oil – a good 5 cm (2 inches) – to smoking point, then add a few prawns at a time and fry quickly until golden, about 2–3 minutes. Drain thoroughly and serve with lemon wedges and *Tarator Sade* (page 25), or *Cousbareyah* (page 28).

Following page (l–r): Cold Fish with Paprika (p. 55), Cumin-Spiced Prawns (p. 68) and Grilled Red Mullet (p. 52)

CUMIN-SPICED PRAWNS

Karidesli Kimyon

An adaptation of a *pilav* with prawns, given to me by a Turkish friend. I think, as he does, that it's better without the rice since you get the full impact of the spicy prawns. But *pilavs* are popular throughout Turkey and Greece, so if you want to make the prawns go further, add about 255 g (8 oz rice), a few tomatoes if you wish, and just over double the quantity of stock. Simmer for 10–15 minutes longer, until the rice has absorbed all the liquid.

Serves 4–6

700 g (1½ lb) prawns, unshelled weight
5 cm (2 inch) piece lemon zest
3–4 parsley sprigs
6 white peppercorns
few celery leaves
45 ml (3 tbsp) olive oil
Maldon or sea salt
1 large onion, skinned and finely chopped
3–4 garlic cloves, skinned and finely chopped
5 ml (1 tsp) cumin seeds, lightly crushed
pinch of sugar
pinch of cayenne pepper
freshly ground black pepper
30 ml (2 tbsp) finely chopped parsley
juice of ½–1 lemon

Shell the prawns, throwing the shells and heads into a large saucepan. Cover well with cold water, add the lemon zest, parsley sprigs, peppercorns and celery leaves. Bring to the boil and simmer for about 45 minutes. Strain, and measure out 225 ml (8 fl oz) of the stock and reserve it. (Keep the rest for making soup, unless of course you are cooking a *pilav*, in which case you'll need about 600 ml (1 pint) of liquid.

Fishing boats moored in the Ionian Islands.

Heat the oil in a large frying pan, add the prawns and sauté quickly, just to colour. Remove with a slotted spoon, and sprinkle generously with salt. Add the onion and garlic to the pan, cook gently for 10 minutes until the onion has softened. Scatter in the cumin seeds, a pinch each of sugar and cayenne pepper, and a good grinding of black pepper. Stir well, then pour in the reserved stock and add the prawns. Bring quickly to the boil, then simmer – on the lowest possible heat – for about 10 minutes until the liquid is considerably reduced.

Transfer to a serving plate, scatter over the parsley and lemon juice to taste. Allow to cool to room temperature before serving, and accompany with hot *Pittas* (page 146).

LOBSTER IN PAPRIKA OIL

Kırmızı Biberli İstakoz

The prize of the Bosporus is its lobster. Delicately sweet and succulent, and perfectly set off in this simple paprika oil dressing.

Serves 4–6
2 lobsters, preferably hen, each weighing about 700 g (1½ lb), not more as they can then be tough
175 g (6 oz) salt (optional)
175 ml (6 fl oz) olive oil
15–30 ml (1–2 tbsp) paprika
Maldon or sea salt
juice of 1 large lemon
To serve finely chopped parsley
lemon juice

If the lobsters are live, bring about 2.3 litres (4 pints) water to the boil, add the salt, then when rapidly boiling again, plunge the lobsters in, head first, then cook for about 15 minutes until bright red and the tail flesh is opaque. Take out of the pan and cool, laying the lobsters on their back so that a little of the liquid is retained in the shell, keeping the flesh succulent.

When cool, or if bought ready-cooked from the fishmonger, split the lobsters in two down the middle with a heavy cleaver – have the lobsters, shell side up, with their heads facing away from you. Then cut off and crack the claws with a sharp blow – keep these to a minimum, you want to be able to extract the flesh but not have too much cracked shell. Remove the little bag visible in the lobster's head – this is the stomach and must be discarded. Then pull out the long thin black vein running from the head to the tail. Now, all that is left which is inedible are the feathery gills which lie between the creamy coloured head meat and the small legs – these should be removed after scraping out the head meat and the liver (or tomally) which is greenish in colour and a great delicacy. The soft pale pink meat under the gills is also edible. All the rest of the flesh (and the coral or roe, if there is any) can now easily be taken out. Cut the large tail meat into pieces, then extract the sweet claw flesh. Mix all the meat together in a large shallow bowl, then whisk the oil with the paprika and a little salt and pour over the lobsters. Sprinkle with the juice of 1 lemon, and leave for 1 hour, turning the meat occasionally. Serve sprinkled with finely chopped parsley and extra lemon juice if you wish. Exquisitely simple but deceptively rich, so rice, or bread, and a plain salad should be the only accompaniments.

Fish Kebabs (p. 54).

EGGS

Baidh

Boil next the eggs, and smear them all in red;
With gold and silver let the wast *be spread.*
Now dust the lines with salt, yet not in haste,
But in appropriate measure, well to taste.

IBN AL-RUMI[1]

Eggs have long held an established place in the Arab kitchen. It is said that the ancient Phoenicians ate ostrich, and even pelican's, eggs but more usual today are hen's eggs – plentiful all over the Middle East. They are believed to symbolize the mystery of life, since they form a circle without an opening, and are often eaten at religious festivals, while egg dishes of one sort or another are nearly always served to break a fast. During the month-long fast of Ramadan, huge dishes of fried eggs and onions are prepared for the evening meal and the smell of the frying onions (which I adore) used to tantalisingly waft up to the verandah where I was trying to go to sleep on those hot summer nights. Even now, when I smell fried onions, I can see a dark blue sky, stars twinkling, and hear the crickets competing with the harsh, gutteral sounds of excited Arabic greetings as the evening meal was being prepared.

For picnics – a favourite Arab pastime – hard-boiled eggs were a must. Wonderfully flavoured, and often coloured by long slow cooking with onion skins, sometimes coffee grounds too, they would then be dipped into a variety of spices and seasonings. Often they had been cooked the day before – buried in a stew so that the dish's flavours had filtered through the egg shells, to give a myriad tastes. This method is also used for eggs that are to accompany stews – the eggs being peeled, once hard-boiled, and returned to the pan for a final few minutes' cooking.

Another important picnic-basket ingredient were the *eggahs*, or *iggahs* – Arab omelettes or egg cakes, rather similar to the Spanish *tortilla*. Whether the Moors took them to Spain, or brought them home again, nobody quite knows but almost every country has their own variation whilst the Persians – as so often in the realm of cuisine – have made them a speciality. The Lebanese too have a rather nice refinement: instead of making one whole *eggah*, to be cut into wedges, most households have a special frying-pan with 10 or 12 circular depressions into which the egg mixture is poured, thus enabling the cook to make individual *eggahs* for a number of people at one time. The Turks tend not to mix their eggs into the vegetable, herb, or meat bases but just to break them on top of the cooked mixture, for poaching and serving whole. This is not to say that they are not a picnic food – in the Middle East, picnics are a very serious affair. The whole family is involved, a little stove is taken, often, too, a huge container with a stew or dish of beans, just needing reheating and, of course, the coffee pot.

Whatever the occasion, whatever the method of cooking, eggs are not merely our breakfast-time 'scrambled, fried, soft-or-hard-boiled?' They are exotically transformed with garlic, mint, lemon, vinegar, yogurt, onions, tomatoes – into dishes to be savoured and relished at all times.

1. Died AD 896/283 Islamic calendar.

Verdant fields surrounded by desert – a typical North African scene.

© Philippe Ploquin

HAMINE EGGS

Baidh Hamine

This method of cooking eggs has been used all over the Middle East since time immemorial, and they are the traditional accompaniment to *Foul Medames* (page 143). Pale café-au-lait in colour with the yolks saffron-tinted and amazingly creamy in texture, people are disinclined to believe when you tell them the eggs have been simmered for as long as six hours. If you have a solid fuel stove, you can leave them on top overnight. And if you are in a real hurry, you *can* cheat and simmer for only two hours – although the result is not quite so creamy, or chestnutty in taste.

Serves 3–6
6 large eggs
the skins of 2–3 onions
coffee grounds (optional)
corn or olive oil

Put the eggs in a fairly deep saucepan into which they will fit quite snugly – if they have too much room to move around, you may find some of the shells splitting. I don't actually mind this since it gives a two-tone effect once the egg has been peeled. Tuck the onion skins in between the eggs (the Turks often add some coffee grounds as well – this produces somewhat darker eggs) and then cover well with cold water. Spoon a layer of oil over the surface, to prevent the water from drying out – do *not* forget to do this – and then cook, on the lowest possible heat for about six hours. Serve with *Foul Medames* (page 143). Lovely, too, dipped into fresh herbs.

HARD-BOILED EGGS WITH CUMIN

Baidh Masluq

A popular street snack in many countries of the Middle East – only the accompanying seasoning may vary. In Morocco they use cumin and salt; in Beirut I had them with cumin, salt and finely chopped fresh mint but I think my favourite was the Iraqi way with cumin and ground coriander – the sweetness of the coriander offsetting the bitter-sharp cumin.

Serves 3–6
6 eggs, hard boiled
15 ml (1 tbsp) Maldon or sea salt
30 ml (2 tbsp) cumin seeds
15 ml (1 tbsp) coriander seeds

Peel the eggs and halve or quarter. Put the salt in a small bowl, lightly crush the cumin seeds in a mortar, and grind the coriander to a coarse powder in a spice grinder, then mix the spices thoroughly with the salt. Either sprinkle over the eggs or let people dip the eggs into the mix.

FRIED, SPICED HARD-BOILED EGGS

Aijet Beythat

Another more refined version, dating from the medieval manuscript of al-Baghdadi, peels the hard-boiled eggs, then fries them in oil before rolling in spices. It uses coriander, cinnamon and cumin but when I was in Iraq they used cinnamon, cumin and turmeric – giving a mild curry flavour.

Serves 3–6
6 eggs, hard boiled
olive oil, for frying
15 ml (1 tbsp) ground cinnamon
30 ml (2 tbsp) cumin seeds, lightly crushed
15 ml (1 tbsp) ground turmeric
15 ml (1 tbsp) Maldon or sea salt
coarsely ground white pepper

Peel the eggs and, using a fine skewer (or large darning needle), prick them all over through to the yolks

– this lets the flavours seep through the eggs and also helps to stop the whites splitting. Just cover the bottom of a small frying pan with a film of oil and heat until not quite smoking. Add the eggs and cook gently for about 5–6 minutes, turning frequently, until golden brown all over.

Mix all the spices together with the salt and a fairly generous grinding of white pepper, then roll the eggs in the mixture while they are still hot. Serve as a *mezze* or with meat and vegetable stews.

DEEP-FRIED EGGS WITH MINT

Baidh ma' Na'na Muhammar

A popular lunch, especially in small Arab villages.

Serves 6
olive oil
6 eggs
fresh mint, finely chopped
fresh marjoram, finely chopped
12–18 spring onions, trimmed
Maldon or sea salt

Fill a large deep pan with the oil until it is about one-third full. Heat until not quite smoking. Break an egg into a saucer, and carefully slide into the pan, and then add the rest, one by one (this allows you to remove each one just as it sets – overcooking results in tough, leathery eggs). Cook for about two minutes until the whites are slightly golden at the edges and the yolks just firm. Remove with a slotted spoon and put on hot individual serving plates. Sprinkle generously with the mint and marjoram, put 2–3 spring onions on each plate, and scatter on a little salt. Serve at once with *Pitta* (page 146) and an assortment of pickled vegetables.

FRIED EGGS WITH LEMON AND GARLIC

Baidh bi Tom wa-Limoun

I had a young Palestinian nanny in Baghdad, whom I thought an angel. Unfortunately, she had a mother who was as demonic as I thought her daughter angelic. On her visits (which were frequent) she used to terrify me and wage continual war with the cook, whom she was convinced was determined to poison her. Finally, his patience ran out and he refused to let her in the kitchen or give her any food. Nothing daunted (and obviously well-prepared for this repeated ritual), she would set up her primus stove in a corner of the flat roof and for the rest of her stay, eat nothing but these eggs. Terror was overcome by curiosity – and the powerful aroma of frying garlic. I would creep upstairs and, sitting as far away as I decently could from that toothless old harridan, partake of the forbidden feast.

Serves 6
40 g (1½ oz) unsalted butter
3 garlic cloves, skinned and finely chopped
30–45 ml (2–3 tbsp) lemon juice
6 eggs
15 ml (1 tbsp) cumin seeds
freshly ground white pepper
salt

Melt the butter in a large frying pan and when barely bubbling, scatter in the garlic. Just as it's turning gold, stir in the lemon juice and then slide in the eggs. Fry them slowly for about 2 minutes until the yolks are set. Quickly grind the cumin in a spice grinder and sprinkle over the eggs, then serve with a good grinding of white pepper and a sprinkling of salt.

FRIED EGGS WITH CHEESE

Baidh bi Gibne

A popular dish all over the Middle East where it is usually served straight from the fire in the little double-handled frying-pan in which the eggs have been cooked. When making this dish for several people, I find it easier though to use one large frying pan. If you can't get the hard Greek cheeses Kasseri, Kephalotyri or the less dry but firm Hallumi, use slices of *Labneh* cheese – well dried out. Gruyère also makes a good substitute, as does a mature Cheddar.

Serves 6
350 g (12 oz) hard cheese
30–45 ml (2–3 tbsp) olive oil or butter
6 eggs
Maldon or sea salt
freshly ground black pepper
cayenne pepper or ground cinnamon

Cut the cheese into six slices. Pour just enough oil to cover the surface of a frying pan large enough to hold the cheese slices snugly and heat until just smoking. Arrange the cheese in one layer and cook for a few minutes until it begins to melt at the edges and bubble, then quickly break an egg over each slice of cheese. Cook for another 2–3 minutes until the eggs are set to your liking. Sprinkle with salt, black pepper and a pinch of cayenne or ground cinnamon. Lightly cut through the whites and cheese with the edge of a fish slice, and serve at once. Some cooks also prick the yolks with a fine skewer to let them spill out over the whites: unless cooking the eggs individually, do this after putting them on the plates.

POACHED EGGS ON YOGURT

Yumurta Çilbir

A surprisingly good combination of eggs with yogurt from Turkey. Although always decorated with paprika in melted butter, the yogurt base often varies from family to family. Some add vinegar instead of lemon juice; some add neither. A little dried mint is liked by some cooks, a pinch of ground cumin by others. So please yourself: I sometimes like a touch of grated root ginger, and fresh tarragon is lovely in the summer.

Serves 6
450 ml (¾ pint) natural yogurt
2–3 garlic cloves, skinned and finely chopped
Maldon or sea salt
juice of 1 lemon
10 ml (2 tsp) white wine vinegar
6 eggs
40 g (1½ oz) unsalted butter
15 ml (1 heaped tbsp) paprika

Beat the yogurt with the garlic cloves and a good pinch of salt, then whisk in the lemon juice and divide between six small bowls. Bring a large pan of water to the boil, and quickly dip in each egg, unshelled, for 20 seconds (hold in a ladle or sieve). This will help prevent the whites from running all over the place when you poach the eggs.

Bring another pan of water – preferably a wide shallow one, a *sauteuse* is ideal – to the boil. Whisk in the vinegar, then break the eggs gently into the pan; don't attempt to cook more than three at once, absolute maximum. Whatever anyone says, poaching eggs is a fine art, which can very easily turn to disaster. If time is of the essence, then use two pans – but not an egg-poaching mould. The whites come out too thick, the eggs look as if they have come off a production line.

Let the water bubble once, then take the pan off the heat, cover and leave for 3–4 minutes, depending on how set you like your eggs. While they are setting, melt the butter in a small saucepan and, when just beginning to sizzle, stir in the paprika. The butter should be tinged quite a deep red, so add a little extra paprika if need be.

Drain the eggs with a slotted spoon, put one into each bowl, and drizzle the butter over each egg in a zig-zag pattern.

GREEN BEAN EGG PIE

Eggah bi Ful

Eggahs, or *iggahs*, are Arabian omelettes. Not the delicate, creamy, pan-to-table omelettes of the French kitchen, but a more solid egg pie omelette, crammed with vegetables, herbs, meat, brains – anything to hand really – and served cut in wedges like a cake. Ideal for the *mezze* table and perfect for picnics and the pilgrimages which are a ritual of the many religious and national holidays, since they can be cooked and left to cool, or even reheated if wished. The sight of bands of pilgrims on their way to Mecca stopping by the wayside and warming up *eggahs* on their little primus stoves was not an uncommon one during my childhood. Nowadays, sophistication has set in and there are special charter flights to the Holy City. The form of travel may have changed; the diet has not, and in nearly every person's hand baggage will be a foil-wrapped bundle – containing two or three *eggahs* to sustain them on the journey. This one was a favourite in Iraq, where green beans grew prolifically – and had to be picked every day, just as the sun was up, while they were still relatively small and tender. For by nightfall, they had almost doubled in size, so fast was their growth rate. In Egypt fresh broad beans would be used instead.

Serves 6
about 350 g (12 oz) fresh green beans, topped and tailed
6 eggs
salt and freshly ground black pepper
good pinch of turmeric

1–2 garlic cloves, skinned and finely chopped
30–45 ml (2–3 tbsp) finely chopped chervil
25–40 g (1–1½ oz) unsalted butter or oil

Cut the beans into 2½ cm (1 inch) lengths, drop into a pan of boiling water and cook until just tender, about 5–15 minutes depending on the freshness and age of the beans. I wouldn't recommend using frozen beans – the texture is wrong, and the end result, to me at any rate, falls short of delicious. (This doesn't apply to broad beans – frozen are fine.) Drain and refresh under cold running water.

Beat the eggs in a large bowl, season with salt and pepper and a pinch of turmeric. Mix the garlic into the beans, then add the beans and chervil to the eggs. Melt the butter in a large frying-pan and just as it starts to sizzle, pour in the egg and bean mixture. Cover the pan and cook, slowly, for about 15–20 minutes until the eggs are set with just a thin film of liquid on top. If you are used to making *tortillas*, put a large plate on top of the pan and invert quickly, then return the omelette to the pan and cook, over a slightly higher heat, to brown the bottom. An easier method is to put the pan under a hot grill for 1 minute or so until nicely golden. Cut into wedges, or small pieces, and serve hot or cold.

ONION EGG PIE

Ajja

Another *eggah* popular in Iraq. In Egypt, leeks would probably be substituted, with the addition of a little lemon juice. In the Lebanon, courgettes are a favourite, sometimes with ground cinnamon or paprika added.

Serves 4–6
2 large onions skinned
small bunch of parsley finely chopped
6 eggs
salt and freshly ground white pepper
pinch of ground ginger (optional)
45–60 ml (3–4 tbsp) olive oil

Either put the onions through a mincer or grate them (a food processor makes this simple), then mix with the parsley. Beat the eggs and add to the onions and parsley. Season with salt and a generous grinding of white pepper and add ginger if using (this is not strictly traditional, but our cook always used it – and I like the 'bite' it gives).

Heat the oil in a large frying pan, pour in the egg mixture and cook, covered, for about 20–25 minutes until firm. Either invert and return to the pan (in which case you may need the extra oil) or place under a hot grill to golden. Eat hot or cold.

POTATO AND TOMATO EGG PIE

Batata wa Tomatim Eggah

The tomatoes we grew in Iraq were enormous – even bigger than beef steak tomatoes. Combined with potatoes and spring onions, they made this a favourite *eggah*. In Persia, they mash the potatoes, omit the tomatoes and add a bunch of finely chopped chives.

Serves 4–6
50–60 g (2–2½ oz) unsalted butter
2 large potatoes, finely sliced
1 bunch spring onions, trimmed and chopped into rings
2 large beef steak tomatoes, finely sliced
3 large garlic cloves, skinned and crushed
6 cardamom pods
salt and freshly ground black pepper
6 large eggs
To garnish 45 ml (3 tbsp) finely chopped parsley

Previous page (l–r): Potato and Tomato Egg Pie (above), Hard-boiled Eggs with Cumin (top, p. 72), Green Bean Egg Pie (p. 75), Fried, Spiced Hard-boiled Eggs (p. 72).

Melt 60 ml (4 tbsp) butter in a large frying pan, add the potatoes and gently fry for about 5 minutes on each side until softened. Add the remaining butter if necessary, then the onions, tomatoes and garlic. Mix everything together, then cook for another 10 minutes, stirring occasionally to prevent sticking.

Crush the cardamom pods, remove the seeds and pound in a pestle and mortar, then add to the pan and season with salt and freshly ground black pepper. Beat the eggs until frothy, then stir them into the pan, whisking around well. Cook slowly for about 15–20 minutes until nearly set, then place under a hot grill until golden. Sprinkle with the chopped parsley and serve cut into wedges.

MEAT EGG PIE

Eggah bi Lahma

Meat *eggahs* are popular all over the Middle East. Lamb is the favoured meat but you can use beef as well. Again the vegetables and herbs vary according to what is in season, and from country to country.

Serves 4–6
30 ml (2 tbsp) olive oil
1 large onion, skinned and finely chopped
2 garlic cloves, skinned and crushed
400 g (14 oz) minced lamb or beef
small handful fresh coriander leaves, finely chopped
5 ml (1 tsp) freshly ground allspice
salt and freshly ground black pepper
6 large eggs
40–50 g (1½–2 oz) unsalted butter
To serve a bowl of yogurt

Heat the oil in a frying pan, add the onion and sauté gently for 5 minutes until softened. Add the garlic and cook for another 2 minutes, then stir in the meat and fry until browned all over. Tip into a bowl, and stir in the coriander, allspice, salt and pepper. Beat the eggs until frothy, then blend into the meat.

Rinse and dry the frying pan and return to the

heat. Melt the butter until just beginning to sizzle, then pour in the egg mixture and cook, covered, for about 20–25 minutes, slowly, until almost set. Pop under a very hot grill until golden on top. Accompany with a bowl of yogurt.

SPICY SAUSAGE EGG PIE

Ojja bil Merguez

In Tunisia they add a highly spiced sausage and dried chillies to the *eggah*, and often stir the eggs until set –

almost like rather firm scrambled eggs. You can also break the eggs whole in the centre of the pan, leaving the *merguez* sauce around the edges, but in this case you must eat the *ojja* hot. Substitute spicy Greek or Italian sausages if *merguez* is unobtainable. I have also used a *chorizo* (the spicy version) very successfully, but then add it with the eggs since it only needs heating up, not cooking.

Serves 4–6
45–60 ml (3–4 tbsp) olive oil
3 large garlic cloves, skinned and crushed
3 medium potatoes, cut into tiny dice
2–3 dried red chillies, seeded and coarsely
    chopped
30 ml (2 tbsp) tomato purée
15 ml (1 tbsp) caraway seeds

Dried fruit market.

© Philippe Ploquin

5 ml (1 tsp) *Harissa* (page 30)
5 ml (1 tsp) paprika
5–6 *merguez* (see page 156), cut into thick slices
Maldon or sea salt
6 large eggs

Fry the garlic for 1–2 minutes in the oil, then add the potatoes and the chopped chillies and gently fry for a further 10 minutes. Stir in the tomato purée, caraway, *Harissa* and paprika, add water just to cover and stew slowly for about 30–40 minutes. Add the sausages and cook for another 15 minutes.

Beat the eggs, then pour into the pan, stirring to mix. Either continue stirring until firmly set but still creamy, or leave to set as if cooking an *eggah*. Serve hot if you have stirred the eggs, warm or cold if not.

HERB AND VEGETABLE EGG PIE

Kuku Sabzy – I

The *kuku* or *kukuye* is the Persian version of the *eggah*. True to Persian perfection, it has been refined to great heights, particularly the herb and vegetable *kuku*, which traditionally appears on the New Year table – the intense greenness symbolising new life in the year to come. *Kuku* are usually baked in the oven in a large rectangular dish, and make their appearance at almost every meal, cut into small squares as a *mezze* or into long, thin strips as a first course or side dish. The vegetables and herbs can be varied depending on what is in season – their freshness and greenness are the essence.

Serves 6 as a first course
225 g (8 oz) fresh spinach, or chard
3 thin leeks
1 small bunch spring onions
45 ml (3 tbsp) finely chopped parsley
30 ml (2 tbsp) of at least three of the following,
    finely chopped:
        fresh coriander leaves
        fresh dillweed
        fresh tarragon
        fresh chives
        fresh chervil
        cos lettuce leaves
salt and freshly ground black pepper
30 ml (2 tbsp) walnuts, chopped (optional)
8 eggs
40–50 g (1½–2 oz) unsalted butter
To serve a bowl of yogurt

Wash and shake dry the spinach, then chop finely, discarding any thick stems. (Chard is popular in Persia but is hard to find in the West unless you grow it yourself – a sad lack, in my opinion.) Trim the leeks, and chop into thin rings. Do the same with the spring onions, using as much as possible of the green tops. Mix together the vegetables with all the herbs, season with salt and pepper then fold in the walnuts if using – they give an interesting texture.

Beat the eggs until frothy, then whisk into the herbs. Liberally grease an ovenproof dish and pour in the egg mixture. Bake in the oven at 180°C (350°F), mark 4, for 45 minutes to 1 hour, until firmly set. Cover the dish for the first 30 minutes, then remove the cover to allow the top to colour. Served both hot or cold, but always with a bowl of yogurt.

WALNUT AND CHIVE EGG PIE

Kuku Sabzy – II

A nuttier, yet more delicate, version of the traditional herb *kuku*, given to me by a Persian friend one New Year's Day in London. Do not be tempted to increase the saffron – too much will turn that delicate honey flavour into a bitter horror.

Serves 4

2 saffron strands
a good handful of chives, finely snipped
a good handful of parsley, finely chopped
45 ml (3 tbsp) fresh coriander leaves, finely chopped
25 g (1 oz) sultanas
50 g (2 oz) chopped walnuts
6 eggs
salt and freshly ground black pepper
25–40 g (1–1½ oz) unsalted butter

Put the saffron strands into a small metal dish, then under a very hot grill for just under a minute. Crumble lightly, then pour over 15 ml (1 tbsp) boiling water and leave for 5 minutes. Mix together the herbs, sultanas and walnuts, then beat the eggs until frothy and whisk into the herbs. Add the saffron and its water, season with salt and black pepper. Grease an ovenproof dish generously, pour in the eggs and cook, covered for the first 15–20 minutes, in the oven at 180°C (350°F), mark 4, for 30–40 minutes until set. Good hot or cold.

AUBERGINE EGG PIE

Kuku Bademjan

Also made as an *eggah* in other countries of the Middle East, where the tomatoes and saffron would be omitted.

Serves 4–6

2 medium aubergines
salt
2 strands saffron
45 ml (3 tbsp) olive oil
1 large tomato, finely sliced
1 small onion, skinned and finely chopped
1–2 garlic cloves, skinned and crushed
30 ml (2 tbsp) finely chopped fresh dillweed
freshly ground black pepper
6 large eggs

Cut the aubergines into chunks, put on a large plate and sprinkle liberally with salt. Leave for at least 30 minutes, then rinse under cold running water to remove the bitter juices which will have risen to the surface. While the aubergines are standing heat the saffron strands under a hot grill, lightly crush, then cover with 15 ml (1 tbsp) boiling water.

Heat the oil in a large frying pan, add the aubergines, tomato, onion and garlic cloves and sauté gently for about 5 minutes, then stir in the saffron, dillweed and season with salt and black pepper. Generously grease an ovenproof dish, mix the eggs into the vegetable mixture and pour into the dish. Cook for about 45 minutes, covered for the first 20 minutes, in the oven at 180C (350°F), mark 4, until set. Leave to cool in the dish, then turn out and cut into small squares or long strips. Serve with yogurt.

MEAT

Laham

Strips of tender meat in slices,
Dipped in oil of finest make,
Tempt anew the flagging palate,
And the appetite awake.

MAHMUD IBN AL-HUSAIN AL-KUSHAJIM[1]

Throughout the whole of this vast region, the word meat is nearly always synonymous with mutton. True, you may be asked 'sheep mutton or goat mutton'? Goat mutton may even be the better choice, but mutton it will be. Anything else and it will usually be specified – and it will usually be lamb, apart from a few pork dishes in Greece and Cyprus. Lamb, or kid, roasted whole, are of course the traditional festive dishes: in Greece, at Easter, when the new young spring lamb is anticipated weeks ahead with much excitement and preparation. Elsewhere, whenever there is cause to celebrate – although occasionally a young gazelle, locally caught, may form the centrepiece of a desert banquet. But for centuries, sheep and goats have happily munched and foraged on the lightly-grassed hillsides and barren mountain tops, leaving the fertile valleys free for cultivation of vegetables. Nowadays, with more land reclaimed with sophisticated irrigation schemes, beef and veal[2] are becoming popular but they will still be cooked according to recipes unchanged through the ages, and lamb certainly still dominates the kitchen.

Since much of this lamb is certainly of an age to be legitimately classed as mutton, but without the advantages of a luscious living, the Middle Eastern cuisine has evolved a number of ways to produce an enormous range of dishes beautifully tender in texture and incredibly varied in flavour. Faced with this one, often very tough, basic ingredient in the meat larder, the ingenuity and the imagination of cooks throughout history, have combined with the multitude of exotic spices and seasonings of the area, to create a spectrum of tastes almost unrivalled in the world.

The methods used to achieve the requisite tenderness are twofold – both very simple. First, the meat is cut into very small pieces, and then it is marinated, sometimes for as long as 24 hours. Let not such simplicity be scorned however. For in these two steps the experience of centuries has been absorbed, refined and polished to great heights. I can remember peeking through my mosquito net (ostensibly safely napping) to the courtyard below where the cook was making his evening preparations. The swish of his long, thin knife – slightly curved at the end – as he honed it on the steel gates, signalled the beginning of his performance. For performance it was. The carcass hanging on a large hook, he would deftly flick the knife across it – a large, fine slice of meat fell on the stone table below. In seconds, it was in long, thin ribbons. Then, moving to the other side of the table, a few more slashes had produced a mound of perfectly even-sized cubes. Minutes later, the carcass was a skeleton. Nerve-wracking – but irresistible – to watch, and I would anxiously check at the finish that he still had all the fingers of his left hand.

The second part of the operation was dull by a child's ghoulish standards, and it was only in latter years that marinades – with all their versatility and glorious combinations – began to fascinate. Olive oil, 'of finest make' of course, was the first necessity. After that, each country, each cook had – and has – their own idiosyncratic additions.

There is a further refinement in the preparation of meat which must be mentioned, since it forms a large – and supremely delicious – part of the Arab table. The meat, once cut, is minced and then pounded to a fine pasty mixture before being formed into small rissoles or patties. Forget though the grey-brown mess of school dinners, the thin breadcrumb-laden slabs that masquerade as beefburgers in Western supermarkets. The meatballs that come out of the Arab kitchen are succulent and tender, sweetly spiced, often subtly sauced, and infinite in their variety.

1. *Astrologer, poet and court advisor on food to Saif al-Daula; lived AD 915–967/303–356 Islamic calendar.*
2. *Veal is mentioned, once, as an alternative to 'meat' in al-Baghdadi's book.*

GRILLED MEAT ON A SKEWER

Şiş Kebab

Şiş kebabs (pronounced *shish*) are the kebabs most familiar to us in the West. In fact we have adopted the word *kebab* to mean anything put on a skewer and grilled, particularly over a barbecue. Whereas, *kebab* in Turkish merely means 'cooked meat' and it is *şiş* that is the skewer. The style of cooking undoubtedly

was born with the bands of nomadic tribes, constantly pushed westwards across the plateaus from Lake Baykal towards Turkey. Precious fighting time could not be lost to the indulgences of *haute cuisine*, yet fighting, and fleeing, was hungry work. So they merely slew whatever animals they came across – usually sheep, cut up the carcasses, impaling the meat on their swords, then cooked it over the camp fire. Through the years, such refinements as marinades, herbs, spices and even vegetables have been added but it is still undoubtedly agreed that for the best flavour the skewers should be grilled over a wood or charcoal fire. The essence of simplicity has not been lost.

Today, this is a dish found all over Greece and Turkey – the subtle differences lie in the marinade seasonings. The recipe below uses a Greek marinade, the two following variations are Turkish.

Serves 4–6
900 g (2 lb) lean lamb, either fillet or boned leg
For the marinade
150 ml (¼ pint) olive oil
30–45 (2–3 tbsp) lemon juice
1 large onion skinned (optional)
15 ml (1 tbsp) rigani or oregano
3 bay leaves, crumbled
5 ml (1 tsp) black peppercorns, crushed
Maldon or sea salt

Cut the meat into small cubes, removing any fat or tough sinews. Mix the oil with the lemon juice in a large bowl, then grate the onion into the bowl if using – some Greeks do, some don't (I like it). Add the rigani, bay leaves and peppercorns then mix in the meat and stir well. Leave covered for at least two hours – in Persia they let it stand for 12 hours, which makes the meat meltingly tender.

To cook, drain the meat and thread on skewers, then put under a hot grill (or over a hot charcoal or wood fire – make sure it's neither flaming nor smoking) for about 7–10 minutes, constantly turning and basting with the marinade. The meat will be done when it is brown and crusty on the outside but still just pink in the middle. Sprinkle with salt, extra lemon if you wish, then serve with *Pitta* (page 146), cucumber and tomato salads.

TURKISH MARINADED KEBABS

Şiş Kebab – II

In Turkey, sweet cinnamon is preferred to the pungent rigani, and paprika is sometimes added as well. Lemon juice is optional while the onion is usually grated and then sieved – just to extract the juice.

Serves 4–6
900 g (2 lb) lean lamb
For the marinade
150 ml (¼ pint) olive oil
juice of 1 large onion
juice of 1 lemon (optional)
5–10 ml (1–2 tsp) ground cinnamon
5 ml (1 tsp) paprika (optional)
5 ml (1 tsp) black peppercorns, crushed

Mix all the marinade ingredients, excepting the salt, with the meat in a large bowl and leave, covered, for 2–12 hours. Cook as for *Şiş Kebab* (page 83), then serve with a sprinkling of salt, lemon wedges to garnish, on a bed of finely chopped parsley.

TURKISH YOGURT MARINADED KEBABS

Şiş Kebab – III

Although not traditional, I also like using this for firm white fish such as cod steaks or monkfish.

Serves 4–6
900 g (2 lb) lean lamb or firm white fish

For the marinade
60 ml (4 tbsp) olive oil
300 ml (½ pint) natural yogurt
juice of 1 medium onion
5 ml (1 tsp) black peppercorns, crushed
5 ml (1 tsp) cumin seeds, crushed (optional)
10 ml (2 tsp) paprika (optional)
Maldon or sea salt
To garnish chopped parsley or dried mint

Mix together the oil, yogurt, onion juice and black peppercorns. Add either the cumin seeds or paprika, then stir in the meat (or fish) and leave for 2–12 hours. Cook in the usual way, sprinkling with salt before serving with *Pitta* (page 146) and a cucumber salad. Garnish the salad with chopped parsley or dried mint.

MEAT AND VEGETABLES ON A SKEWER

Şaşlik

Pronounced 'shashlick', this is a very popular dish in Turkey. It's more substantial than the plain *şiş kebab* but for the *mezze* table you can make a miniature version by chopping the meat and vegetables into quite small pieces, using cherry tomatoes if possible, but nice firm ones. The only disadvantage, to my mind, to this dish is that the tomatoes cook quicker than the onions or peppers, which obviously will still be fairly crunchy. But it is delicious. One other point, onions quartered will be difficult to thread on the skewers, so cut them into five by cutting each curved side off, leaving a square central core.

Serves 6–8
900 g (2 lb) lamb, cubed
marinade (either of the previous two)
4 small tomatoes, quartered
4 small onions, skinned and cut into 5 pieces

1 large green pepper, seeded and cut into 16
   pieces
175 g (6 oz) button mushrooms
salt and freshly ground black pepper
To serve lemon wedges
onion slices

Marinade the meat in whichever marinade you prefer
– traditionally it would be an oil and lemon juice one.
Then thread the meat on skewers, alternating each
piece with a vegetable, dispersing the vegetables as
evenly as possible. You may have a few pieces of
onion left over – these are cook's perks in my house,
otherwise give them to onion lovers.

Baste with the marinade and cook under a hot
grill for 7–10 minutes, then sprinkle with salt and
freshly ground black pepper. Serve with lemon
wedges, slices of raw onion and a cucumber and
tomato salad.

THE REVOLVING
KEBAB

Döner Kebab

All over Turkey there are small eating places, with just
a few bare tables, and the huge vertical spit with an
apparently enormous hunk of meat slowly, but
endlessly, revolving around a three-sided charcoal fire.
Dön means to 'turn around', hence the name for what
is now a familiar sight in the West, and a food that we
take very much for granted. But it takes a great deal of
expertise to prepare this outlandish sausage, and it is a
technique I find fascinating although I have not yet
been brave enough to try it. I was sorely tempted one
day, after a demonstration in a small Turkish restaurant in London. Like all experts, they made it look so
dreadfully simple but I'm afraid reality set in once
back in my own kitchen. However, for those fearless
cooks who wish to try it, an ordinary rôtisserie spit
can be used (although the meat will take longer to
cook), and I think it is interesting anyway to see how

the Turks have evolved the *kebab* into this difficult but
particularly delicious dish. The meat from the
hindquarters of the lamb (the loin and chump chops
in English butchery) is cut into long, fine strips, all fat
and tough sinews removed, then pounded until almost
paper-thin and marinated for 24 hours in oil, milk,
lemon and finely sliced onions. After draining, each
slice is spread with warm lamb fat and then (this is the
tricky bit) tightly wound round an enormous skewer,
beginning at the middle, then up to each end, strip by
strip building up that huge sausage, enormously fat in
the centre and tapering off at each end, the whole
being continually pressed, then trimmed at the finish
to make a smooth and neat shape. The spit is fixed
vertically in front of a three-sided, many-tiered charcoal brazier to begin its perpetual pirouette. As the
meat on the outside becomes crusty and browned, it is
carved off, to be eaten instantly with fresh mint or
parsley, *raki* of course, while the rest continues its
slow dance, the next customers impatiently waiting.
Until nothing is left.

In Syria, there is a dish similarly made with veal.
Called *shawmirmah*, the meat is marinated in a huge
range of spices, including fenugreek, cardamom,
coriander, mastic and often a whole head – or two –
of garlic.

MINCED MEAT

Kofta

Here, in *köfte*, minced meat rissoles or meatballs,
grilled or fried, steamed or poached, have the Arabs
displayed their greatest inventiveness in transforming
the otherwise tough and inedible into a supreme delicacy. Despite the same basic recipe, the ways of
preparing them are legion. Once, when I had tasted
seven – very different – *köfte* in as many days, I asked
'How many *köfte* are there?' Our cook, who was a
poetic soul and devoured Arabic poetry much as I
devoured his food, replied 'They are as numerous as
the stars in the firmament'. It became my favourite
phrase for weeks thereafter.

I am still discovering new variations, and I have given a goodly number below, not only because I think they are delicious but they are simple to make, requiring only time (and even that is banished if you have a food processor), a decently stocked spice cupboard and a little imagination. Lamb is the meat usually used but all are equally good with beef, or a mixture of both. Veal is sometimes used in Syria, although it seems a little extravagant when it is so expensive in England but pork could well be substituted – though this would of course be forbidden in the Middle East. Of paramount importance to the tenderness and succulence of this dish, is the texture of the meat. You must pound it until absolutely pasty – in a food processor this takes a matter of minutes. Otherwise, put the meat through a mincer even if you buy it already minced, at least once, if not twice, then bash it with a wooden spoon against the sides of a large bowl until you have a really pasty mass (I know this sounds rather horrid but it is descriptive, and you will be rewarded with the glorious smell of the spices, and the delicious end result). Keep your hands wetted with cold water while forming the rissoles, for the minimum of mess and the neatest of shapes. And if you flatten them into beefburgers, even the most timid of children (gastronomically, that is) will eat them – and ask for more. Keep the seasonings simple at first, then experiment to find those you like best.

Serves 6
900 g (2 lb) lamb, beef or a mixture, minced and
    pounded
2 large onions, skinned and minced or grated
salt and freshly ground white or black pepper
5 ml (1 tsp) ground cinnamon
    plus 5 ml (1 tsp) paprika
OR 5 ml (1 tsp) cumin seeds, crushed
    plus 5 ml (1 tsp) ground allspice or dried mint
OR 5 ml (1 tsp) coriander seeds, ground
    plus 30 ml (2 tbsp) finely chopped parsley
1–2 garlic cloves, skinned and crushed or finely
    chopped
To serve *Pittas* (page 146)
chopped parsley
lemon wedges

Mix everything together in a large bowl, having pounded the meat first. Or whizz the meat in a food processor, then add the onion and spices of your choice (white pepper will give a slightly spicier taste than black), and whizz again. Form the meat into small balls and thread on a skewer (the flat-edged type are best) or shape like a sausage round the skewers. Lightly oil the grill grid or barbecue grid to avoid the meat sticking, then cook under a high heat (non-smoking, glowing barbecue) for about 4–7 minutes until nicely browned and crisp on the outside but still tender and juicy within. Serve tucked into warm *pittas*, with chopped parsley, lemon wedges and a selection of salads.

SPINACH AND LAMB MEATBALLS

Kufta Isbanish Kharouf

Spinach, or chard, is a much loved vegetable in Iraq, Persia and Syria. I have also used fresh beetroot tops very successfully as a substitute, but fresh is the word.

Serves 4–6
700 g (1½ lb) fresh spinach
700 g (1½ lb) lamb, minced and pounded
2 slices of white bread, crusts removed
2 eggs, beaten
salt and freshly ground white pepper
1½ ml (¼ tsp) ground fenugreek
5 ml (1 tsp) freshly ground allspice
60 ml (4 tbsp) olive oil
juice of 1 large lemon
juice of 2 limes

Wash and trim the spinach, then cook until softened in a large pan with 30 ml (2 tbsp) of water to prevent sticking. Drain, chop and mix with the meat. Soak the bread in cold water for 5 minutes, then squeeze dry, crumble and pound well into the meat mixture. Beat in the eggs and seasonings until pasty, then form into small balls or, as our cook used to do, long slender fingers.

Heat 45 ml (3 tbsp) oil in a frying pan, add the meatballs and cook for 3–4 minutes until browned all over. Drain the pan of the used oil, add the remaining fresh oil, the lemon and lime juice and enough water to not quite cover the meatballs, about 100–150 ml (4–5 fl oz). Bring quickly to the boil, then simmer very gently, covered, for about 10 minutes, until the liquid is absorbed and the meat is quite tender.

MEATBALLS WITH PINE NUTS AND TOMATOES

Daoud Pasha

Pine nuts, with their sweet, delicate flavour, are much loved, and much used, in Syria. Meatballs stuffed with these nuts were a firm family favourite when we were in Damascus, where they were cooked, unusually, in the northern Syrian fashion – in the oven. When we moved to Kirkuk, in the north of Iraq, their sudden absence from the menu was loudly – and somewhat unreasonably – lamented by me. For Kirkuk, although spectacular in its 'burning fiery furnace'[1] into which King Nebuchadnezzar threw Meshach, Shadrach and Abednego, had little to offer in the way of food, except, surprisingly enough, tomatoes. Our cook made wonderful sauces from these, particularly for meatballs, which I had to concede were very good, but . . . Then, the blissful day arrived. Visitors from Aleppo, bearing gifts – of pine nuts. I later discovered that this marriage of pine nuts, tomato sauce and meatballs was a traditional dish of the Lebanon as well as Egypt, although tomato purée is used rather than whole tomatoes. For me, however, the dish will forever be Kirkuk.

1. The effect of the 'fiery furnace' is actually produced by the gases, escaping from the oil wells below, igniting on contact with the air. There is a slight gap between the earth and the flames – giving the impression that the fires are burning in mid-air. Although we were obviously some miles away, it was a dramatic spectacle – and visible from most of the windows of our house.

Serves 6

75 ml (5 tbsp) olive oil
100 g (4 oz) pine nuts
900 g (2 lb) lamb or beef, minced and pounded
1 large onion, skinned and grated or minced
60 ml (4 tbsp) finely chopped parsley
5 ml (1 tsp) freshly ground allspice
2½ ml (½ tsp) ground ginger
Maldon or sea salt
freshly ground white pepper
1 large beef steak tomato, or 225 g (8 oz) plum
    tomatoes, or 60–75 ml (4–5 tbsp) tomato purée
pinch of sugar
juice of 1 lemon

Heat 30 ml (2 tbsp) oil in a frying pan, add the pine nuts and sauté gently for 2–3 minutes until they turn golden-pink. Drain. Mix the meat with onion, parsley, allspice, ginger, a good pinch or two of salt, and freshly ground white pepper, until quite pasty. Form into balls a bit smaller than a small egg, then push your finger through to the centre of each one, moving it around a little in the middle to make a pocket. Pour a scant 5 ml (1 small tsp) pine nuts into each cavity, then firmly close the meat up again. (If wished, reserve some pine nuts so that each meatball can be garnished with one stuck into the top, after cooking).

Heat the remaining oil, until nearly smoking, then cook the meatballs for 4–5 minutes until browned all over. While they are cooking, blanch the tomato or tomatoes (if you can, get fresh plum tomatoes – or use canned ones, and weigh them after draining), then blend to a purée with about 30 ml (2 tbsp) water. When the meatballs are cooked, add the tomato purée to the pan, with a pinch of sugar and half the lemon juice. Add a little more water to the pan if necessary to come just about level with the meatballs, then season lightly and simmer gently for about 15–20 minutes until the sauce has been absorbed. Add another spoonful of water or so, if the sauce evaporates too quickly. Sprinkle over the extra lemon juice, and a bit more chopped parsley if you wish. Traditionally served hot, with rice, but very good cold.

MEATBALLS WITH YOGURT

Khoreshe Mast

From Persia, subtly spiced meatballs, in a creamy yogurt sauce delicately tinged with saffron.

Serves 6

800 g (1¾ lb) lamb, minced and pounded
2 large onions, skinned
salt and freshly ground black pepper
5 ml (1 tsp) dried dillweed
large pinch of ground fenugreek
45 ml (3 tbsp) olive oil
8 cardamom pods
10 ml (2 tsp) cumin seeds
10 ml (2 tsp) coriander seeds
6 whole cloves
5 cm (2 inch) piece cinnamon bark
3 saffron strands
juice of 1 lime
175 ml (6 fl oz) natural yogurt
2½ ml (½ tsp) cornflour

Put the meat into a large bowl, then add one of the onions, either grated or minced. Season fairly highly with salt and freshly ground black pepper, add the dillweed and fenugreek and mix thoroughly. Form into small meatballs and keep aside. Heat the olive oil in a frying pan, meanwhile grind the spices – having taken the cardamom seeds out of their pods – then add to the pan and cook for about 1 minute until they start to smell aromatic. Slice the remaining onion finely and add to the pan. Let it fry for 6–7 minutes until softened.

Crumble the saffron strands into a measuring jug, then pour on 175 ml (6 fl oz) boiling water and let it stand for 5 minutes. When the onions are soft, add the meatballs to the pan – push the onions to the sides – and cook, constantly turning until browned all over, about 4–5 minutes. Pour on the saffron water (and the strands), and the lime juice, mix together, then simmer gently for about 20–25 minutes until the water has been almost absorbed.

While the meatballs are cooking, stabilise the yogurt by first whisking in a pan until smooth and 'thin', then mix the cornflour with a little cold water. Stir into the yogurt with a good pinch of salt, and constantly stirring with a wooden spoon in the same direction (this is vital), bring gently to the boil. Leave to simmer, uncovered, for about 10 minutes until it is fairly thick. Then remove from the heat – it is now ready to be used and can be cooked, even boiled, for as long as necessary, without curdling. The yogurt we had in the Middle East was made from salted goat's milk, as it has been from time immemorial, and so never curdled. But homemade, or bought, yogurt which is made from cow's milk will, unless stabilised. It makes no difference to the taste of the dish but it does slightly mar the appearance.

When there is a scant 15 ml (1 tbsp) liquid left in the pan, stir in the yogurt and cook, gently, for another 5–15 minutes depending on how much sauce you want left with the meatballs. I like a little, very thick, sauce, especially if serving cold. Others prefer to have more sauce particularly when serving hot, with rice.

STUFFED MEATBALLS

Kufteh Mo'alla

Another superb variation from Persia – an extremely sophisticated version of Scotch eggs. A few tablespoons of tomato purée are sometimes added to the broth in other countries, with the prunes, split peas and pistachios omitted. In Persia, mint tea is often used to soak the prunes, and if the dish is to be served as a main course, the quantity of broth would be doubled, to give a small bowl of soup as a starter.

Serves 4–8

75 g (3 oz) yellow split peas, soaked overnight
900 g (2 lb) lamb, minced and pounded
1 onion, skinned and minced or grated
45 ml (3 tbsp) finely chopped dillweed

Maldon or sea salt
freshly ground black pepper
5 ml (1 tsp) ground cinnamon
about 25 g (1 oz) pistachios (unshelled weight)
8 prunes, stoned and soaked for 2 hours in cold
    water or tea
4 eggs, hard-boiled and shelled
450 ml (¾ pint) light stock, preferably veal
2–3 strands saffron
about 45–60 ml (3–4 tbsp) flour
60–75 ml (4–5 tbsp) olive oil
juice of 1 large lemon
pinch of sugar
15 ml (1 tbsp) finely chopped fresh mint
15 ml (1 tbsp) finely chopped fresh basil

Rinse the split peas, put in a pan with water to cover by a good 5 cm (2 inches) and bring to the boil, then gently simmer until the peas are quite soft but not mushy. This will take about 30 minutes to 1 hour, depending on the age and freshness of the peas. Drain and mix with the meat, onion, dillweed, a generous seasoning of salt and pepper and the cinnamon. Shell the pistachios, drain the prunes and stuff each with 3–4 nuts. Divide the meat into four, rolling each piece into a large ball, then push your thumb through to the centre and make a good cavity in the middle. Insert a prune, then an egg, then another prune, and close up again, making sure the join is well sealed.

Bring the stock to the boil, pour over the saffron strands and leave for 5 minutes. Lightly flour the meatballs, heat the oil in a large shallow pan until nearly smoking, and cook the balls, turning gently but constantly until golden all over. Drain off any oil in the pan, then pour in the stock and saffron, the lemon juice and add a pinch of sugar. Bring slowly to the boil, then simmer for about 25–30 minutes, until the meatballs are thoroughly cooked and the sauce much reduced. Either serve hot, sprinkled with the mint and basil, or transfer into a dish, pour over the sauce and the herbs and cool, before cutting into thick slices.

COURGETTE AND LAMB MEATBALLS

Kabak ve Köfte

From Izmir, on the Aegean coast of Turkey, comes this unusual combination. It was not far from here, near Ephesus (Efes, in modern day Turkey) that the Virgin Mary settled to spend a peaceful old age. A simple chapel stands as a shrine on the site of her house, while a few miles away are the ruins of the ancient Greco-Roman town which must have been magnificent.

Aubergines are sometimes substituted for the courgettes. If you use aubergines don't peel or grate them, just cut into small chunks before salting them. And you may need a little extra oil for the cooking.

Serves 6–8
700 g (1½ lb) courgettes, peeled
salt
30–45 ml (2–3 tbsp) olive oil
2 medium onions, skinned and finely chopped
1–2 garlic cloves, skinned and crushed
700 g (1½ lb) lamb, minced and pounded
75 g (3 oz) Feta cheese, grated
15 ml (1 tbsp) dried mint
2 eggs
freshly ground black pepper
plain flour
vegetable oil, for frying

Cut the courgettes in half, lengthways, sprinkle with salt and leave for 1 hour. Rinse thoroughly, squeeze, then grate them. Heat the oil in a large frying pan, add the onions and gently sauté until softened, about 5 minutes. Add the garlic and the grated courgette, and cook, gently, for 10–25 minutes, until tender. Remove from the heat and cool, then mix with the meat, cheese, mint and eggs. Season with salt and freshly ground black pepper, then pound until pasty.

Form into little balls, and roll quickly in flour. Heat a little oil, enough to cover the surface of the frying pan, until nearly smoking, then, on a very low heat, cook the meatballs for 10–15 minutes, turning them frequently until golden on the outside and cooked through. Very good hot, even better cold.

LADIES' THIGHS

Kadın Budu

The Turks have the most picturesque names for their dishes – Ladies' Navels, Girl's Fingers, Liar *Dolma* . . . These soft, juicy meatballs with their crisp outer shells are first simmered in a little water to trap the juices, then quickly fried in hot fat – a reversal of the process used elsewhere. There is another similar dish, *summakli köfte* (meatballs with *sumac* – with the added spice, for some reason, they cease to be ladies' thighs!) which substitutes grated potato for the rice, and serves them on toasted bread, covered in yogurt with a little *sumac* sprinkled over. Both are good.

Serves 4–6
700 g (1½ lb) lamb, minced and pounded
50 g (2 oz) rice
1 or 2 large eggs
5–15 ml (1–3 tsp) olive oil (optional)
1 medium onion, skinned and grated or minced
15 ml (1 tbsp) coriander seeds, lightly ground
2–3 garlic cloves, skinned and crushed
salt and freshly ground black pepper
5 ml (1 tsp) dried mint
OR 5 ml (1 tsp) finely chopped fresh parsley
    plus 5 ml (1 tsp) finely chopped fresh dillweed
oil or unsalted butter, for frying
plain flour (optional)
To serve lemon wedges

Mix the meat with the rice. Then either whisk one egg until frothy, with or without 5 ml (1 tsp) olive oil – this is purely a matter of personal taste – then mix well into the meat. Or, add 15 ml (1 tbsp) oil to the meat, and no egg. Recipes vary greatly on this point – I have even seen some without egg or oil, but I think one or the other adds to the succulence of the meatballs. Add the onion, spices and herbs of your choice, again mixing thoroughly, then leave the mixture to stand for 1 hour, to let the flavours permeate.

Form the meat into small balls, wetting your hands as necessary, then arrange in one layer in a large shallow pan. Put just enough water to cover the bottom of the pan, about 1 cm (½ inch), 150–175 ml (5–6 fl oz), cover and cook gently for 15–20 minutes until the water has all been absorbed and the meat looks cooked. Remove from the pan and cool.

Beat the other egg, again until frothy, and dip the meatballs quickly into it. Heat enough oil or butter to cover the surface of the pan, about 30–45 ml (2–3 tbsp) and when hot, quickly dip the meatballs in flour if you wish (I don't, but many like the extra crispness it gives) and put into the pan. Cook for a few minutes until browned and crisp all over. Serve with lemon wedges, rice, *Pittas* (page 146) and salads.

GREEK MEATBALLS

Keftedhes

In Greece, they add breadcrumbs to the meat rather than rice, also the typical Greek seasoning, rigani. You are more likely, too, to find a mixture of meats than in the other countries.

Serves 4–6
700 g (1½ lb) lean meat, minced
40 g (2½ oz) fresh breadcrumbs
1 small onion, grated
2 small eggs
45 ml (3 tbsp) finely chopped parsley
2½ ml (½ tsp) rigani
salt and freshly ground black pepper
oil, for deep frying

Pound the minced meat until pasty or whizz in a food processor. Soak the breadcrumbs in cold water for 5 minutes, then squeeze dry. Mix into the meat, with the onion, and the eggs – beaten first – then add the spices and season quite highly with salt and black pepper. Form into small balls.

Heat a good 5–7½ cm (2–3 inches) oil in a deep fat fryer until nearly smoking, then carefully drop in the balls and cook for 2–3 minutes until crisp and golden.

BROCHETTES

In Morocco, the French influence is again revealed in their name for *köfte* – *brochettes*. Miniature versions, laden on tiny skewers, and spiced with a pinch of almost everything the spice cupboard has to offer, but so subtly there is just one glorious rich flavour – the component parts almost impossible to identify so well blended are they. *Felfla soudania* is a ground spice from exceedingly hot peppers, native to North Africa and Senegal – use *Harissa* (page 30) instead unless a kind friend (kind only if you happen to love hot chillies!) can bring some back from Morocco for you. *Ras el hanout* I found once in Paris, but never, so far, in England. It is an incredibly complex blend of spices, including cardamom, mace, nutmeg, several types of peppers (hot and sweet), ginger, cloves, cinnamon, ash-tree fruits, something I found translated as 'belladonna berries' – obviously *not* what we would mean by belladonna, and several other spices which I have, as yet, not been able to equate with anything we know in the West. Do not attempt to make it, simply omit.

Serves 6–8
900 g (2 lb) lamb or beef, minced and pounded
75 g (3 oz) lamb or beef fat, chilled then minced
1 large onion, skinned and grated
1 small bunch parsley, finely chopped
1 small bunch fresh coriander leaves, finely
    chopped
10 ml (2 tsp) paprika
5 ml (1 tsp) cumin seeds, ground
good 5 ml (1 heaped tsp) ground cinnamon
pinch of *felfla soudania* or 1½–2½ ml (¼–½ tsp)
    Harissa (page 30)
2½ ml (½ tsp) *ras el hanout* (optional)
Maldon or sea salt
4–5 sprigs fresh mint, very finely chopped

Mix the pounded meat with the minced fat, blending evenly (the fat melts during the cooking, making these extraordinarily succulent). Then mix together the grated onion with all the herbs and spices – this helps to distribute them throughout the meat – and add to the meat, stirring quite thoroughly. Season fairly generously with salt. Then take a lump of meat,

about the size of a small egg, and shape into a thin sausage on a skewer – or into long thin fingers, if you haven't skewers. Lightly oil a grill grid and cook under a high heat for 3–5 minutes until browned on the outside. Traditionally served with mint tea.

MINCED MEAT WITH BURGHUL

Kibbeh

The national dish of Syria and the Lebanon in whatever form, and it has many. Raw (the Arab answer to steak tartare) is one of the most popular, although in Syria tray *kibbeh* is almost equally loved. Then, so are the long 'fingers' of *kibbeh* stuffed with a few pine nuts – Syrian women are said to be endowed by the gods if they have a long finger favoured for the making of these rissoles. And to watch them at work is fascinating. First, the pounding, even more dramatic than normal. I can remember hearing the hammering – which invariably began as poor Mademoiselle Dupont was vainly trying to instil the three 'R's into her class of small multi-nationals who gathered in our flat in Damascus each morning. The instant it began, our attention was lost. For, when silence fell, we knew we would be allowed to go and watch the cook's young and very beautiful wife making the *kibbeh*. With a swift, deft movement a handful of that pasty mixture would be whipped around her middle finger, caressed into an elongated smoothness, then slipped off, ready to be filled with the exquisitely sweet nuts. Ten minutes later, row upon row of slim, perfectly shaped and even sized 'shells' were lying on the long brass tray. She would present it to her husband, give a small bow (and a shy but wide smile as she bent her head) to us wide-eyed children and the Mam'selle and quietly disappear into the nether regions. It was the only time I ever saw this beautiful girl, who cannot have been more than seventeen – if that, and who was much renowned for her prowess at *kibbeh* making. Her husband, of course, greatly enjoyed the reflected glory that it gave him, and he would stand, arms folded across his chest, smiling indulgently while she made them, nodding enthusiastically as the tray was filled. For this also betokened a happy occasion, *kibbeh* never being served at times of sadness, like a funeral or when a member of the family was going away – both events frequent, alas.

RAW KIBBEH

Kibbeh Nayye

Serves 6–8
125 g (4 oz) burghul (cracked wheat)
450 g (1 lb) lamb, minced and well pounded
1 large onion, skinned and grated
Maldon or sea salt
freshly ground black pepper
freshly grated nutmeg
freshly ground allspice
cayenne pepper
cos lettuce, washed and drained
finely sliced onion rings
olive oil

Put the burghul in a bowl, cover with cold water and leave to soak for about 10 minutes, then squeeze thoroughly to dry. Mix the burghul with the meat, grated onion, and the seasonings. The quantity here is very much a matter of taste. Traditionally it is fairly highly spiced, which I like, but it is advisable to begin with a little, adding a pinch of this, and a pinch of that, until you find what is right for you – this is half the fun of making *kibbeh* anyway! Pound, or whizz in a food processor until the mixture is really pasty – on a very hot day, I find it helps to add 15 ml (1 tbsp) or so of iced water. Then divide into 6 or 8 portions and pat into a neat, round shape, slightly domed in the middle.

Make a fan of cos lettuce leaves on individual plates, put a portion of meat into the middle of each, then make an indentation in the domes with your thumb. Place the onion rings around the meat, and pour a dribble of olive oil into each hollow just before serving.

TRAY KIBBEH

Kibbeh bi Sanieh

A mixture similar to that used for *kibbeh nayye*, but with double the amount of burghul, is often formed into small cakes, or shaped round skewers, and then either fried or grilled to be served crisp and hot. Even more delicious, and ideal for the *mezze* table since it is equally good hot or cold, is the popular Syrian tray *kibbeh* – the basic mixture sandwiching cooked lamb, onions and pine nuts.

Serves 8–10
225 g (8 oz) burghul (cracked wheat)
450 g (1 lb) lamb, minced and well pounded
1 large onion, skinned and grated
Maldon or sea salt
freshly ground black pepper
freshly grated nutmeg
freshly ground allspice
cayenne pepper
For the stuffing
1 small onion, skinned and finely chopped
15 ml (1 tbsp) olive oil
225 g (8 oz) lamb or veal, minced
75 g (3 oz) pine nuts
salt and freshly ground black pepper
2½ ml (½ tsp) ground cinnamon
5 ml (1 tsp) dried mint (optional)
100 g (4 oz) unsalted butter, melted
60 ml (4 tbsp) lamb or veal stock

Soak the burghul in cold water for 10 minutes, then squeeze dry. Mix with the meat, grated onion and seasonings to taste, pounding until quite pasty.

To make the stuffing: sauté the onion in the oil until soft, spread the meat on top and stew gently for about 10–15 minutes, until lightly browned, adding the pine nuts, salt and freshly ground black pepper, cinnamon and mint after 5 minutes.

Brush a baking tin with a little of the melted butter, spread half the raw *kibbeh* mixture over the bottom, cover with the cooked meat, onions and pine nuts, then put the remaining *kibbeh* over the top. Run a knife round the edge of the tin, then cut the pie into lozenge shapes, small or large according to how you want to serve it. Sprinkle on the rest of the butter, and bake for 45 minutes to 1 hour in the oven at 190°C (375°F), mark 5, dribbling on 15 ml (1 tbsp) stock every 10 minutes, until golden and crisp. Serve hot or cold with a large bowl of chilled yogurt.

STUFFED KIBBEH

Kibbeh Mahshi

These are the ultimate in *kibbeh* – long, thin, crisp shells filled with sweet, sweet pine nuts or, even more difficult to stuff perfectly, with a juicy meat filling. I must confess such is my addiction to pine nuts, that I always use them, but you can, if you wish – and are adept – use the stuffing for *Kibbeh bi Sanieh* (see previous recipe). Wet your hands thoroughly both to make the shells and to stuff them, patching up any cracks with your thumb – again constantly dipped in cold water. At pottery classes years later, I was always reminded of *kibbeh*. Suffice to say my *kibbeh* shells are more elegant than my vases. However, if you are a good potter, you will probably be a superb *kibbeh* maker. The movements are not dissimilar.

Serves 5–6
225 g (8 oz) burghul (cracked wheat)
450 g (1 lb) lamb, minced and well pounded
1 large onion, skinned and grated
Maldon or sea salt
freshly ground black pepper
freshly grated nutmeg
about 5 ml (1 tsp) ground cinnamon
50–75 g (2–3 oz) pine nuts
olive oil, for frying

Soak the burghul in cold water for 10 minutes, then squeeze out, and mix with the meat, onion and seasonings. Pound until thoroughly pasty, then with both hands wet take a small lump of meat, a little less than a medium-sized egg, and shape it around your middle or forefinger to an even thickness all over, wetting the shell if necessary to close up any cracks. Drop about 5 ml (1 tsp) of pine nuts into each shell, closing up the ends in a smooth oval shape.

Heat a good 5 cm (2 inches) oil in a deep pan until nearly smoking, then carefully roll in two or three shells and fry for about 5 minutes, until browned and crisp all over. Do the cooking in small batches, until you get deft at it – if there are too many in the pan, they can stick together and then crack. Drain thoroughly and serve hot or cold with yogurt, tahina salad and vegetable salads.

GRILLED LIVER WITH GARLIC

Mi'Laaq Mashwi bi Toum

I never liked liver much as a child – until the summer we went to Beirut. Persuaded to try this dish (the smell of garlic was, once again, the appetite-whetter!) it became a daily ritual. Grilled, as here, it is usually served hot, but there is an equally good cold version, in which the liver is quickly fried in hot oil – though for no more than a minute or so else it becomes dry and leathery. Turkey also has her version of this, called *çiger kebab* (liver kebab) but the liver is merely salted and brushed with oil before cooking, to be served with raw sliced onions, chopped parsley, tomatoes and lemon wedges.

Serves 4–6
4–6 slices of liver, each about 1 cm (½ inch) thick
3–4 garlic cloves, skinned
Maldon or sea salt
60 ml (4 tbsp) olive oil
freshly ground black pepper
15 ml (1 tbsp) dried mint
juice of 1–2 lemons

Cut the liver into small pieces and put in a bowl. Crush the garlic with about 2½ ml (½ tsp) salt, then mix with the oil, lots of black pepper and the dried mint. Pour over the liver, stirring well, and leave, covered, for about 1 hour. (Purists say you should rub the crushed garlic into the liver pieces but I find this a bit too messy for my liking and I defy anyone to notice a difference in taste.)

Thread the meat on skewers and grill under a medium heat for 3–4 minutes until nicely browned on the outside but still a bit pink inside. Baste after a couple of minutes with the marinade. Sprinkle with lemon juice and serve with almost anything you like except, say the Lebanese, yogurt which they believe to be incompatible with liver. It is almost the only time yogurt does not appear on the table.

GRILLED KIDNEYS WITH MUSHROOMS

Kalwat Mashwi

Kidneys are popular throughout the Middle East, sometimes interspersed with liver on skewers and grilled or, as below, with mushrooms. In Iraq, they also gently stew kidneys and mushrooms in stock sharpened with a little vinegar.

Serves 4–6
700 g (1½ lb) lamb's kidneys
15 ml (1 tbsp) vinegar
salt
juice of 1 lemon
225 g (8 oz) button mushrooms, wiped with a damp cloth
100 g (4 oz) butter, melted
freshly ground white pepper
finely chopped fresh mint, or dried mint
lemon juice

Wash the kidneys thoroughly, carefully take off the outer membrane and cut away the cores in the centre, then soak in cold water mixed with the vinegar, for 1 hour. Bring a pan of lightly salted water to the boil, drop in the kidneys and blanch for 3–4 minutes, then remove and rinse. Cut into pieces – about four to a kidney, then thread on skewers, alternating with the mushrooms and dipping each mushroom into the melted butter as you thread. Sprinkle the skewers with freshly ground black pepper and a little salt,

then brush all over with more melted butter and grill under a medium heat for about 3–5 minutes, turning every minute or so and brushing again with a little butter. When they are well coloured on the outside but still tender in the middle they are done. Sprinkle with lemon juice and mint and serve with hot pitta.

CORIANDER SAUSAGES

Coriander'li

In Cyprus the smell of sausages cooking is enhanced by the coriander seed flavouring, sweet and orangey. Sometimes chopped fresh coriander leaves are added, as is finely chopped or crushed garlic. Saltpetre is available from chemists. If unobtainable, omit. But in that case you must eat the sausages the day of making.

Makes about 24 sausages
700 g (1½ lb) belly of pork, cut into strips, rinds removed
700 g (1½ lb) lean pork, preferably hand and spring
30 ml (2 tbsp) salt
freshly ground white pepper
22½ ml (1½ tbsp) sugar
1¼ ml (¼ tsp) saltpetre
30 ml (2 tbsp) coriander seeds, finely ground
2 garlic cloves, skinned and chopped or crushed (optional)
30 ml (2 tbsp) finely chopped coriander leaves (optional)
sausage skins (optional)
lard, for frying

Cut all the pork into chunks and then put through the fine blade of a mincer twice or whizz for a few minutes in a food processor until very finely chopped. Mix in a large bowl with the remaining ingredients, except the skins and lard, making sure all the seasonings are well and evenly distributed. Either put into the skins – or get your butcher to do it for you, twisting them every six inches or so, then hang in a dry, airy place for 1–2 days. This improves the flavour enormously but is not essential; then dip into boiling water for one second before grilling or frying in a very little lard.

If you can't get – or cope with – the sausage skins, leave the mixture overnight in the refrigerator, then form into sausage shapes or small patties and again, either grill or fry in a little lard. Cook slowly for about 15–20 minutes – longer than you would bought packaged sausages as the meat content is 100%, as opposed to about 70% in even the best bought sausage – many even less, and much of it not pure meat. I am, of course, talking about packaged brands, not the local butcher who makes his own sausages.

POACHED BRAIN SALAD

Salata Mukh

Possibly because the choice of meat has traditionally been so limited, no part of the animal is wasted – from top to toe, although the much-talked about sheep's eye is rarely actually on the menu. That other delicate part of the anatomy – the testicles – is certainly considered a fine dish though. It was one of the most expensive, and popular, items at the luscious Cairo restaurant, Hati's, during the first half of this century. However, back to brains – where there are two schools of thought. One says that they are possibly the finest food for feeding one's own intelligence. The other, particularly in more remote, rural areas, regards them as taboo, saying that they will make one as stupid as the animal from which they came. The terrifying mother of my Palestinian nanny firmly held the latter view – which possibly explains her constant battles with the cook for whom this was a firm favourite! Nonetheless, brains are popular all over the Middle East, both poached, and fried as in the following recipe.

Serves 4

4 sets lamb's brains, or 2 sets calf's (see method)
salt
15 ml (1 tbsp) vinegar
juice of 1½ lemons
5 ml (1 tsp) turmeric
75–90 ml (5–6 tbsp) olive oil
3 spring onions, finely sliced
freshly ground black pepper
45 ml (3 tbsp) finely chopped parsley or chervil

Always buy brains from a reputable butcher and ensure they are very fresh, then use them on the same day. Frozen brains are occasionally available and can be substituted but I never find them quite so tender. Soak them for half an hour in a large bowl of cold water into which you have stirred the vinegar. Then rinse under cold running water, very carefully removing the thin outer membranes – try not to break up the flesh when doing this.

Put the brains in a small pan, squeeze over half the lemon juice, then just cover with water and sprinkle on a little salt, and the turmeric. Bring the water gently to the boil, then simmer for about 10–15 minutes. When they are firm they are ready, so watch them, as overcooking will dry them out.

Drain and leave for 5 minutes, then cut into slices and arrange in a shallow dish – the turmeric will have coloured them a beautiful pale yellow. Spoon over the olive oil and the rest of the lemon juice, then stir a little. Scatter on the chopped spring onions, season with a pinch of salt and quite a good grinding of black pepper, then garnish with the parsley. Serve with warm pittas. Really – they are good.

FRIED BRAINS

Mukh Muhmmar

In Turkey and Iraq particularly, fried brains are popular. I find this a good way, too, to introduce people to brains – many are prejudiced against them due to the very softness of their texture. Here, the crisp crunchy outside forms an ideal contrast.

Serves 4
4 sets lamb's brains or 2 sets calf's
15 ml (1 tbsp) vinegar
salt
juice of ½ a small lemon
about 45 ml (3 tbsp) plain flour
1 egg
freshly ground white pepper
5 ml (1 tsp) freshly ground allspice
5 ml (1 tsp) paprika (optional)
75–90 ml (5–6 tbsp) homemade, dried finely
    ground breadcrumbs
olive oil, for frying
To serve chopped parsley
lemon or lime wedges

Soak the brains in cold water, into which you have stirred the vinegar, for 1 hour. Rinse under a cold tap and carefully take off the thin membranes. Then put into a pan, cover with boiling water, add a good pinch of salt, the juice of ½ small lemon and simmer for 3–4 minutes until beginning to firm up. Immediately remove and dry on absorbent kitchen paper.

Sprinkle the flour on a shallow plate, beat the egg with freshly ground white pepper, the allspice and paprika if using, and spread the breadcrumbs on another plate. Cut the brains into small pieces, roll each one in the flour, dip into the egg, then roll in the breadcrumbs, making sure they are well coated. Heat a good 5 cm (2 inches) olive oil in a deep pan until nearly smoking, then cook a few pieces at a time for about 4 minutes until nicely golden all over. Drain thoroughly and serve, generously sprinkled with chopped parsley, with lemon wedges. Or, even nicer, as we had in Iraq, with lime wedges. Good hot or cold.

STEAMED MUTTON

Choua

Steamed mutton, or lamb, is an unusual and delicate speciality of Morocco. Simply flavoured with salt and cumin seed, the lamb is beautifully tender and juicy.

Serves 4–6
900 g (2 lb) boned leg of mutton or lamb
Maldon or sea salt
15 ml (1 tbsp) cumin seeds, lightly crushed

Cut the meat into small cubes, trimming off all fat and sinews. Bring plenty of water to the boil in the bottom part of a steamer, put the mutton (or lamb) in the top, cover tightly and steam gently for 1¼–2 hours. If you don't have a steamer with a hermetic seal, stretch a clean tea towel over the top of the steamer and then fix the lid on firmly (tie the ends of the towel over the pan lid so they don't burn on the cooker). When the meat can be pulled apart with the fingers, it is done. Pile on a serving platter, sprinkle lightly with salt and about 5 ml (1 tsp) cumin. Serve with rice, or *Pittas* (page 146) and salads, with a bowl of salt and the remaining cumin in a little bowl on the table so that people can help themselves to extra if they wish .

SKEWERED LAMB WITH PERSIAN RICE

Chelo Kebabs

The art of the *kebab* has been turned into a fine ritual in Persia, where there are restaurants devoted entirely to serving this dish. Two points distinguish this from all else. First, the *Chelo* or Persian rice (page 140), which is parboiled then steamed to produce a wonderful golden crusty bottom, or *tah dig*. These pieces are scraped out last and served separately at the side of the dish, traditionally offered to any guests of the house as a delicacy. Secondly, the meat is not minced but pounded, after marination, until very thin and elastic so that it can be shaped on skewers in a long sausage. This is then 'nipped in', as it were, to make four or six rounds per skewer. I am afraid that I do cheat here, and mince the meat first. Despite pounding with a ferocity that set my entire kitchen trembling, I have never managed to get quite enough elasticity to produce those neat shapes without some of the meat dropping off very unceremoniously half-way through cooking. However, I try to redeem my heresy by carefully observing the rest of the ritual – fine timing is of the essence here, but one soon falls into a smooth routine. And it is much appreciated by guests – large and small!

Serves 4–6
450 g (1 lb) basmati rice (see page 140)
900 g (2 lb) lamb, minced
5 ml (1 tsp) turmeric
5 ml (1 tsp) cinnamon
2½ ml (½ tsp) cumin seeds, crushed
Maldon or sea salt
freshly ground black pepper
120 ml (8 tbsp) olive oil
75 g (3 oz) unsalted butter
8–12 small, very firm tomatoes
To serve 1–2 large onions, finely sliced
2½ ml (½ tsp) dried mint (optional)
100–175 g (4–6 oz) unsalted butter, chilled
4–6 large eggs
small bowl of *sumac* (see page 157)

Put the rice in a large bowl, cover with cold water and leave to soak for 6 hours or overnight if possible. (I have actually only soaked the rice for 2 hours on certain occasions, but it is not quite so fluffy in the end). Mix the meat with the turmeric, cinnamon, cumin seeds, a goodly pinch of salt and grinding of black pepper, and half the oil. Cover and leave to marinate for at least 2 hours. Or you can prepare the meat when you soak the rice – it can only do good.

Half an hour before you wish to eat, prepare the serving ingredients. Put the onions in a shallow bowl, sprinkling with mint if wished (this varies from cook to cook). Cut the butter into 25 g (1 oz) pieces (one per person) and arrange on a small dish – if your kitchen is very hot, put back in the refrigerator. Otherwise, cover and just leave to one side. Fill a small tea bowl with two or three tablespoons of *sumac* – you won't actually need more than a pinch per person but you want to be able to see the stuff. Then break the eggs, individually, keeping the whites for another recipe, and returning each yolk to its half shell. I then put these on a snail dish, perfect for keeping them upright, but if you don't have such a thing, either crumple foil in a shallow plate so that the shells can stand up, or simply pop each half-shell into an egg cup and arrange these on a flat platter or small round tray. I can still see in my mind's eye a set of exquisite rock-crystal egg cups, held in brightly-coloured enamelled filigree holders – perfect for this dish. Maddeningly, I can't remember where. Perhaps in the Topkapı Palace, Istanbul, where I can certainly

© Françoise Peuriot

Roasting ducks and woodcocks after the hunt.

Following page (l–r): Grilled Liver with Garlic (p. 93), Köfte (p. 85), Raw Kibbeh (p. 92) and Tray Kibbeh (p. 92).

recall lusting after some rock-crystal teaspoons of a similar ilk. This may all sound like a dreadful performance, but it is actually quickly done. Drain the rice, and cook as in recipe for *Chelo* (page 140).

While the rice is cooking, either mince the meat, then pound it, or whizz for a couple of minutes in a food processor – it must be really pasty. Pat the meat into a long sausage on each of 4–6 skewers, then take 6–4 'nips' in each sausage to produce nicely rounded shapes. Put 2 tomatoes on the end of each skewer. (Incidentally, don't be tempted to make up the skewers too much ahead of time. I did, once, and all the meat fell off before it even reached the grill!) Check the rice, and rinse under cold water when done. Continue as in recipe for *Chelo* (page 140).

Put the grill on – it must be really hot, then serve the onions, for people to nibble on while waiting. Once the rice has been steaming for 5 minutes, brush the remaining oil over the kebabs, then put the

skewers on to cook for 6–10 minutes until crisp and browned on the outside. Turn the skewers after 2 minutes.

Meanwhile, put the butter on the table, with the plate of egg yolks, and the bowl of *sumac*. Turn the *kebabs* again, and after 2 minutes turn again. Tip the rice into a large dish, scraping out the crusty pieces then placing them around the edge, and serve. Each person helps themselves – the guest of honour being offered the *tah dig*. Then they each mix an egg yolk into their rice, a piece of butter, and a sprinkling of *sumac*. Now the skewers are ready to be taken off the grill, quickly put on a long platter, and rushed straight to the table – still sizzling. This is one dish which must be served as soon as it is cooked, and traditionally, with small rounds of flat bread, *nane sanjak*, also hot from fresh baking. I am still on the search for that particular recipe, so substitute hot pittas straight from the oven.

A village, fields and palms in Morocco.

© Françoise Peuriot

CHICKEN AND POULTRY

Dajaj

Next a chicken, full and tender,
Fattened many moons agone
And a partridge, with a fledgling,
Roast with care, and nicely done.

MAHMUD IBN AL-HUSAIN AL-KUSHAJIM[1]

Not a little poetic licence went into those lines, I feel, unless the chicken of a thousand years ago had a vastly different life style from today's. Reading through the hundreds of different stuffings, exquisite spicings, and careful cooking methods recommended by the medieval chefs, I suspect that the creature was as scraggy as the ones we knew. So, the Arab imagination once again comes into play and chicken is lusciously married to all the exotic seasonings of the area. Scented and sweetened with rose-flower water, oranges, mulberries or plums; spiced with cinnamon, ginger, turmeric, cardamoms; enhanced by vinegar, lemons, pomegranates; softened with yogurt, garlic and oil; made fruity with quinces, apples and rhubarb; nutty with pistachios, hazels, almonds, poppy seeds, pine or walnuts; earthy with chick peas and onions; freshly green with parsley, coriander, mint, marjoram, and savoury – you could eat a chicken dish 'for eighteen moons' without a repetition of recipe. That repertoire exhausted, there is still the rest of the feathered world to choose from. Wild duck from the Caspian Sea and the Iraqi marshes; partridge, loved by the Greeks, Cypriots and Moroccans; pigeons, a favourite everywhere; woodcock, quail, snipe, sandgrouse. The poet spoke truly of the 'partridge, with a fledgling', for even the tiniest birds are viewed in

relation to the kitchen, many of which our softer, Western hearts would regard as sacrosanct. Particularly, I suspect, the minute *beccaficio* (*becfigue, beccafichi, beccafico,* or *beccaficca* in kitchen Arabic). This little creature, the figpecker to us, is so tiny that in Cyprus it is pickled whole, even the bones softening in the vinegar made from their sweet fine wine, Commanderia. Each bird only provides one mouthful of that favoured delicacy. Trapped as he sits fattening himself on grape juice, or his favourite fruit the fig – sucking out flesh and seeds, this little bird was popular with our ancestors, known as the *oiselet de Chypre* in the Middle Ages. The Lebanese still cook them as we did, threaded on skewers and spit-roasted, often wrapped in vine leaves to heighten their fruity flavour. For those of us with tenderer susceptibilities, there is always the turkey, to be seen scratching his living on every village high street. A veritable spindleshanks compared to the smug fat creatures I used to ride past on cold December mornings in East Anglia. Never daunted, however, the Arabs marry the scrawny bird to a spiced, minced lamb stuffing. The result: delectable.

1. *AD 915–967/303–356 Islamic calendar.*

GRILLED CHICKEN WITH GARLIC

Dajaj Mashwi bil Zait wa Tom

Popular everywhere, this simple but garlicky marinade totally transforms even the most boring of English chickens – or scrawny Arab ones. In the Lebanon, we had a favourite restaurant which served divinely tender baby poussin (highly nurtured by the owner, I suspect), and I often use these now for a dinner *à deux*. For the *mezze* table, though, I make miniature *kebabs*, using the skinned breasts only, but you could equally well use a jointed chicken, or just the legs. Turn this into a Turkish dish by adding the juice of an onion, a little ground cinnamon and lots of freshly ground black pepper.

Serves 6
6 chicken breasts, skinned and boned
4–6 garlic cloves, skinned
Maldon or sea salt
juice of 1–1½ lemons
90–120 ml (6–8 tbsp) olive oil
finely chopped parsley

Cut the breasts into bite-sized cubes and put in a shallow dish. Crush the garlic with salt until quite pulpy. Mix in the lemon juice, then whisk into the oil. Pour over the chicken, turning everything over, and leave, covered, for 1–4 hours, turning the pieces once or twice during that time.

Put a large amount of chopped parsley on a plate. Thread the chicken on small skewers – I use small bamboo ones soaked in lemon juice (soaking stops them burning when grilling and the lemon juice gives a wonderful tang to the middle of each piece of chicken; but water will do just as well). Roll each skewer in parsley then cook under a hot grill – better still over a hot barbecue, oil the grid first – for about 4–6 minutes, turning them to golden all over, and basting with the marinade, or extra oil if necessary. Wonderful.

GRILLED CHICKEN WITH SPICES

Dajaj Mashwi bil Baharat

Back home in Baghdad, our cook produced his own version of chicken *kebabs*, gloriously spiced with cardamom, turmeric and allspice. 'Even more wonderful,' I pronounced.

Serves 6
6 chicken breasts, skinned and boned
3 garlic cloves, skinned
Maldon or sea salt
8–10 cardamom pods, husks removed
2½ ml (½ tsp) turmeric
freshly ground allspice
freshly ground white pepper
juice of 3 limes or 1–1½ lemons
90–120 ml (6–8 tbsp) olive oil

Cut the meat into small pieces and put into a bowl. Crush the garlic well with some salt. Grind the cardamom seeds in a spice grinder, then mix with the turmeric, allspice and a good grinding of white pepper and whisk into the lemon juice. Add the garlic and oil and pour over the chicken. Leave for 2–4 hours, turning occasionally.

Thread on small, soaked, skewers, as for last recipe, and grill for 4–6 minutes until golden all over, basting occasionally.

GRILLED CHICKEN WITH GARLIC AND YOGURT

Dajaj Mashwi bil Tom wa Laban

On our second trip to Beirut, I had these and immediately, and utterly disloyally, preferred them to all else. The yogurt does not flavour the chicken so

Fried Partridge (p. 114) on a bed of Rice with Nuts (p. 139).

much as tenderise it and make it succulent and juicy. In Egypt, they were prepared with cardamom pods and yogurt – also very good. And in Greece, a pot of yogurt is often poured over grilled chicken, simply marinaded in oil, lemon and garlic – with maybe a touch of marjoram or rigani added. I tend to use the leftover legs from the chickens whose breasts have already contributed to other dishes (the wings kept for later) but you can use breasts, or chicken pieces if you prefer.

Serves 6
6 chicken legs
2–3 garlic cloves, skinned
Maldon or sea salt
5 ml (1 tsp) paprika
5 ml (1 tsp) cinnamon
1½–2½ ml (¼–½ tsp) cayenne pepper
juice of 1 lemon
90–120 ml (6–8 tbsp) olive oil
90–120 ml (6–8 tbsp) natural yogurt
freshly ground black pepper
To serve lemon wedges (optional)

I don't usually skin the chicken legs but sometimes make the odd gash here and there in the deepest part of the flesh, particularly if they are large. Crush the garlic with a little salt, then mix with the paprika, cinnamon and cayenne to taste. Stir in the lemon juice, then add the oil and yogurt. Put the chicken legs into a deep dish and cover with the marinade. Turn several times to cover them completely, then leave for 3–5 hours – overnight in the refrigerator is even better. Add a little more yogurt or oil if necessary.

Sprinkle with salt and lots of freshly ground black pepper then cook under a high heat on the grill for about 20–40 minutes, turning constantly and brushing with the marinade until very crisp and deeply golden – I like them almost charred on the outside. Eat hot or cold, gorgeous, with lemon wedges.

CHICKEN WINGS WITH LIME JUICE AND GARLIC

Ajniha al Dajaj bil Limoun Hamidh wa Tom

This was another hot contender for 'favourite' whenever we went to Beirut. My only problem on those wonderful holidays was too much choice – and eyes considerably bigger than tum. I always buy chickens whole and then joint them at home – usually using the breasts for one dish, then the legs for another (sometimes leaving them on the bird – merely filleting off the breasts – and then simply roasting the chicken with a stuffing under the skin where the breasts would have been). The wings however are always instantly snipped off and added to my collection in the freezer. Then, when I have lots, we can have a huge plate of these . . . You can now, conveniently, buy bags of frozen chicken wings in many supermarkets. Even better.

Serves 4–6
12 chicken wings
2–3 garlic cloves, skinned
Maldon or sea salt
juice of 3–4 limes, or 2 large lemons
pinch of cayenne pepper

Wash the wings, and singe off any lingering feather ends. Crush the garlic well with about 1½ ml (¼ tsp) salt until really pulpy, then rub a little on each chicken wing. Put into a bowl and squeeze over the lime or lemon juice. Leave for at least 1 hour, preferably 4–5, turning them occasionally so all parts get impregnated with the juice. Put the wings into a pan, preferably sitting in one layer. Pour the marinade over and then just enough water to cover. Bring quickly to the boil, then lower the heat and simmer for 12–15 minutes, uncovered, until the chicken is done and most of the sauce reduced. Transfer to a serving dish, scraping up all the juices in the pan and pouring them over. Wonderful eaten immediately and, if there should be any left-over, even better cold.

GRILLED CHICKEN WINGS WITH SESAME SEED

Ajniha al Dajaj Ma' Buzur Simsim

Returning home, once again our poor cook was inundated with tales of wonderful foods. I suppose it was not very diplomatic of me to keep regaling him with stories of all these glories I ate on holiday but he always seemed to rise to the occasion. The next day I was given a plate of these and, of course, he had regained my affections. I have not met them elsewhere in the Middle East so have tried to recreate them from memory. Even if time has played a few tricks, I think they are very good.

Serves 6
12 chicken wings
45 ml (3 tbsp) sesame seeds
1–2 garlic cloves, skinned and crushed
Maldon or sea salt
freshly ground white pepper
pinch of fenugreek
juice of 1 lemon
45–60 ml (3–4 tbsp) olive oil
To serve finely chopped parsley

Wash the wings and singe off any feather ends. Dry fry the sesame seeds for 1–2 minutes until golden but not burnt, then tip into a bowl. Mix in the crushed garlic, salt, pepper, fenugreek and lemon juice. Then beat in the oil, little by little, until well emulsified. Pour all over the chicken wings and leave to marinate for 4–5 hours, turning occasionally. Grill under a high heat for 5–9 minutes, turning once, and basting with the marinade, until crisp and golden. Serve sprinkled with parsley. Heaven.

Right: Chicken Wings with Lime Juice and Garlic (above) and Rice with Broad Beans (p. 138).

FRIED CHICKEN BALLS

Koftit Ferakh Muhmmar

Chicken is popular, too, minced and made into miniature *köfte*, seasoned variously with turmeric, ginger, fenugreek or sweet cinnamon and paprika. Nuts are often added to the mixture, pistachios in Iraq, pine nuts in Syria and the Lebanon. Driving from Damascus to Baghdad, we stopped quite late at a tiny roadside café – one table and four chairs outside the flat-roofed two-roomed dwelling – to 'have a little something to eat and stretch our legs.' By the time I had asked my innocent, and childishly logical question, 'Why? Are they too short?' bowls of steaming hot chick peas topped with these crisp meatballs were being handed out through the glass-less window (when the shutters were closed, so was the café). There was no choice – and we needed none. Sitting, singing 'Twinkle, twinkle little star' at the brilliant sparkles in that dark night and tucking into those succulent rissoles, I solemnly announced that I was the happiest person in the world! I think my parents would have been happier without the endless serenade – Damascus to Baghdad is a long drive. Thankfully this dish is still a family favourite – if not the nursery rhyme.

Serves 4–6
3 chicken breasts, minced
2 slices white bread, crusts removed
50 g (2 oz) pine nuts
45 ml (3 tbsp) finely chopped parsley
1½ ml (¼ tsp) turmeric
1 egg, beaten
Maldon or sea salt
freshly ground black pepper
plain flour
olive oil, for frying
juice of 1 lemon

Put the chicken into a large bowl. Soak the bread in a little water for 5 minutes, then squeeze dry and crumble into the chicken. Add the pine nuts, parsley and turmeric and mix. Beat in the egg, then season

with salt and pepper and mix very thoroughly until the mixture is quite soft and smooth. With wet hands, form into small balls no bigger than a walnut, and I sometimes make them as small as a hazelnut, literally 'bite-sized'. Lightly sprinkle with flour, then heat a good 2½ cm (1 inch) oil in a deep pan, and when nearly smoking, drop in a few balls. Cook for a few minutes until golden-brown and crisp. Drain on absorbent kitchen paper and cook the rest the same way. Lovely hot, and cold, both sprinkled with lemon juice – lots.

CHICKEN BALLS

Koftit Ferakh

Another popular variation. Although cooked chicken can be used in the previous recipe, I prefer to use raw, it seems to be more succulent. But for this dish, already cooked chicken is a must if you don't want to fry the meatballs and I think they are best unfried, the crunchiness of the nuts contrasting pleasantly with the soft chicken.

Serves 4–6
350 g (12 oz) cooked chicken meat, off the bone
2 slices white bread, crusts removed
milk
75 g (3 oz) pistachios, shelled and very finely
    chopped
1½ ml (¼ tsp) ground cinnamon
pinch of paprika
15–30 ml (1–2 tbsp) olive oil
juice of ½–1 lemon
Maldon or sea salt
freshly ground black or white pepper
finely chopped parsley

Mince the chicken or put in a food processor and whizz until very finely chopped. Soak the bread in a little milk, then squeeze dry and crumble finely. Mix into the chicken, then add the pistachios, cinnamon and paprika. Stir in half the oil and lemon juice and season lightly. Knead until the mixture is thoroughly amalgamated, adding a little more oil or lemon if it's too thick, and according to taste. Adjust the seasoning if necessary, then roll thickly in the chopped parsley and chill slightly before serving.

CHICKEN WITH PRUNES, HONEY AND ALMONDS

Dajaj Ma' Khokh, Asl wa Lauz

Visiting a Moroccan friend in London, the day after she had given a huge family party, I sampled this. Traditionally served hot, it was absolutely wonderful cold, the sauce having set to a sweet-spicy glaze. Persia, too, cooks prunes, not to mention apricots and sultanas, with chicken, and there are several references to the combination in old cookery books, but the countries in-between seem to have lost the habit – a pity, for it is good.

Serves 6–8

1 large chicken, weighing about 1.6 kg (3½ lb),
   jointed (see below)
Maldon or sea salt
freshly ground black pepper
5 cm (2 inch) piece of cinnamon bark
2 large onions, skinned and grated or minced
75–100 g (3–4 oz) unsalted butter
2–3 saffron strands
225 g (8oz) prunes, soaked overnight
2½ ml (½ tsp) ground ginger
2½ ml (½ tsp) ground cinnamon
15 ml (1 tbsp) clear honey
30 ml (2 tbsp) peanut oil
75 g (3 oz) blanched almonds
30 ml (2 tbsp) sesame seeds

Have the butcher joint the chicken into 6 or 8 pieces, and ask for the liver if possible. If you do get the liver, wash it and cut out all yellowish bits – one trace of them and the sauce will be quite bitter. I usually keep the wings back for other recipes but you can, of course, include them here. Rub the pieces all over with salt and lots of freshly ground black pepper (the recipe given to me states: '1 heaped soupspoonful pepper,' but I feel that a bit *too* much for most people's taste), then arrange in a large heavy-based pan. Bury the cinnamon bark, and the liver if you have it, in the middle, then sprinkle over the onions. Cut the butter into small pieces and put on top, then bring about 350 ml (12 fl oz) water to the boil and pour over the saffron. Stir to start its colour running, then pour over the chicken. Cover the pan, and cook over a moderate heat until you hear the liquid bubbling. Turn the heat down and simmer for 30–40 minutes until the chicken is quite tender. Turn it over several times during the cooking, adding more boiling water if necessary. Remove chicken pieces and reserve.

Drain the prunes and add to the pan, together with the ginger and ground cinnamon (take out the cinnamon bark) and cook for 15 minutes. Then stir in the honey and boil the sauce hard until it is quite syrupy, about 4–7 minutes but this does vary. Check to see if it needs more salt and pepper (unlikely) then gently lay the chicken pieces on top of the sauce. Cover the pan and reheat chicken.

Heat the oil and quickly fry the almonds for 2–3 minutes until nicely golden, then drain well. Dry roast the sesame seeds or, wipe out the almond pan and fry them in that until coloured. Arrange the chicken on a large platter, pour over the sauce, then scatter almonds and sesame seeds on top. Excellent eaten immediately – even better the next day.

CHICKEN SOFRITO

Dajaj Sofrito

Sofrito, a word of Spanish origin, is used to describe a method of cooking chicken, veal or fish, much loved in the southern-eastern band of Mediterranean countries. Like so many things, the end result belies the essential simplicity of this dish: poaching in oil, water, lemon and turmeric to give a chicken softly touched with gold, sitting in its lightly jellied sauce of a pale primrose hue. A great favourite in Alexandria when I visited with my grandfather. And I have since met a Turkish variation, *Tavuk Jölesi*, which omits turmeric but actually makes aspic of the chicken stock. Pieces of the meat are then set between layers of the aspic mixed with parsley and slivered almonds. Very pretty.

Serves 6–8

1 large chicken, weighing about 1.6–2 kg (3½–4½ lb)
juice of 1 lemon
30–45 ml (2–3 tbsp) olive oil
2½ ml (½ tsp) turmeric
1 garlic clove, skinned and crushed
5 cm (2 inch) piece cinnamon bark
Maldon or sea salt
freshly ground white pepper

Rinse the chicken inside and out and place in a large saucepan. Mix the remaining ingredients with about 300 ml (½ pint) water and pour over the chicken. Bring to the boil quickly, then turn the heat to low and gently simmer, covered, for 50 minutes to 1¼ hours. This will depend on your chicken, and if you should be lucky enough to get a real boiling fowl, then of course it will be much longer. But in England they are hard to find, so I tended to use a free range roasting chicken. Turn the chicken quite frequently during the cooking time, and add a little more water if necessary, but don't swamp the animal. Once the chicken is quite tender, remove the pan from the heat and check the seasoning, adjusting if necessary, then leave until cool enough to handle.

Carve the meat into nice chunky pieces and arrange on a platter – not too shallow, you want room for the sauce to set around the meat. If the sauce has started to jell you may need to warm it a little, then pour all over the chicken and let it get quite cold – in cool climates, overnight in a cold larder is fine. If chilling, then bring to room temperature before serving, unless it's blazing hot, in which case remove from the refrigerator about 10–15 minutes before serving. Excellent with all sorts of salads, and particularly good with any of the nut sauces – walnut for my choice.

STUFFED CHICKEN

Piliç Dolması

The first Turkish party I attended was quite an overwhelming affair, even by Middle Eastern standards. And in the middle of the table was a circle of eight golden, tantalising chickens. When our hostess came to carving them, she cut straight through. Aha, I thought, boned chickens – impressive at the best of times. This was even better though, for the chicken flesh had been cooked, minced and mixed with veal and pistachios and then stuffed into the skin, for its final sautéeing. My first attempts to recreate this at home perforce had to omit the final stage since, by then, my chicken skin looked like an unsolvable jigsaw puzzle, so I merely rolled the whole thing into a huge sausage and cooked that. It tasted excellent although it didn't look quite so awe inspiring. Then I learnt that there was the cheat's way. I still cheat, I'm afraid, whenever I can get to my friendly butcher. He does the whole job superbly, in about 1 minute flat. I am getting better, and I give his instructions – they sound so foolproof – below. With a word of warning, go slowly at first – whenever I try to ape his performance, the wretched skin catches on some protruding bone I didn't know existed, and rips. But it can be done. And yes – it is worth it.

Serves 8–12

1 large chicken, weighing about 1.8 kg (4 lb)
Maldon or sea salt
freshly ground black pepper
1–2 celery sticks
3–4 parsley sprigs
2 onions, skinned and quartered
450 g (1 lb) lean veal, minced
125 g (4 oz) pistachios, shelled
1 garlic clove, skinned and finely chopped
5 ml (1 tsp) ground cinnamon
juice of ½–1 lemon
75–90 ml (5–6 tbsp) finely chopped parsley
45 ml (3 tbsp) olive oil

Rinse the chicken, then chop off the wings (keep for another recipe) and the tips of the drumsticks. Rub the chicken all over, quite roughly, to start loosening the skin from the flesh, and then, using a boning knife or one with a small thin blade, loosen the skin from the breast membrane by carefully running between the skin and the breasts. Be very gentle over the top of the breast bone as it can easily tear here, but if you have rubbed well, it should slide through easily enough. Now, sit the chicken on its 'tail' end and start pulling the skin down, from the neck, over the wing gaps, the body and finally the legs. It will be inside out when you have pulled it right off – and, hopefully, more or less in one piece. Wash, and turn the right way out.

The rest is easy. Put the chicken into a large pan, add a little salt and pepper, the celery, parsley and onions. Bring to the boil, skim, then simmer gently for about 1 hour until the chicken is beautifully tender. Let it cool in the stock until easily handled, then take out and cut off all the flesh. Strain the stock and reserve.

Mince the chicken, then mix with the veal, pistachios, garlic, cinnamon and juice of ½ lemon. Stir in the parsley and make sure everything is evenly distributed, then season, quite highly, with salt and pepper.

If you should be unfortunate enough to have any holes in your skin, darn them, and all other openings except the largest. Spoon the stuffing in, not too tightly – you don't want it to burst in the cooking after all this, then sew up the cavity. Mould it roughly into a chicken shape.

Heat the oil in a large pan, add the 'chicken' and fry on all sides until browned, about 4–5 minutes, then add a couple of ladles of the reserved stock and the remaining lemon juice. Cover the pan, and stew gently for about 1 hour, adding more stock by the ladle, when the last lot has almost disappeared. At the finish, you should have about two ladles of liquid, almost a glaze, left. Transfer to a serving dish. Leave to cool. To serve, cut into thick slices – at table. After all that hard work, a little showing-off is quite permissible.

CIRCASSIAN CHICKEN

Çerkez Tavuğu

Another very famous Turkish dish and one of the most splendid ways of serving chicken cold. It was, according to legend, named after the Circassian girls in the Sultan's harem – reputed to be among the most beautiful. Other countries of the Middle East have adopted this recipe with alacrity, simply using the nuts available in their locality. Walnuts are the Turkish choice, hazelnuts, almonds or even pine nuts are used elsewhere. I wouldn't recommend mixing nuts, except pine nuts and almonds, because I think the flavours become too jumbled, but many people do.

Serves 6–8
1 chicken, weighing about 1.6–1.8 kg (3½–4 lb)
2 onions, skinned
2 cloves
2 leeks
few celery leaves
Maldon or sea salt
freshly ground black pepper
1 thick slice white bread, crusts removed
150 g (5 oz) walnuts
1–2 garlic cloves, skinned and crushed
15 ml (1 tbsp) walnut oil
paprika

Rinse the chicken, then put in a large pan with one onion quartered, one stuck with the cloves. Add the leeks, celery leaves, a pinch of salt and freshly ground black pepper and bring to the boil. Skim off any scum, then simmer gently, covered, for about 1 hour until the chicken is quite tender. Remove the chicken and strain the stock. Carve the chicken into large pieces, then put in a shallow dish covered with a little stock. Let cool, the stock keeps the chicken juicy.

Soak the bread in a little stock for 5 minutes. Grind the walnuts until quite fine, then put in a pan with the bread, crumble it a bit, and add a scant 600 ml (1 pint) of the strained stock. Add the garlic and bring to the boil stirring constantly, and bashing

the bread until it's completely pulverised. Cook until the sauce has thickened, almost to the consistency of a good mayonnaise – you can add a little more stock if necessary. Season with a little more salt and pepper.

Drain off the stock in which the chicken pieces are cooling, then arrange the chicken on a large serving platter. Completely cover with the sauce, then leave to cool, covered, and, unless it's very hot, preferably not in the refrigerator because it kills the development of the flavours. Just before serving, mix the walnut oil with a little paprika and drizzle all over the top.

STUFFED TURKEY

Habash Mahshi

Turkeys, of course, come from North and Central America – not Turkey at all. First brought back to Europe by the *conquistadores* from Mexico, they were quickly adopted into the European kitchen. The French called them *coq d'Inde* (bird of India) later shortened to *dinde* or *dindon* (the male bird). The Turks were equally logical in their name, *hindi*, also meaning from India. The sixteenth-century English were, however, somewhat confused both in their geography, and their fowls. Firstly, East and West Indies were thought for a while to be the same place; secondly guinea fowl, known since the previous century, came via agents of the East India Spice Company through Turkish domains from Guinea (in West Africa) to Europe. The new bird was merely in their eyes a larger version of the old, Turkey was near India, and thus was a great confusion born. Notwithstanding its origins, turkeys are popular and abound in the Middle East. Small and scratching around for their living, they tend to be tougher and gamier in taste than the English birds – plump and cosseted. With spicy stuffings, and slow simmering or pot-roasting, however, they make a delicious dish, often served as the centrepiece of a buffet, cut into small pieces and piled dramatically over their stuffing.

Previous page (l–r): Sweet and Sour Leeks (p. 117), Greek Mushrooms in Oil (p. 124), Spiced Carrots (p. 120), Stuffed Onions (p. 122) and Burghul Salad (p. 135).

The Turks usually roast their birds, the Lebanese simmer them in stock, and often add cayenne and paprika to the stuffing.

Serves 10–12
3.6 kg (8 lb) turkey, dressed weight, liver reserved
juice of 2 lemons
120 ml (8 tbsp) olive oil
450 g (1 lb) lamb, minced
50 g (2 oz) blanched almonds
50 g (2 oz) pistachios, shelled
50 g (2 oz) walnuts
50 g (2 oz) sultanas
225 g (8 oz) long grain rice
small bunch fresh parsley, finely chopped
5 ml (1 tsp) freshly ground allspice
5 ml (1 tsp) ground cinnamon
Maldon or sea salt
freshly ground black pepper
175–225 ml (6–8 fl oz) turkey or chicken stock
To garnish 50 g (2 oz) pine nuts

Wash the turkey inside and out, and squeeze over the juice of 1 lemon. Discard any yellowish bits from the liver, then finely chop and reserve. Heat 15 ml (3 tbsp) oil in a large pan, add the mince and stir fry for 3–4 minutes until coloured all over. Add the nuts and fry for another 3 minutes, add the sultanas and then stir in the rice and cook until all the grains are gleaming. Take off the heat and mix in the parsley, spices and salt and pepper, then the liver and the remaining lemon juice. Stuff the turkey with the mixture – not packing too tightly for the rice will swell up, then brush all over with the remaining oil. Put the turkey in a large roasting tin, pour the stock in the bottom and cover loosely with foil. Cook in the oven at 190°C (375°F), mark 5 for 25–30 minutes to every 450 g (1 lb), plus an extra 25 minutes or so until the bird is quite tender. If you want the skin golden, remove the foil for the last 40 minutes but many people prefer the flesh to remain pale. Remove from the oven when done and leave, covered, to cool. Carve the flesh into bite-sized pieces, discarding the skin if you haven't browned it, then pile the stuffing on a serving platter and arrange the turkey meat on top. Just before serving, fry the pine nuts in a little oil and scatter over. An excellent treatment for what is, all too often, a rather dull bird.

MOROCCAN GRILLED PIGEONS

Hammam Mechoui

There was a restaurant near the Pyramids famous for its pigeons, which, alas, to me was only a legend. But again my grandfather 'told all' and a favourite supper of ours was fresh pigeon breasts, grilled according to his precise requirements, 'no, no, no, not enough lemon juice; a touch more pepper – more, and lots of chervil. Is it finely chopped? Good, that's good.' I must say I never once in my life saw him cook anything – but he always seemed to know how to cook everything, down to the last detail. Pigeons don't hold the same inhibitions for the English as the other birds favoured by the Middle East, so are widely available. But rarely fresh, except in the country where I used to find the neighbouring farmers were only too happy to slip me as many as I wanted – and more! And for the Egyptian dish, they were perfect – a little brushing with oil, sprinkling of lemon and pepper, then a quick grilling with salt and finely chopped chervil, or parsley. Done. Frozen birds simply will not do. I have tried marinating them overnight in oil but they still lacked that marvellous tenderness. So if you haven't fresh pigeons but want 'to go Egyptian' – use baby poussins. I was overjoyed then to be given a Moroccan recipe which gently stews the pigeons first, before grilling. The answer to my problems – and to the *mezze* table. For the initial cooking can be done hours ahead, leaving only the final grilling before serving.

Serves 4–6

4 pigeons, cleaned
50 g (2 oz) unsalted butter or 60 ml (4 tbsp) oil, if serving cold
10 ml (2 tsp) paprika
5 ml (1 tsp) cumin seeds, crushed
1 garlic clove, skinned and crushed
pinch of cinnamon
Maldon or sea salt
freshly ground black pepper

Wash the pigeons inside and out and put into a large pan, preferably sitting them snugly side by side tilted on one breast. Melt the butter if using, then mix with half the paprika and cumin seeds, the garlic, and cinnamon. Oil can just be stirred into the ingredients, then poured over the pigeons with about 600 ml (1 pint) water: the birds should barely be covered. Bring to the boil, then cover the pan and simmer gently for 1½–2 hours until quite tender, adding a little more water if necessary, and turning the birds on to the other breast halfway through cooking. When they are done, remove from the pan and boil the sauce hard until much reduced – you'll need a scant 150 ml (¼ pint). Cool the sauce and birds.

About 10 minutes before serving, stir the remaining paprika and cumin into the sauce. Cut the breasts off each bird (keep the remainder of the carcass for a glorious soup) and brush each breast, on both sides, with a little of the sauce. Sprinkle with salt and pepper and grill under a high heat for 2–3 minutes on each side until crisp. Cut each breast into three slices on the diagonal, and serve hot or cold.

ROASTED 'STOLEN' PARTRIDGES

Partridges Klephti

Klephtis, from the Greek 'to steal' was a term originally applied to the Greek brigands who waged guerrilla warfare against the occupying Turks. Soon it came to mean their method of cooking – meat, usually stolen, and particularly birds, stuffed with mountain herbs, wrapped in paper, then buried in an earthenware pot to cook over a glowing pinewood fire. However scrawny the creature may have been in the beginning, the end result was delicious, and the technique is still popular in Greece today. So are partridges. In England these little birds, akin to a mildly gamey chicken, are protected, their season being 1st September to 1st February. At their best however, during October and November, they respond well to this treatment. I like them quite well hung but if you prefer a milder flavour, three days is sufficient. Or substitute guinea fowl or baby poussin if inclination and/or availability dictate.

Serves 4–6

2 young partridges, hung, then dressed
juice of 1 lemon
6 sprigs fresh thyme
6 sprigs fresh marjoram
Maldon or sea salt
freshly ground black pepper
4–6 rashers streaky bacon
butter or olive oil

Wash the birds inside and out, then rub lemon juice all over them. Stuff the birds with 3 sprigs each of the herbs, then season with salt and black pepper and wrap in the bacon.

Liberally butter or brush with oil (the latter if the birds are going to be left to cool) 2 pieces of foil or baking paper large enough to completely envelop the birds. Put a bird in the centre of each paper, and seal firmly. Cook in the oven at 170°C (325°F), mark 3, for about 1–1½ hours – this will depend on the age and size of the birds. Check after 1 hour by piercing the breast – if the juices are clear, it's done. Or wiggle one of the legs: if it moves very easily, again it's ready. Take out of the oven, remove the bacon and discard the herbs, then joint into four pieces and serve with the juices poured over. If you want to serve them cold (I think very good) leave to cool in their papers before jointing them. Excellent with cucumber and yogurt salad.

FRIED PARTRIDGES

M'hammer Durraj

M'hammer is actually one of three basic sauces which provide many subtle variations on a theme for the Moroccans. This is 'red' sauce, traditionally made with butter, paprika and cumin as the constants. I have two variations of this recipe, very similar, except that one calls for a quarter of a pickled lemon. Which

gives a delicate, but distinct, difference. A difference I like. But if you haven't any pickled or preserved lemons (or limes) omit – using juice will not produce the desired effect. Again, poussins can be substituted – and it's amazing what respectability this recipe gives to a frozen battery hen.

Serves 6

3 partridges, cleaned
2½ ml (½ tsp) cumin seeds, crushed
2½ cm (1 inch) piece fresh root ginger, peeled and grated
5 ml (1 tsp) paprika
5 ml (1 tsp) coriander seeds, ground
1 medium onion, skinned and minced or grated
1 garlic clove, skinned and crushed
Maldon or sea salt
freshly ground black pepper
100 g (4 oz) unsalted butter
60–75 ml (4–5 tbsp) peanut oil
2–3 strands saffron
bunch of coriander leaves
bunch of fresh parsley
¼ preserved lemon or 3 slices *Limoun Hamadh Makbouss* (page 127)

Wash the partridges inside and out and pat dry. Mix the spices with the onion and garlic, pounding until quite pulpy. Rub all over the partridges, smearing a little on the inside as well, then sprinkle on some salt and lots of freshly ground black pepper. Melt half the butter and 15 ml (1 tbsp) oil in a large pan or flame-proof casserole dish, add the birds, breast side down, and fry for 3–4 minutes until golden all over. Pour 600 ml (1 pint) boiling water over the saffron strands and stir until the colour starts to run, then pour over the partridges. Add a little more water if necessary, the birds should be three-quarters covered, then tie the coriander and parsley together and tuck into the middle. Bring to the boil, then simmer, covered, for 30–45 minutes until the birds are tender. Older partridges may need a little longer – do the leg pull test: if it moves easily, they're done. Take the birds out of the pan and cut each in half, using a cleaver or a good, heavy sharp knife.

Cut the peel away from the flesh of the lemon, then squeeze the flesh hard to extract as much juice as possible. Add to the sauce with the lemon zest, and boil hard to reduce to about 150 ml (¼ pint). If you want to make the dish to this stage in advance, don't reduce it quite so much, to allow for reduction on reheating.

About 15 minutes before serving, heat the remaining butter and oil. When very hot, add the partridge halves – you probably won't be able to do more than two at a time – and fry until deeply golden. Drain and cook the rest. Reheat the sauce, discard the herb bunches, and pour over the partridges. Serve with lots of Arab bread, large napkins and bowls of rose-water. This is gutsy finger food.

GRILLED QUAIL

Assafeer Meshwi

Sentiment, I'm afraid, does not rule the Mediterranean heart when it comes to the autumn flocks of migrating birds. From Italy and Greece to North Africa, almost all birds are considered fair game, and many have their journey rudely ended in the cooking pot. These tiny creatures, *assafeer* to the Egyptians, are much loved as a *mezze*, seasoned and grilled over charcoal braziers served sprinkled with lemon juice. Once I had overcome my initial qualms as to their very small size – I too enjoyed them. English quail are gutsier in flavour, which I like. But you could substitute baby poussins. One will do 2–4 people.

Serves 6–12
12 quail, cleaned
1–2 garlic cloves, skinned and very finely chopped
Maldon or sea salt
10 ml (2 tsp) cumin seeds
10 ml (2 tsp) coriander seeds
30 ml (2 tbsp) fresh coriander leaves
juice of 1 onion
pinch of cayenne pepper or two of paprika
120 ml (8 tbsp) olive oil
finely chopped parsley
To serve parsley
lemon wedges

Wash the quail and put in a deep dish. Lightly bash the chopped garlic with a little salt – you don't want it completely crushed but you do want to release some of the juice. Grind the cumin and coriander seeds in a spice grinder and mix into the garlic, then quickly grind the coriander leaves and add them too.

Mix in the onion juice, the cayenne or paprika, then stir in the oil to make quite a thick paste. Smear all over the birds and leave to marinate for 1 hour.

Thread on 2 large skewers (otherwise you'll be forever turning birds) and grill under a high heat for about 5–7 minutes, turning constantly, until they are done and slightly charred on the outside. Serve on a bed of parsley with lemon wedges. Good hot or cold.

VEGETABLES

Khudar

Lances we have, the tips whereof are curled,
Their bodies like a hawser turned and twirled,
Yet fair to view, with ne'er a knot to boot,
Their heads bolt upright from the shoulder shoot,
And, by the grace of Him Who made us all,
Firm-fixed in soil they stand, like pillars tall.

MAHMUD IBN AL-HUSAIN AL-KUSHAJIM[1]

Thus was the noble asparagus poetically described at the famous banquet held by the Baghdad Caliph Mustakfi.[2] The gathering had been called to discuss the great dishes of the Arab kitchen, each one present to read a poem, thereafter all to feast on the fare so lyrically portrayed. Even then asparagus was a rare delicacy, and it was the one poem not translated into reality, the Caliph calling for someone to write to his neighbouring ruler to 'request him to send us such asparagus from Damascus.'[3] Ten centuries later its appearance in the market place of Baghdad was still cause for excitement, and I well remember the morning when I woke to the cook's shouts of '*yallah, yallah, yallah*' (hurry, hurry, hurry) echoing through the house. He had just received word that the long awaited 'caravan' from Damascus had been spotted on the outskirts of the city – and there was a large consignment of asparagus. I begged to be allowed to go to the market and soon was safely ensconced high up on the shoulders of my favourite member of the household, Mahmoud-Ali. Affectionately known as Ali-horse (in honour of many hours spent playing that role), he was of Nubian descent and stood at a majestic six foot six. In his immaculately white, flowing *djallaba* and tasselled scarlet *tarboush* he was a

colourful and commanding figure in the market place, and we moved swiftly through the packed crowds surging and jostling to reach the lorry laden with the magic vegetable. I was momentarily disappointed it was not a camel – 'caravans' being synonymous with that disdainful beast – but it was too exciting to mind for long. Ali's hand had gracefully tossed a coin high up in the air, and almost simultaneously caught three precious bundles bound in plaited straw, just like the poem 'With links of gold so twine they, waist to waist.'[4] Clasping our burdens tightly, the urgency was over and now we could wander gently through the market. From my point of view, it was a dazzling sight. I had only recently read the story of Aladdin's Palace: now here it was before me – jewels strewn in every direction. Mountains of huge ruby radishes, encircled by their emerald leaves, were flanked by long, dark and glossy aubergines – in their turn offset by tiny pearl rounds of turnip. Peppers were arranged as on the salad plate, in a fan of alternate yellow, red and green; beside were large fair-skinned onions, then their small, deeply purple Italian cousins. Above hung a fringe of plaited ropes of garlic – their fat cloves shining faintly pink through the papery covering. Huge bundles of coriander leaves flopped behind a pool of lemons while bright, shining oranges were quietened down by the soft green of long, pointed okra, quaintly but aptly named 'ladies' fingers'. Everywhere I looked there were different colours and shapes, each trader setting up next to another who would offset his wares to the best advantage. And all the time, the shoppers – men as well as women – were prodding and sniffing, was it the right shape for stuffing? Were the pomegranates juicy? Who had small courgettes today? And where was the water carrier? The sun was midway on the horizon and we were hot. At last, we came across the watermelon stall. A slice of that – dark pink, cool and crisp – would do to quench our thirst. Happily, we trotted home, Ali to deliver the treasured asparagus; I to breakfast, then to school. It was going to be a wonderful day.

1. *AD 915–967/303–356 Islamic calendar.*
2. *Caliph from AD 944–946/333–335 Islamic calendar, when he was cruelly ousted and 'had his eyes put out' by the Buyid Ahmad ibn Abi Shuja. He died in AD 949/338 Islamic calendar.*
3. Meadows of Gold *by Mas'udi, translated into French* Les Prairies d'Or, *by Barbier de Maynard and Pavet de Courteille.*
4. *Mahmud ibn al-Husain al-Kushajim.*

ONIONS MARINATED IN VINEGAR

Basal Mamqur

Onions were grown in the 'gardens of kings' and the 'gardens of the gods' in ancient Mesopotamia, and one of the earliest written codes of law, the *Hammurabi*, states that bread and onions shall be given, monthly, to the very poor. Perhaps that is why onions are so denigrated in Arabic folklore – yet the reality contradicts the myth. Everyone enjoys eating them. They play a vital role in the Arab kitchen, particularly raw. Even the Prophet Mohammed, despite his strictures not to attend prayers with the smell of onions (or garlic) on the breath, enjoyed eating them. Alas, I know of no foolproof way of avoiding the raw onion's lingering aroma, but the Persians, once again, have introduced a

subtle refinement to soften the burning rawness of its taste. On the homeopathic principle, the two potent flavours – onion and vinegar – react with each other to produce this sweetly delicious dish.

Serves 4–6
2 very large onions, skinned and finely sliced
45 ml (3 tbsp) white wine vinegar
7½ ml (½ tbsp) dried mint
2½ ml (½ tsp) cumin seeds, crushed
Maldon or sea salt

Toss the sliced onions in a large bowl with the vinegar, mint and cumin seeds. Sprinkle with salt and leave for 1–2 hours, turning every now and again. Wonderful as an appetiser, good too as a side dish with *şiş kebabs* and *köfte*.

SWEET AND SOUR LEEKS

Kurrat Hamidh

The essence of sweet-sour dishes is not confined to the Chinese. Yet, strangely, this technique in cooking often seems to go hand in hand with a dualist religion or philosophy. In China, they have the elements *yin* and *yang*, male and female. In ancient Persia, it was the very old belief of Zoroastrianism. Here, the opposites of good and evil have to be in a state of balance in order for the world to exist. In their cuisine too, perfect harmony is always strived for. So you have the balance of sour and sweet, the mild with the strongly spiced, the crisp and crunchy with the softly fluffy – as in their rice.

Curiously, of all the other Middle Eastern countries, only Morocco seems to have kept a repertoire of sweet-sour dishes. Elsewhere, the taste seems to have been lost though al-Baghdadi gave several recipes.

Leeks we had in profusion in Damascus (Syrian leeks are mentioned several times in al-Baghdadi's medieval manual, so that hasn't changed) and, after a family friend had visited from Tehran, this dish appeared regularly on the menu.

Serves 6
900 g (2 lb) leeks
60 ml (4 tbsp) olive oil
2 garlic cloves, skinned and crushed
15 ml (1 tbsp) soft pale brown sugar
juice of 1 sour pomegranate, or 1–1½ lemons

Wash and trim the leeks – I like to keep as much green as possible, although traditionally only the whites are used. The leeks we had in Syria seemed always to be very pale and elegantly thin. Cut them in half lengthways.

Heat the oil in a pan large enough to fit the leeks in one layer – I use a large shallow baking tin; add the garlic and sugar and stir constantly until slightly syrupy. Add the leeks and cook until lightly golden, then pour in the pomegranate or lemon juice and cover the pan (use a baking or metal tray if cooking in a baking tin, covered with foil). Turn the heat to the lowest possible setting and stew slowly until the leeks are tender but not mushy – about 10–20 minutes. Lovely hot, better cold.

CELERIAC STEWED IN LEMON

Karafan wa Limoun

Celeriac, the celery brainwashed by botanists to grow like a turnip. It has survived this brutal treatment remarkably well to give us the sweetness of one, and the smoky pepperiness of the other – a lovely vegetable, and a perfect partner to lemon. A good Lebanese marriage.

Serves 4–6
2–3 large celeriacs
60–75 ml (4–5 tbsp) olive oil
pinch of cinnamon
pinch of paprika
tiny pinch of cayenne
juice of 1½–2 lemons

Maldon or sea salt
freshly ground black pepper

Peel the celeriacs – they are often quite pitted so you may need to peel deeply, don't feel too guilty. Cut into slices, then into long thin matchsticks. Heat the oil in a large shallow pan, add the celeriac and fry, turning constantly, until lightly golden all over. Pour in about a wineglass of water, sprinkle on the spices, then the juice of 1½ lemons. Simmer for about 20 minutes, then taste the liquid – if it needs more lemon, add it. Season with salt and black pepper if you wish – not too much though, the cayenne is quite spicy and you don't want to kill the delicate balance of tastes. Cook for another 10 minutes or until the celeriac is tender. I think best cold, although often served hot.

GREEN BEANS WITH ONION AND TOMATO

Fassolakia Freska

Beans, beans, everywhere. All over the Middle East they grow. And there are countless ways of preserving them, and cooking them. We had them in salads, we had them as a vegetable, we had them in *eggahs*. Packed in huge jars and salted – they stared at us balefully through their glass in the winter. I still love green beans and used only to lament at the eccentricities of the English summer which sometimes gave me a glut or, as one year, only five. Not pounds – beans. In Sri Lanka, we have wonderfully exotic beans: yardlong, pale yellow, dark purple, and the delightful, frilled wing bean – all excellent for this dish.

A Greek recipe this, but popular also in Turkey – with cinnamon and coriander; the Lebanon – with cinnamon, paprika and cayenne; Persia – with dillweed and garlic; Iraq – with garlic and fresh coriander. I like it too with garlic and fresh pineapple mint.

Serves 6
1 kg (2¼ lb) fresh green beans
60 ml (4 tbsp) olive oil
2 large onions, skinned and finely sliced
1 garlic clove, skinned and finely chopped
30 ml (2 tbsp) tomato purée
15 ml (1 tbsp) dried rigani or oregano
Maldon or sea salt
freshly ground black pepper
To serve lemon wedges (optional)

Top and tail the beans, then cut into long diagonal slices. Heat the oil in a large shallow pan, add the onions and fry for 10 minutes until soft. Add the garlic and cook for another minute. Mix the tomato purée with about 2 wineglasses of water and stir into the pan. Add the beans – the water should cover them; if not, add a little more. Sprinkle with rigani, salt and pepper (white in Iraq – which I still favour), cover the pan and simmer, very slowly, for about 20–40 minutes, depending on the age and the origin of your beans. Serve hot or cold, with lemon wedges if wished.

COURGETTES BAKED WITH TOMATOES

Chourba wa Tomatin

Courgettes are a much used vegetable all over the Middle East – and great care is taken when buying them. For stuffing, they should be large and oval. For salads, long and thin. For this dish, slim and fairly small. It is quite an art – the only thing that would flummox the Arab housewife would be the English prize marrow. And yet this recipe, particularly loved in Turkey, is the perfect answer to those whoppers.

Serves 6
900 g (2 lb) courgettes
90 ml (6 tbsp) olive oil

2–3 garlic cloves, skinned and finely chopped
450 g (1 lb) fresh small tomatoes, blanched, skinned and halved
15 ml (1 tbsp) coriander seeds, crushed
Maldon or sea salt
freshly ground black pepper
To serve finely chopped parsley (optional)
lemon juice (optional)

Top and tail the courgettes – if they are small, merely cut down the middle, lengthways, otherwise cut into thick slices. Heat the oil, add the garlic and sauté for ½ minute – careful here, garlic burns very easily. Add the courgettes and fry for another 2–3 minutes, turning fairly frequently to colour them. Add the tomatoes, stir for 1 minute, then bash slightly with a wooden spoon to release their juices. Sprinkle over the coriander seeds, salt and black pepper, cover the pan and simmer, very gently, for about 10–15 minutes until the courgettes are done – but not slushy, they should still just have a bite to them. Put into a serving dish, allow to cool, then sprinkle with parsley and lemon juice if wished.

OKRA WITH TOMATOES AND ONIONS

Bamia bi Tomaten

Strangely I did not meet okra – or ladies' fingers as they are evocatively called – until I met the Sudanese. Then I was hooked. But the Arabs love, grow and cook them too – perhaps they were considered just a bit too sophisticated for a child's taste. Shame, for they are delicious. A word of advice though; when preparing, do not cut the tip end right off – this will release the glutinous juices, loved by aficionados but overpowering to the beginner. And, aficionado that I am, I still prefer to enjoy the full impact of their flavour when I bite into them. (You can buy canned okra but, whatever anyone says, they are not the same.)

Serves 6–8

900 g (2 lb) fresh okra
90 ml (6 tbsp) olive oil
225 g (8 oz) pickling onions, peeled and halved
4 garlic cloves, skinned and finely chopped
30 ml (2 tbsp) coriander seeds, crushed
3 large beef steak tomatoes, or 450 g (1 lb) small
    tomatoes, blanched, skinned and sliced or
    halved
Maldon or sea salt
freshly ground black or white pepper
juice of 1–2 lemons

Wash the okra, cutting off any excess stalk but leaving the tips intact. Heat the oil in a large pan, add the onions and cook for 10 minutes, stirring frequently, to colour them. Add the okra, stirring gently, and fry for another 5 minutes, then add the garlic and coriander – push the okra and onions to the sides of the pan, and cook until the aroma starts to rise, about 3–4 minutes, before putting in the tomatoes. Season with salt and pepper (a mixture of black and white for my taste) then add a wineglass or two of water – just to cover the okra, and cook, very slowly until the okra are really tender – 45 minutes to 1 hour. Add the juice of 1 lemon, and simmer for another 10 minutes, then turn on to a serving plate, and leave to cool, covered. Sprinkle on more lemon juice if wished and serve.

ARTICHOKE HEARTS WITH BROAD BEANS

Baklalı Enginar

Artichokes are beloved of the Greeks and Turks. Also, interestingly, of the Copts – who observe the most devout Lenten fast. It reminds me of medieval Venice – no meat, no milk, no butter, no eggs, no cheese. Much ingenuity was needed to produce interesting food during those 40 days. And it was given. This dish is almost too good for the *mezze* table. It

should be appreciated on its own. Certainly the English climate is not kind enough to provide it in Lent. So enjoy it in early summer, as the Greeks and Turks do.

Serves 6

6 fresh artichokes
juice of 2 lemons
45 ml (3 tbsp) olive oil
2–3 garlic cloves, skinned and finely chopped
pinch of sugar
700 g (1½ lb) fresh broad beans, shelled
15 ml (1 tbsp) finely chopped marjoram
Maldon or sea salt
freshly ground black pepper

The fresher the artichokes the better. If you can pick your own, you will be able to prepare them easily the traditional way – removing the leaves, then scraping out the choke to leave just the heart. If you have to buy your artichokes, I find it easier to throw them into a pan of boiling water and cook for 5–7 minutes. This makes light work of peeling the leaves and pulling out the choke. (Do not throw the leaves away – once peeled, cook them for a further 5 minutes and enjoy them – dipped into a mustardy vinaigrette – cook's perks!) Put the hearts into a large pan with the lemon juice, oil, garlic, sugar and about 175 ml (6 fl oz) of water. Bring to the boil, then add the shelled broad beans, marjoram, salt and black pepper. Turn the heat low and simmer for about 20–40 minutes, depending on age and size of the vegetables, until tender, by which time the liquid will be much reduced. Transfer vegetables and liquid to a serving dish – leave to cool to room temperature.

SPICED CARROTS

Jazar Atariyah

My English friends are amazed when I mention carrots as a Middle Eastern vegetable. There is something indescribably British about carrots, solid, respectable, slightly sweet, always there – usually overcooked. Yet in Persia, and Tunisia – the Moorish arm was long and broadly swept – they are a favourite, sweetly seasoned in the one country, hotly in the other. Their native habitat of course is Afghanistan – not surprising when one remembers how beautifully India treats them: as a heavenly sweet – regally decorated with pure silver leaf.

Serves 6
900 g (2 lb) carrots
30 ml (2 tbsp) olive oil
3 garlic cloves, skinned and finely chopped
15 ml (1 tbsp) cumin seeds, crushed
OR 15 ml (1 tbsp) caraway seeds
    plus 1–2 dried red chillies
Maldon or sea salt
pinch of sugar (optional)
15 ml (1 tbsp) rose-water (if using cumin)
To serve lemon juice (optional)

Top and tail the carrots, scrub them and cut into long thin fingers. Heat the oil in a large pan, add the garlic and sauté for 1 minute, then add the cumin (or, for the Tunisian dish, caraway and chilli) and carrots. Toss for a couple of minutes to glaze slightly, then add a wineglass of water, salt, sugar if the carrots are old, and the rose-water (omit this if making with caraway and chilli). Cook over a medium heat, covered, until the carrots are just done – still with a bite – and the liquid absorbed. Put into a serving dish, let cool slightly, and serve. Some like lemon juice – I think it kills the rose-water, so suit your taste. But go gently if using it.

STUFFED AUBERGINES

Imam Bayıldı

One of the most famous of the Turkish *mezeler*, its name literally means 'the Imam fainted' – some say with pleasure at the deliciousness of the dish, others claim the poor priest was horrified at the amount of oil the dish used. I prefer the first theory, especially as you can overcome the problem of aubergines soaking up too much oil by salting them first. This also draws out much of the bitter juices which would otherwise spoil the dish. There are many other versions of stuffed aubergine – *badinjan mahshi* to the Arabs, some using minced lamb, or beef, and pine nuts (particularly popular in Syria and Lebanon), cheese and minced lamb (Turkey), or rice with minced meat, or nuts (everywhere).

Serves 4–8
4 medium-sized aubergines, preferably long and
    slim
Maldon or sea salt
150 ml (¼ pint) olive oil
2 large onions, skinned and finely chopped
3 garlic cloves, skinned and crushed
good bunch parsley, finely chopped
3 large tomatoes, blanched, skinned and coarsely
    chopped
1 bay leaf
2½ ml (½ tsp) ground cinnamon
freshly ground black pepper
2½–5 ml (½–1 tsp) caster sugar
juice of 1 large lemon
To garnish 50 g (2 oz) black olives, stoned and
    halved

Cut the stems off the aubergines, then slice each aubergine in half lengthways and scoop out some of the flesh – make a deepish hollow but leave a little flesh around the edges of the skins or they can break very easily. Sprinkle the insides – and the pile of scooped-out flesh – with salt, and leave for at least 30 minutes.

Heat 45 ml (3 tbsp) oil in a frying pan, add the onions and sauté for about 10 minutes until soft and golden. Add the crushed garlic and fry for another 2 minutes, then stir in the parsley, tomatoes, bay leaf and cinnamon. Season with salt and black pepper and cook for another 5 minutes, until the tomatoes are soft. Pile into a bowl and cool slightly.

Wash the aubergines gently to remove the salt, put the flesh into a sieve and rinse in cold water, then squeeze to dry. Drain the aubergine shells, and pat dry as much as possible. Add another 30 ml (2 tbsp) oil to the frying pan, and quickly cook the flesh for 2–3 minutes. Add to the onion mixture. Pour in another 30 ml (2 tbsp) oil to the pan and sauté the shells, skin sides, for a couple of minutes, then carefully arrange, side by side in a pan into which they fit snugly. Spoon some stuffing into each one, then mix the remaining oil with about 150 ml (¼ pint) of water and the sugar and lemon juice and pour, carefully, over the aubergines. Add a little more water if necessary – they should be just covered.

Cover the pan, and simmer very gently until the aubergines are quite soft, about 30–45 minutes. Take off the heat and let them cool in the pan, then transfer, with care, to a serving dish and garnish with black olives. Can be kept in the refrigerator up to 6 hours, or the freezer for a week. Either way make sure to bring to room temperature to serve.

STUFFED ONIONS

Basal Malfoul

Onions are not just used as a basic flavouring ingredient, or eaten raw, alone and in salads. They are also candidates for stuffing, appearing with different fillings in almost every country. I particularly like the mixture we had in Baghdad though I think it has Turkish overtones. The sweetness of the sultanas, pine nuts and mint complements the onions perfectly but any of the traditional stuffing mixtures are good. In Saudi Arabia they turn this into a truly regal dish, which is well worth doing once in a while – but be warned, you need time and patience. For the onions are slashed through to the centre once peeled, then boiled for 10 minutes until softening and the layers starting to separate. Each 'leaf' is then stuffed, rolled and tied with string, lightly sautéed and then simmered until soft. Perfect for the *mezze* table. But for small gatherings, or if time is of the essence, the version below is quicker and simpler. Still delicious.

Serves 6–12
12 medium onions, skinned
100 g (4 oz) pine nuts
30 ml (2 tbsp) olive oil
75 g (3 oz) long grain rice, well rinsed and drained
50 g (2 oz) sultanas or raisins
2 medium tomatoes, blanched, skinned and chopped
60 ml (4 tbsp) finely chopped parsley
30 ml (2 tbsp) finely chopped fresh mint
1½ ml (¼ tsp) freshly ground allspice
Maldon or sea salt
freshly ground white pepper
lemon juice

Boil the onions in a large pan of water for about 10 minutes until fairly soft. Drain and leave until cool enough to handle, then cut a small slice off the stem end, and pull out the centres. Give yourself a decent-sized hollow but leave a thick shell so they don't fall apart. Keep the scooped out flesh for flavouring another dish.

Fry the pine nuts in the oil until they turn pink – about 2 minutes, then mix with the rice, sultanas or raisins, tomatoes, herbs and allspice. Season lightly with salt and pepper, then mix everything together very thoroughly. Three-quarters fill each onion – you need room for the expansion of the rice, then arrange side by side in a large pan. Pour in water to come half-way up the onions, then sprinkle in a little lemon juice. Cover the pan and simmer slowly for about 25–40 minutes until the filling is cooked and onions perfectly tender. Check from time to time to see if more water is needed, adding if necessary. Allow to cool in the pan, then transfer to a serving dish.

STUFFED QUINCES

Dolmeh E Beh

It was a quince apparently, not an apple, that lured Eve into temptation, and the quince is certainly one of the oldest cultivated fruits, now sadly neglected in the West. But not in Iran, where it is highly regarded and served gloriously stuffed with a mixture of minced meat and split peas. Peppers and tomatoes are also stuffed with this mixture, as are apples (*Dolmeh Sib* or *Teiffah bil-forno*) – here sometimes the meat is omitted and a filling of rice and sultanas used instead. So all is not lost if you have no quinces, but should somebody offer you these pale golden fruits (apple or pear shaped) accept with alacrity. They are as delicious as the heady perfume which indicates their readiness to be cooked. If using apples, make sure they are large and crisp – Bramley's will not do as the flesh will always collapse. Cooking time can be reduced to about 20 minutes – but check with a fine-pointed knife. Tomatoes should be of the beef variety – again check after 15 minutes; peppers will take 'quince-time'.

Serves 6

6 large quinces, about 225 g (8 oz) each, or 12 smaller ones
45 ml (3 tbsp) yellow split peas
30 ml (2 tbsp) olive oil
1 onion, finely chopped
350 g (12 oz) lean lamb, minced
Maldon or sea salt
freshly ground black pepper
2½ ml (½ tsp) ground cinnamon
butter
90 ml (6 tbsp) white wine vinegar
60 ml (4 tbsp) sugar

Wipe the quinces with a damp cloth – they are very slightly furry, but do not peel. Boil the peas in a small pan well covered with water for about 25–30 minutes until soft, then drain. Heat the oil, then fry the onion until soft and barely coloured. Add the lamb and stir until browned all over. Season with salt, pepper and the cinnamon and cook for another few minutes.

Cut a small slice off the top of each quince, then core out a good hollow using an apple corer. Finely chop the hollowed flesh (discard the cores) and add to the stuffing. Pack as much as possible into each quince, pushing well down (chopsticks again are useful here, the blunt end), then top each one with its 'hat'. Arrange, snugly side by side, in a flameproof dish. Scatter over a few slivers of butter and pour in water to come halfway up the quinces. Cover, bring to the boil over a medium heat, then simmer gently for 30–45 minutes until the quinces are tender. Mix the vinegar with the sugar and 45–60 ml (3–4 tbsp) water and pour over, then simmer for another 10 minutes. Serve hot or warm, traditionally with a plain meat or rice dish, but good too with salads.

STUFFED POTATO BALLS

Batata Mahshi

Potatoes are not a particularly Middle Eastern vegetable. However they do exist and are occasionally transformed into something quite magical, as here. There is an even more spectacular dish in which a hollow is cored out of the whole potato and the stuffing put therein. These I was given, once – I must have been unusually angelic that day. But they are tricky to get quite right, and I find these 'surprise' potato balls go down so well that I confess that after the first attempt I have not faced the difficulty again. For brave souls, bake the stuffed spuds in the oven – medium setting, half covered with a tomato sauce, for about 1 hour. Until they are soft but not disintegrating – that's the clever bit. I had these in Iraq incidentally, although Syria has her version, but not Persia, where potatoes were until recently called 'Malcolm's plums' after the man who introduced them, and where they are still regarded with some trepidation. In the Lebanon, they use a mixture of soft cheese, meat and fresh herbs for the stuffing.

Serves 6

900 g (2 lb) potatoes
Maldon or sea salt
1 large egg, beaten
30 ml (2 tbsp) plain flour
30 ml (2 tbsp) olive oil, plus extra for frying
1 large onion, skinned and minced or grated
125 g (4 oz) pine nuts
50 g (2 oz) sultanas or raisins
small bunch of parsley, very finely chopped
1½ ml (¼ tsp) ground ginger
1½ ml (¼ tsp) freshly ground allspice
homemade dried breadcrumbs, finely ground
To serve chopped parsley (optional)

Peel the potatoes, cut into even-sized pieces and boil in salted water until soft. Mash thoroughly and then return to the pan over a medium heat to dry out for 1 minute. Stir in the egg, then sift on the flour and beat in well to mix. Season with a little more salt. Heat the oil, add the onion and sauté for 15 minutes until very soft and golden. Push to the side of the pan, add the pine nuts and cook for 1–2 minutes until pink, then stir in the sultanas, or raisins, and parsley. Season with ginger and allspice, and cook for another minute, then pour in 60 ml (4 tbsp) of hot water. Lower the heat and simmer for 4–5 minutes until the liquid is completely absorbed.

Take lumps of the potato about the size of a small plum, roll into small balls. Then poke a finger through to the centre of the potato, swivelling your finger slightly to make a good hollow. Fill with a little of the stuffing, then close the potato over the hole, smoothing over so that it doesn't burst.

Cover the balls with breadcrumbs, rolling them well in, then heat a good 2½ cm (1 inch) olive oil in a deep pan until just smoking. Put 2 or 3 balls into the pan, and cook quickly, constantly turning, until deeply browned and crisp all over. Drain and cook the rest as quickly as possible. Keep warm in a hot oven while cooking the remainder. Serve, with extra chopped parsley if wished. A pepper mill on the table is a must.

BEETROOT STEWED WITH THEIR LEAVES

Pancar Yemegi

One of the things that used to amaze me as a child visiting England on holidays were the bits and pieces not used in the kitchen. Orange rind was the first example that horrified me, since I adored the crystallised peel – one of my few childhood 'sweeties'. Then, as I got older beetroot and radish tops – these last are particularly good chopped and strewn on salads. Beetroot leaves remind me of spinach, only slightly sweeter, and make this dish superb. I'm afraid you'll have to grow your own – even if they haven't

been shorn by the greengrocer, the leaves wilt too quickly to be any good. From plot to pot within two hours is the ideal.

Serves 6–8
900 g (2 lb) raw beetroot with their leaves
150 ml (¼ pint) olive oil
1 large onion, skinned and finely chopped
1–2 garlic cloves, skinned and cut in half (optional)
Maldon or sea salt
freshly ground black pepper
lemon juice

Cut off the leaves about 2½ cm (1 inch) above the beetroot, rinse quickly then shake dry, and chop coarsely. Peel the beetroot and slice thickly.

Heat the oil in a large pan, add the onion and fry for 3–4 minutes to soften slightly. Add the garlic if using (sometimes I do, sometimes not – especially if I have baby beetroot, then I simply let their own sweet flavour dominate), and add just enough water to cover the beets. Season with salt and black pepper (white in Iraq), and cook gently until the beetroot is tender, 25–45 minutes – depending on size and age of beetroot. Pour into a dish, cool to room temperature, then sprinkle on a little lemon juice. Particularly good with a bowl of chilled yogurt.

GREEK MUSHROOMS IN OIL

Manitaria

Mushrooms *à la grecque* must be one of the most famous *mezze* dishes in the world. Unfortunately, too often it suffers from over-designing. It is at its best when simple – nice firm mushrooms, good olive oil, lemon, garlic, parsley and thyme. Water is used in the simplest versions, white wine in the more sophisticated. Either is good, but you need nothing else.

Serves 6–8

600 g (1¼ lb) tiny button mushrooms
150 ml (¼ pint) olive oil
200 ml (7 fl oz) white wine, or water, or a mixture
Maldon or sea salt
freshly ground black pepper
1 sprig fresh thyme
2 garlic cloves, skinned and very finely chopped
small bunch parsley, finely chopped
juice of 1–1½ large lemons

Wipe the mushrooms with a damp cloth. Mix together all the remaining ingredients, except the juice of the extra half lemon, in a large pan and bring to the boil. Turn the heat down, add the mushrooms, stir well, then simmer very gently for 6–10 minutes until the mushrooms are tender. Taste the juice after 5 minutes, adding extra lemon if need be. Transfer to a serving dish and let them completely cool – vital for the flavours to mellow. Serve with good bread to mop up the delicious juices.

FRIED AUBERGINES WITH CHEESE

Patlıcanli Hellim

Aubergines come in all shapes and sizes in the Middle East – and a rainbow of colours from the palest ivory to the glossiest purple-black. Heavily speckled, pale purple and dark, dark black aubergines are sometimes regarded as bad luck for young women, said to cause sterility should they touch one. Yet in Syria, and I believe, in Egypt, to walk slowly round, and through, a plot of growing aubergines is said to cure that same sterility. Strange how folklore develops. In Turkey they are enjoyed as the delicious food they are. Particularly good, though rich, in this dish.

Serves 6–8

2 large aubergines, long and thin
Maldon or sea salt
60–120 ml (4–8 tbsp) olive oil, plus extra for
    frying
225 g (8 oz) Feta or Hallumi cheese
4 eggs, beaten
freshly ground black pepper
60 ml (4 tbsp) finely chopped parsley
15 ml (1 tbsp) dill seeds, crushed
homemade dried breadcrumbs, finely ground
To serve lemon wedges

Cut the stem off the aubergines, then cut in half lengthways chopping each half into three or four pieces. Put on a plate, sprinkle with salt and leave for 30–45 minutes, then rinse thoroughly and pat dry.

Heat the oil (the lesser amount) in a large frying pan, add the aubergines and fry quickly on both sides just to colour. Add more oil if necessary when turning them. Drain on absorbent kitchen paper.

Grate the Feta into a bowl, add 2 of the eggs, freshly ground black pepper, the parsley and dill and mix well. Sandwich two slices of aubergine with a little of the cheese mixture – don't worry they won't fall apart, then dip each parcel into the remaining eggs, and coat very well with breadcrumbs. Heat a good 5 cm (2 inches) oil in a large pan until just smoking, add 2 parcels and fry for 2–3 minutes until golden and crisp. Drain very well, cook the rest and serve at once. Lemon wedges to accompany.

PICKLED TURNIPS

Torshi Lift

Of all the pickles prepared in the Middle East – and there are many – this is one of the most spectacular looking and, to me, evocative of both Baghdad and Cairo. Huge jars of sliced turnips, brilliantly coloured by the added beetroot, sit in every shop window, on every café counter. And in winter, there were barrows of hot turnips – pink and steaming – on every street corner, the vendors' cry of *mayyi, mayyi* tempting you to a plate at all times of day, to ward off the cold and keep you going until the next meal. Beetroot and turnips were boiled together until soft, then taken out of the huge vat with a slotted ladle, sprinkled with a little salt, to be eaten on the spot. Sometimes people would ask just for a cup of the broth – a good digestive, say the Iraqis. I often make this as a winter (in Sri Lanka – monsoon!) vegetable to accompany roast lamb. Then, with the cold lamb next day? Pickled turnips, of course.

Fills about four ⅓ litre (¾ pint) kilner jars

800 g (1¼ lb) small turnips

250 g (9 oz) raw beetroot, preferably not much larger than the turnips – 4 should give about the right weight

100 g (4 oz) fresh dates, stoned and halved (optional)

4 small garlic cloves, skinned and very finely chopped

handful celery leaves

62½ ml (4½ tbsp) Maldon or sea salt

350 ml (12 fl oz) white wine vinegar

Peel the turnips and slice in half crossways. Peel the beetroot and slice fairly thinly. Pack the turnips into sterilised jars alternating with a layer of beetroot slices every now and again, and sprinkling on the dates (used in Iraq, not in Egypt), chopped garlic and a few celery leaves between each row. Bring 900 ml (1½ pints) water to the boil with the salt, then stir in the vinegar. Pour over the vegetables, making sure they are completely covered by the liquid. If there is not quite enough, add a little more vinegar – you could equally well add a little more brine if you prefer, use 22½ ml (1½ tbsp) salt to 300 ml (½ pint) water. Seal the jars and leave in a warmish spot – I don't mean the airing cupboard: a warm kitchen will do, a cold larder will not. Ready to eat in 10–12 days, check after 10, will keep in a cool place for 4–6 weeks. I have never had any last that long, so more-ish are these.

PICKLED CAULIFLOWER AND CABBAGE

Torshi Arnabeet wa Karoum

Another brilliantly coloured pickle – this time a deep, episcopal purple. I am always tempted to buy too large a red cabbage, so enticing are those glossy shining orbs, providing myself with a good excuse to make this. It is as popular in England as in the Middle East.

Fills about four ⅓ litre (¾ pint) kilner jars

1 very fresh firm cauliflower, about 450 g (1 lb) in weight

½ smallish red cabbage, about 450 g (1 lb) in weight

2 large garlic cloves, cut in half

4 sprigs fresh dillweed

5–10 ml (1–2 tsp) dill seeds

67½ ml (4½ tbsp) Maldon or sea salt

350 ml (12 fl oz) white wine vinegar

1 dried red chilli (optional – see below)

Break the cauliflower into small florets, then rinse thoroughly. Cut the cabbage into thick chunks – discard the thick central stem, and do not separate the cabbage leaves. Pack in layers in sterilized jars, putting a half garlic clove, a dillweed sprig and a few dill seeds in each jar. Bring 900 ml (1½ pints) water to the boil, stir in the salt to dissolve, then mix with the vinegar in a jug, and pour into each jar, covering the vegetables. In Iraq our cook used to bury a dried chilli in the middle of the jar but, unless you are putting all the pickle into one very large jar, I wouldn't recommend doing this as it will be very hot indeed. Cover and leave in a warm place for 10–12 days. The vegetables will have mellowed beautifully, and the cauliflower blushed deeply purple. Keeps 4–6 weeks.

PICKLED LEMONS

Limoun Hamadh Makbouss

In actual fact in Iraq we made this with limes – utterly wonderful. But since one rarely suffers from a plethora of limes in England, I have used lemons – also commonly used in the Middle East, and very good. Morocco also has her version of pickled lemons. Quartered but still attached at one end, they are then sprinkled inside with salt, about 5 ml (1 tsp) per lemon, shut tightly, packed into jars, and weighted with 'a perfectly clean stone'. The whole is covered with lukewarm water, tightly sealed and left for 3–4 weeks. The zest is used for flavouring *tagines* or the lemons (flesh scraped out) may be finely chopped and added to the salads. This is also excellent with limes – so, on second thoughts, why not be a little extravagant? Make some of each.

Fills four ½ litre (¾ pint) kilner jars
8–12 lemons, slightly more limes
Maldon or sea salt
10 ml (2 tsp) paprika
pinch of cayenne pepper or chilli powder
15 ml (1 tbsp) cumin seeds, ground
peanut oil

Wash the lemons thoroughly – particularly important if using bought lemons, as nowadays most have been sprayed with chemicals. Cut into fine slices and arrange in circles around the sides and bottom of a colander, leaving the first circle of holes uncovered. Sprinkle well with salt and leave for 24–36 hours (limes need the lesser time, lemons won't hurt if left longer). Pack in layers in sterilised jars, sprinkling on a little paprika, a mere touch of cayenne or chilli, and some ground cumin seeds between each layer. Cover completely with oil – in my original recipe, it calls for olive oil but I find this rather dominates the soft lemony taste. I have, however, mixed olive and peanut oil very successfully. Seal the jars tightly and leave for 3–4 weeks when the lemons will have deeply coloured and become soft and only mildly tangy. One of the best of all pickles.

SALADS

Salatat

Flowing and ebbing like a swelling sea,
Oil decks them out in cream embroidery
Which, as it floods and flecks them fold on fold;
Twists latchets as of silver or of gold.

MAHMUD IBN AL-HUSAIN AL-KUSHAJIM[1]

I suppose the popular myth of the Middle East as one vast barren desert, with the odd palm tree dotted here and there, is the reason so many people think salad has no place in the Arab kitchen. It is a myth which was obviously firmly lodged in the mind of the new young, and excessively smug, teacher who once told me to be a good girl, and eat up my salad, finishing rather haughtily, 'Of course, I know you couldn't have such things where you've just come from, that dreadful climate, and all that sand.' I stared at the limp, brown-tinged lettuce leaf, the wrinkled half-tomato and the grey hard-boiled egg. All 'healthily' undressed, naturally. Tears welled up as my mind's eye flashed back to the country I had so recently left. How could I explain to this alien being the salads of my lunches last week?

The wonderful variety and freshness of their ingredients: tiny courgettes, picked 10 minutes before eating, the lemon and orange picked on the way back to the kitchen for the dressing; baby beans still warm in golden olive oil; crunchy white cabbage gleaming and green from oil, parsley and fresh coriander; lettuce leaves so crisp you could use them as a spoon to scoop up lashings of tahina dip. How to explain – to this dull grown-up, who always wore grey – the feeling, and enjoyment, of bright colours:

the circles of yellow, green and red pepper slivers; radishes – red and white – strewn on oranges, multi-coloured mounds of minutely chopped tomato, cucumber and onion mixed with myriad green herbs. At that age, and knowing nothing else, how could I verbalise the Middle Eastern imagination in pairing unlikely allies, in daring to use the unexpected. Who realised that olives would lend themselves so well to a salad – not as a garnish but as the main protagonist? How did the orange and the onion come to be so happily married? Chance discoveries maybe, but there are so many of them. Simple and gutsy, rich yet delicate, lightly refreshing – there seems to be a salad to suit every whim of the most capricious taste bud. The only golden rule is unblemished freshness – vegetables are coldly crisp when raw, firm even when cooked. Herbs are used lavishly, but thoughtfully. From the palest gold, to conifer green and the dusty brown of the peasant's home-made brew, oil – in the main – is olive, but always the best one can afford. Its richness is sharply offset by lemons, small, juicy and plentiful. So, at every meal there is salad. Sometimes, only one. Often, many; very occasionally, almost too many. But, yes, we had salads in the Middle East.

1. AD 915–967/303–356 Islamic calendar.

PEPPER SALAD

Salata Pimento

One of the most popular Middle Eastern salads, not least because it allows the Arab cook to indulge his passion for colour. Yellow, green and bright red peppers are commonly used together, then arranged in circles, alternating strips, fans – anything to show off the colours to their best. The Turks have their version of this dish, in which the peppers are gently sautéed, then tossed in yogurt with a few drops of olive oil.

Serves 6
1 large green pepper
1 large red pepper
1 large yellow pepper
1–2 garlic cloves, skinned and very finely chopped
45–60 ml (3–4 tbsp) olive oil
juice of ½–1 lemon
Maldon or sea salt
freshly ground black pepper
To garnish finely chopped parsley

Cut the peppers in half – choose them as long and evenly sized as possible, it makes the grilling and arranging easier – then discard the seeds, core and pith. Flatten them slightly if necessary, then put under a very hot grill and cook until the skin is completely charred and blistering all over. Remove the peppers, wrap in a clean tea towel and leave for 5–10 minutes, then pull off the blackened skin, rubbing under cold running water any places which have charred through to the flesh.

Cut the peppers into long thin strips and arrange on a platter in any design you like, or you can mix them up to make a rainbow salad. Scatter over the garlic, then pour on the oil and sprinkle with lemon juice, salt and black pepper. Leave for 30 minutes to 1 hour, at room temperature, for the flavours to mellow sweetly, then add a little more lemon if wished. Serve sprinkled with finely chopped parsley.

MIXED SALAD

Salatit Khodar Meshakel

Since time immemorial this has been known as 'little salad' in our house because all the ingredients are chopped into tiny pieces – a technique so simple, yet powerful in its ability to alter the flavours, which amalgamate not only with each other but with the dressing. I have even tried it simply with tomatoes and onions (especially in the winter when tomatoes can be quite tasteless) and it produces quite a different effect to the same salad conventionally made with sliced onions and tomatoes. The ingredients vary from country to country, and from season to season. Tomatoes, cucumbers, large or spring onions are usually the basics with cos lettuce, spinach or chard, beetroot tops added for greenery. Radishes, celery or sweetcorn kernels can also be added, but keep the varieties to a maximum of five or six (a minimum of three). With fresh herbs and the dressing, that is quite enough. You want the flavours to marry – not fight.

Serves 6–8
3–4 tomatoes
1 large onion or small bunch spring onions
1 small cucumber
1 small cos lettuce
8 radishes or 3 sticks celery
60 ml (4 tbsp) finely chopped parsley
30 ml (2 tbsp) finely chopped fresh coriander
    leaves
30 ml (2 tbsp) finely chopped fresh mint or
    marjoram
60 ml (4 tbsp) olive oil
Maldon or sea salt
juice of 1 lemon
1–2 garlic cloves, skinned and finely chopped
freshly ground black pepper

Chop the tomatoes into small dice, discarding the seeds and excessive juices. Cut the onion or spring onions (use as much of the green tops as possible), the lettuce and radishes or celery into tiny dice, and mix everything together in a salad bowl. Sprinkle on the herbs, then the oil and salt. Stir and leave for 30 minutes to let the flavours meld but don't leave it for too much longer if you have included lettuce or it can horribly wilt. Squeeze on lemon juice to taste, then scatter with the finely chopped garlic and season liberally with freshly ground black pepper.

CABBAGE SALAD

Sarmalahana Salata

Turkey combines raw cabbage with Feta cheese and olives to make this salad – ideal for the English winter table. Other countries also use cabbage, either red or white, often salted and weighted for 30 minutes to soften the cabbage, before dressing simply with oil and lemon juice. And in Egypt there is a popular variation on the Turkish salad, using cucumbers instead of cabbage, onions instead of olives, to give a cool-hot contrast to the salty Feta. All are good.

Serves 6
1 small white cabbage, central stalk removed
175 g (6 oz) black olives, stoned
175 g (6 oz) Feta cheese
90 ml (6 tbsp) olive oil
juice of 1 lemon
juice of 1 tangerine
freshly ground black pepper

Shred the cabbage finely. Put into a large bowl, add the olives – halved if very large, then crumble over the Feta. Lightly whisk the oil, lemon and tangerine juices together, pour over and toss. Season with pepper – no need for salt, the cheese provides that. Serve within 2 hours else the cabbage will be limp.

COURGETTE AND FRESH CORIANDER SALAD

Salata Chourba wa Kuzbari Taza

In Baghdad we had a marvellous irrigation system of little canals with gates, all over the garden. When we wanted to water a particular patch, the gate was simply opened and in poured the water. Basking in the hot sun, with their daily drink, courgettes grew apace and I would rush down in the afternoons, after my compulsory siesta, to see how many had 'grown-up' since the day before. We still picked these 'grown-ups' very small, since by the morrow they would have already been too large for the cook's pleasure. With fresh coriander leaves, they make one of the nicest summer salads I know.

Serves 6
450 g (1 lb) courgettes, as small as possible
90–120 ml (6–8 tbsp) fresh coriander leaves, finely
    chopped
45–60 ml (3–4 tbsp) olive oil
juice of ½–1 lemon
squeeze of fresh orange juice
Maldon or sea salt
freshly ground white pepper

Top and tail the courgettes, then slice fairly finely. Strew over the coriander leaves then just before serving, sprinkle on oil, lemon juice and a touch of orange juice. Season with salt and pepper. Excellent.

SPINACH SALAD

Salata Ispanakh

To the Arabs there are no distinctions between vegetables and 'salad vegetables' – if it tastes good cold, why not a salad? Spinach is a prime candidate, popular everywhere. We used to have it in Iraq, raw when very young, lightly stewed when older, with onions and lime juice. The Turks marry it with yogurt, the Persians with nuts, the Lebanese with a simple oil and lemon dressing. Perpetual Beet, also called New Zealand Spinach, is the easiest of plants to grow and flourishes throughout the winter, making this a dish for all seasons. If picking your own spinach to use raw, you will only need half the quantity given below.

Serves 6

900 g (2 lb) fresh spinach
1 large onion, skinned and very finely sliced
juice of 3–4 limes
30 ml (2 tbsp) olive oil
Maldon or sea salt
freshly ground white or black pepper

Wash the spinach quite thoroughly, discarding any tough stems and tatty leaves. If using raw, shake dry, then merely chop finely and put into a bowl. Otherwise, put the chopped spinach, still moist, into a large pan with 15–30 ml (1–2 tbsp) water at the bottom and let it stew gently for about 7–10 minutes. It should be tender but not sloppy. Drain well and put in a bowl. Add the onion, then sprinkle with the lime juice and oil. Season with salt and pepper and allow to cool before serving.

CUCUMBER AND YOGURT SALAD

Cacık

One of the most cooling salads of the region, very similar to the Indian *raita*. This is from Turkey; the Lebanese omit the cucumber and add huge amounts of fresh mint; in Persia they substitute fresh dill for the mint and add sultanas, while in Iraq we used fresh coriander leaves. Popular whatever the variation.

Serves 6

1 large cucumber
Maldon or sea salt
3–4 garlic cloves, skinned
450 ml (¾ pint) natural yogurt
45–60 ml (3–4 tbsp) olive oil
30 ml (2 tbsp) dried mint.

Peel the cucumber and cut into small dice, then put in a colander and sprinkle with salt. Leave for 30 minutes, to drain off the excess fluid. Crush the garlic with a little salt until quite pulpy then mix into 30–45 ml (2–3 tbsp) of the yogurt, before beating in the rest. Stir in the oil, then quickly rinse the cucumber and shake well. Mix in, then add half the mint. Taste to see if more salt is needed, adding if necessary. Sprinkle with the remaining mint then serve as soon as possible.

ORANGE AND ONION SALAD

Munkaczina

Oranges are widely used in salads all over the Middle East – another example of the versatility of the Arab kitchen. One of the simplest – and most exquisite – is the Moroccan recipe which thinly slices the oranges, then brushes them with a little olive oil. A sprinkling of orange-blossom water and ground cinnamon completes this perfect dish. Very good with the highly spiced Moroccan *brochettes*. Additions include grated young carrots or long white radishes, both salads being served well chilled. A gutsier version, popular along the Eastern Mediterranean coast, includes onions and olives with the local favourite fresh herb. I love it with mint but in winter – the ideal time for this salad when oranges are sweet and juicy, and plentiful – window-sill mint is precious. So then use parsley, marjoram, a few thyme leaves stripped off the stalk, fennel if having fish, or – best of all – lemon balm. All are evergreen: even under the heaviest snows a few leaves will still lurk. And any are good. In the tropics, we have the mint – yards of it – at all times of year, but not the oranges! Then I make it with *Limoun Hamadh Makbouss* (page 127). Excellent, particularly at Christmas – with all its rich foods.

Serves 4–6
2 large oranges
1 large onion, skinned and finely sliced
100 g (4 oz) black olives, stoned
Maldon or sea salt
pinch of cayenne pepper
30–45 ml (2–3 tbsp) olive oil
either finely chopped fresh parsley, mint, chervil,
    dillweed, lemon balm or whatever is available

Peel the oranges, holding them over the salad bowl to catch any juice. Remove all traces of pith, then slice the oranges as thinly as possible and nick out the pips. Arrange in overlapping circles in the bowl. Layer the onions on top and then scatter on the olives – cut them in half if they're huge. Sprinkle with salt and a touch of cayenne, then dribble over the oil. Strew, fairly liberally, with the fresh herb of your choice – very finely chopped.

TUNISIAN MIXED SALAD

Salata Meshwiya

Popular all over North Africa but especially Tunisia. Whether it spread with the Moors through to the south of France or was brought back again, I do not know but it bears a remarkable similarity to the French 'salade Niçoise', only spicier – no self-respecting Tunisian would omit the chilli!

Serves 6
1 large green pepper, seeded and coarsely chopped
2 large firm tomatoes
1 large onion, finely chopped or small bunch
    spring onions, chopped, using as much green
    top as possible
50 g (2 oz) small black olives, stoned
5 ml (1 tsp) caraway seed, crushed
1–2 garlic cloves, finely chopped
1 dried red chilli, seeded and finely chopped
175 g (6 oz) canned tuna fish, drained
45 ml (3 tbsp) olive oil
15–30 ml (1–2 tbsp) lemon juice
a drop of *Harissa* sauce (optional)
Maldon or sea salt
freshly ground black pepper
45 ml (3 tbsp) finely chopped parsley

Put the chopped peppers into a large bowl. Chop the tomatoes, discarding seeds and excess juice, then add to the bowl with the onions, olives, caraway seed, garlic and chilli. Crumble the tuna fish and add that too. Whisk the oil lightly with the lemon juice (I like the greater amount, others use less) and a touch of *harissa* if you like it spicy and pour over the salad. Toss well, then season with salt and black pepper and decorate with the parsley.

MUSHROOM SALAD

Borani Garch

A lovely, and unusual, combination from Persia, also excellent with large fresh horse (or field) mushrooms.

Serves 4–6
500 g (1¼ lb) fresh mushrooms
45 ml (3 tbsp) olive oil
1 sweet onion, skinned and finely chopped
1–2 garlic cloves, skinned and finely chopped
Maldon or sea salt
freshly ground black pepper
juice of 1 lime
300 ml (½ pint) natural yogurt
30 ml (2 tbsp) dried mint or dried dillweed

Wipe the mushrooms with a damp cloth. Trim off and discard any tough stalks, then slice the mushrooms quite thickly. Heat the oil in a large pan, add the onion and fry gently for about 10 minutes until softened but only very lightly coloured. Add the garlic and sauté for another 2–3 minutes, then toss in the mushrooms and cook for 2–4 minutes, constantly moving them around. They should still have a slight bite to them. Pour into a bowl, season with salt and pepper then stir in the lime juice. Leave to cool. Just before serving, toss the mushrooms in the yogurt and sprinkle with dried mint or dillweed.

BEETROOT SALAD

Pancar Salatasi

All over the Middle East beetroot salads are popular, usually tossed in oil and lemon, sometimes with a few coriander or cumin seeds. In Turkey they serve it in this yogurt dressing – and I love it like this, the beetroot juices gradually staining the yogurt a wonderful deep pink.

Serves 6–8
60 ml (4 tbsp) olive oil
45–60 ml (3–4 tbsp) lemon juice
1–2 garlic cloves, skinned and crushed
450 ml (¾ pint) natural yogurt
Maldon or sea salt
freshly ground white pepper
450 g (1 lb) cooked beetroot, skinned and cut into chunks
60 ml (4 tbsp) finely chopped parsley
1–2 pinches of ground cinnamon

Whisk the oil, lemon juice and crushed garlic together, then gradually beat in the yogurt to make a smooth dressing. Season with salt and coarsely ground white pepper, then pour over the beetroot. Toss quite thoroughly until the sauce is nicely blushing. Sprinkle with parsley and a little cinnamon.

GREEN BEAN SALAD

Salatit El Loubdieh

Very simple – and like all things simple, very good. Popular all over the Middle East where French beans are the ones traditionally used. I also use home grown runner beans, picking them when really tiny and pencil slim. If you grow peas, you can substitute those too at the mange-tout stage when they are quite flat – all pod and no pea! Broad beans are often used in Egypt, and this is the one instance where the frozen article can also be successfully used though baby, garden-picked ones are still best.

Serves 4–6
450 g (1 lb) young French beans
60 ml (4 tbsp) olive oil
Maldon or sea salt
juice of 1 lemon or 2 limes
1–2 garlic cloves, skinned and very finely chopped
45 ml (3 tbsp) very finely chopped parsley or fresh coriander leaves

Top and tail the beans – if they need stringing they are no good for this salad. Coat a wide shallow pan with 15 ml (1 tbsp) oil, then put in the beans. Just cover with water and sprinkle on a little salt. Cook from 5–10 minutes, shaking the pan from time to time to prevent sticking. I like beans still with a good bite to them and my baby creatures only take a few minutes. Larger, bought ones will obviously take longer, so check to suit your taste. Drain and put in a serving dish. Toss in the rest of the oil and lemon or lime juice while still hot, then leave to cool slightly – this salad is at its best tepid. Sprinkle with the garlic and parsley – best of all, fresh coriander.

HARICOT BEAN SALAD

Kuru Fasulya Piyazi

Popular everywhere, particularly in Turkey. Other dried beans can be used but haricot beans are, I think, the best – small and sweetly earthy.

Serves 6–8
225 g (8 oz) dried haricot beans, soaked overnight
120 ml (8 tbsp) olive oil
juice of 1–1½ lemons
Maldon or sea salt
freshly ground black pepper
1 onion, skinned and finely sliced
3–4 hard-boiled eggs, sliced
100 g (4 oz) black olives, stoned
1 large tomato, finely sliced
finely chopped parsley or mint

Rinse the beans and bring to the boil in a large pan of unsalted water, then simmer until tender but not overcooked – this will take from about 40 minutes to over 1 hour depending on the beans, so check fairly frequently. Drain and put into a bowl. Dress with the oil and lemon juice, then season while they are still warm. Leave to cool. Taste to see if they need more

salt or pepper, then arrange the onion slices on top, then the eggs, a scattering of olives, and finally the tomato slices and lots of finely chopped parsley or mint.

AUBERGINE SALAD

Melitzanes Salata

There are many variations of this. In Egypt they fry green peppers with the aubergines and spice with coriander and garlic. In other countries, tomatoes, and onions too, are cooked with the aubergine, making a dish similar to *ratatouille*. I particularly like this Greek version though – the crunch of raw onion and tomato contrasting nicely with the softness of the cooked aubergine.

Serves 4–6
2–3 large aubergines, sliced
90–120 ml (6–8 tbsp) olive oil
juice of 1–1½ large lemons
1 medium onion, skinned and finely chopped
2 large tomatoes, finely chopped
Maldon or sea salt
freshly ground black pepper
5 ml (1 tsp) fresh marjoram or 2½ ml (½ tsp) rigani or oregano

Put the aubergines in a colander, sprinkle with salt and leave for 30–45 minutes, then rinse under the cold tap and pat dry. Heat 45 ml (3 tbsp) oil in a frying pan, add the aubergines and cook until tender, about 10 minutes. Add a little more oil if necessary. Tip into a serving bowl, sprinkle with the juice of 1 lemon. Add the rest of the ingredients, except the remaining oil, then gradually pour that over, tasting to see how much oil it needs. Toss thoroughly and serve quite cool: 15–20 minutes chilling should be quite sufficient.

BURGHUL SALAD

Tabbuleh

One of the glories of the Middle East: Lebanese in origin, everyone now firmly claims it as their own. Recipes are varied and highly individual but it should be very green, so lots of fresh herbs. Tangy but sweet, rich yet light, earthy but refreshing, it has all the perfect dish needs.

Serves 6
175 g (6 oz) burghul
1 small cucumber, finely chopped
6 spring onions, finely chopped, or 1 large onion, skinned and finely chopped
1 bunch parsley, very finely chopped
45 ml (3 tbsp) finely chopped fresh coriander leaves
8 sprigs fresh mint, very finely chopped or 30 ml (2 tbsp) dried mint
60–90 ml (4–6 tbsp) olive oil
juice of 1–2 lemons
Maldon or sea salt
freshly ground black pepper
To serve blanched vine leaves, raw cabbage or cos lettuce leaves (optional)

Soak the burghul, covered with water, in a large bowl for 30 minutes. Put the cucumber into a colander, sprinkle with salt and also leave for 30 minutes.

Squeeze the burghul hard in your hands to thoroughly drain it of moisture, then mix with the onions using a fork, and lightly smashing some of the onion to release the juices – these will be deliciously absorbed by the cracked wheat. Rinse the cucumber and squeeze hard – in a tea towel if you find this easier, then add to the burghul and onion. Add the herbs, 60 ml (4 tbsp) olive oil and the juice of 1 lemon. Season quite highly with salt and black pepper, then mix well. Taste. It should be quite sharply lemony but delicately balanced, so add more lemon – or oil – if necessary. Serve, either dramatically piled into a tall cone, or on individual plates, traditionally lined with blanched vine leaves, or raw cabbage or cos lettuce leaves. Either way, there should be a bowl with more leaves for people to use as scoops.

BREAD SALAD

Fattoush

Originally a peasant dish, now much loved by all in Syria and the Lebanon. I had it once in a small café in Beirut – one of those secret sojourns with my grandpapa – and was full of it when we returned home to Damascus, somewhat to the horror of our cook. He could not believe that a restaurant, however simple, should be so cheeky as to serve what was, in his eyes, very much a family snack. Family and friends alike get it in my house, and all come back for more. If you can't get *sumac*, substitute lemon juice.

Serves 6
2 *Pittas* (page 146)
15 ml (1 tbsp) *sumac* seeds (see page 158) or juice of 2 large lemons
1 cos lettuce, shredded, or 1 cucumber, chopped, sprinkled with salt and left for 30 minutes
1–2 large tomatoes, chopped coarsely
1 large onion, skinned and finely chopped
small bunch of parsley or handful of celery leaves, finely chopped
6–8 sprigs fresh mint, finely chopped
few sprigs fresh coriander leaves, finely chopped
2–3 large garlic cloves, skinned and finely chopped
Maldon or sea salt
freshly ground black pepper
120 ml (8 tbsp) olive oil

Break the pittas into small pieces – if they are a bit stale I find it a good idea to warm them slightly before soaking – it helps them absorb the *sumac* water or lemon juice. (Some books say that dry toast can be substituted for the pitta – frankly I find the flavour so different as to be almost disappointing, and I would rather make something else. There is, after all, no shortage of choice in the Arab kitchen.)

Crush the *sumac* seeds lightly in a spice grinder then soak in about 120 ml (8 tbsp) warm water. Leave for 15–20 minutes, then sieve, pushing the seeds hard to extract all the juice. Pour over the pittas with 15 ml (1 tbsp) water, or lemon juice if using, and leave for 5 minutes.

If using cucumber instead of the lettuce, rinse off the salt and shake thoroughly dry. Otherwise, simply add all the ingredients to the soaked pittas, tossing thoroughly. Taste to see if any of the seasonings need adjusting – you may want a little more lemon or oil.

OLIVE SALAD

Meslalla

Whilst olives of all possible shape and size appear on tables everywhere, two countries – interestingly enough, at opposite ends of the geographical spectrum – also turn them into a salad. In Turkey, very fresh green olives are stoned, then mashed with crushed garlic and coriander seed, while in Morocco the North African love of spiciness is married to finely chopped preserved olives. Both these salads I discovered in London, with Turkish and Moroccan friends respectively, and I must admit I did feel they might be a little overwhelming. Slightly illogical as, it was gently pointed out to me, I can happily devour a whole bowl of olives in a not inordinate length of time – so, why not an olive salad? Why not, indeed. It is excellent, particularly with pitta and grilled meat. If you buy olives in brine rinse the brine off thoroughly before chopping the olives. Olives soaked in oil can be prepared straightaway – you will merely need less oil in the dressing.

Serves 6–8

450 g (1 lb) large green, black or violet olives
1 large garlic clove, skinned
2½ ml (½ tsp) cumin seeds
5 ml (1 tsp) paprika
pinch of chilli powder or cayenne pepper
peanut oil
juice of 2 lemons
Maldon or sea salt
To garnish finely chopped lemon verbena or fresh
    parsley

Stone the olives, then chop finely. Crush the garlic with the cumin seeds, then mix with the paprika, and chilli powder or cayenne. Moisten with about 15 ml (1 tbsp) oil then stir into the olives, mixing in very thoroughly. Add the juice of 1 lemon, again stirring in well, then a pinch of salt (many olives are already very salt, so take care). Taste, and add more oil, or lemon juice until the balance is right – there should be a distinct tang without it being too sharp. Pile into a serving dish and sprinkle with lemon verbena if you grow it – this is the traditional herb, and it lends a wonderfully sweet lemony flavour, or parsley, also used by many Moroccans.

I also sometimes put the whole lot into the food processor (having stoned the olives first – of course) and whizz, briefly. Chilled, served with Melba toast – and a bone dry sherry, on the rocks – it makes a superb summer snack.

RICE AND PULSES

Riz wa Ful

O glorious aruzza![1] What a boon,
Thou cook as lovely as high heaven's moon!
Purer than snow that hath been furrowed twice
By handiwork of wind and frosted ice.

MUHAMMAD IBN AL-WAZIR[2]

Rice may be an everyday dish in the Middle East, accompanying most meals in one form or another (save Morocco, Tunisia and Algeria, where *couscous* is the favoured grain), but that does not mean it is to be taken lightly. Indeed, this basic ingredient – once an exclusive province of the rich[3] – is accorded a deal of respect, and a certain amount of ritual surrounds its cooking. Nowhere more so than in Persia, where even their 'plain' rice is half-cooked, then steamed to give a lovely crisp crust before being most extravagantly served with butter, egg yolks and the delicately astringent *sumac*. Its preparation will often have been started the previous day – the Persians always soaking their rice for at least six hours. And before the soaking the rice must be bought. This, too, demands care and expertise. When first researching this book, I was told by a rice grower from that country that, though there is only one species of the plant, varieties run into thousands – each paddy field displaying slightly different characteristics, discernible to the expert eye. More importantly to the Persian cook, there will be available in the market at least ten differing qualities of rice. The selection of one will reflect its appropriateness to the dish – and the guests to be served. The best rice we can easily obtain in the West, *basmati*, is only about half-way up the Persian scale. It makes one realise just how perfected is the Persian kitchen.

Thus, though served almost daily, the main role of rice is not so much that of an accompanying staple as a dish important in its own right. Either to be accompanied by meat, fish or vegetables or, particularly in Persia, by one of the superbly blended and seasoned sauces called *khoresh*. It also forms the base of *pilavs*, extremely popular all over the Middle East. Nuts, herbs and/or fruits and vegetables may be added, golden tints given by saffron or turmeric and the presentation is often elaborate, ring moulds being especially favoured for festive occasions – the top of the rice liberally encrusted with nuts of all sorts.

In the curious way that history has of reversing roles, pulses – once very definitely a food of the poor – are now enjoyed as much by the rich. None more so than *Foul Medames* (page 143), proclaimed by the Egyptians as their national dish. Those wonderfully nutty, little brown beans, no doubt gratefully enjoyed as their one meal of the day by the ancient pyramid builders (apparently also given onions to improve their strength) are now eagerly devoured at the highest tables in the land. So too, presumably, was the ancient marriage between rice and lentils, nicknamed 'Esau's Mess', since it appears in al-Baghdadi. The Caliphs had good taste. And even the nomad Bedouin did not neglect his rice – a fertile imagination plucking the one ingredient available from the infertile desert: the date. That indeed is a memorable partnership.

PLAIN RICE

Riz

Although the minutiae of cooking rice will certainly vary from family to family, there are basically three ways of preparing plain rice (apart of course from the special Persian *chelo*). These differ in the fat used, and at what stage it is added. For everyday rice, I use the Iraqi version, given below, also common in Syria. In the Lebanon, they add the butter to the water, so the rice cooks simultaneously in the two, while in Egypt, oil is preferred and the rice is fried for a minute or two first, until just gleaming, before the water is added. This method I find particularly good when you want to serve the rice cold as, say, in a salad, although I do sometimes cook it the Iraqi way, then add oil at the end instead of melted butter. Choose whichever method suits you best, but always measure the volume of the rice before you start – that means even before you wash it.

Serves 6–8
450 g (1 lb) long grain rice
Maldon or sea salt
75 g (3 oz) unsalted butter

Measure out the rice in a jug or teacup, then put the same quantity of water in another jug, and reserve. Put the rice in a large bowl, pour over boiling water, then stir for about 1 minute. Pour into a colander and then thoroughly rinse the rice under cold water until it runs quite clear.

Bring the reserved water to the boil in a large pan, with a pinch of salt, dribble in the rice and bring back to the boil. Let it roll vigorously for 2 minutes, then turn the heat as low as possible, cover the pan tightly and simmer for about 20 minutes, until the rice is

tender and all the water absorbed. The grains should be separate and fluffy and there will be pit holes all over the top of the rice. Turn off the heat and leave for 10 minutes, still covered. (This applies to whichever method you choose to cook the rice. In the other versions, the rice will then be ready to serve.)

Meanwhile, gently melt the butter in a small saucepan, and drizzle it all over the surface of the rice. Leave for 1–2 minutes to allow the butter to be absorbed, then pile on a warm serving dish.

RICE WITH BROAD BEANS

Riz bil Ful

Staying for the first time with my grandfather in Cairo, the smell of frying garlic drew me to the kitchen. It was in fact garlic and coriander, the much loved Egyptian combination, that was on the stove. Added to fresh broad beans, and then stirred into rice, the cook was preparing his family's lunch. Thereafter, I celebrated trips to Cairo with a bowl of this delicious mix.

Serves 6–10
450 g (1 lb) long grain rice, volume measured
90 ml (6 tbsp) corn oil
Maldon or sea salt
2 medium onions, skinned and finely chopped
700 g (1½ lb) fresh broad beans, or 450 g (1 lb)
    frozen broad beans
freshly ground black pepper
5–10 ml (1–2 tsp) coriander seeds
2–3 garlic cloves, skinned and crushed
1½ ml (¼ tsp) ground cinnamon

If you have packaged rice, it will not need washing. Otherwise rinse under cold water, drain and dry out as much as possible. Heat 30 ml (2 tbsp) oil in a large saucepan, add the rice and stir fry gently for 2 minutes until all the grains are translucent and gleaming. Add water to the same volume as the rice measured, a good pinch of salt and bring to the boil, then boil hard for 2 minutes. Cover tightly, and simmer on the lowest possible heat for 20 minutes. Then turn off the heat and leave for another 10 minutes.

Meanwhile, heat half the remaining oil in another pan, add the onions and fry gently for 10 minutes. Shell the beans, then add to the onions and sauté for another 5 minutes, stirring constantly. Pour in just enough water to barely cover the beans, season with a little salt, lots of black pepper, and simmer until the beans are tender; 10–20 minutes, depending on size and whether the beans were fresh or frozen.

When the beans are cooked, fry the last 30 ml (2 tbsp) oil in a small frying pan. Quickly grind the coriander seeds in a spice grinder – coarsely. Tip into the pan, add the garlic and sauté over a medium heat for 1–2 minutes until the aroma is tantalising. Tip into the beans, stirring thoroughly to blend well in, then add the beans to the rice. Mix, then pile on a serving platter. Gorgeous as it is, but good too with *şiş kebabs*, *köfte*, fried *kibbeh*, et al.

RICE WITH NUTS

Riz bil Lauz

Strangely, I don't ever remember eating broad beans in Iraq, though I'm told we did have them. Perhaps this incredible golden rice, tinted with saffron and crowded with nuts, superseded all other memories. At any rate, I can remember shelling the nuts – a job that seemed to take ages, no doubt because so many of them went into my tummy rather than the bowl!

Serves 6–8
450 g (1 lb) long grain rice, volume measured
2–3 strands saffron
about 450 ml (¾ pint) chicken stock
Maldon or sea salt
freshly ground white pepper
30–45 ml (2–3 tbsp) olive oil
50 g (2 oz) sweet blanched almonds
50 g (2 oz) shelled fresh hazelnuts
50 g (2 oz) pine nuts
50–75 g (2–3 tbsp) unsalted butter
15 ml (1 tbsp) cumin seeds, crushed

Wash the rice by pouring boiling water over, stir for 1 minute, then rinse under a cold running tap, until the water is clear. Crumble the saffron, pour over 15 ml (1 tbsp) or so of boiling water, stir and leave for 5 minutes.

Put the rice in a saucepan, with the saffron and its liquid, and a good pinch of salt. Pour in the stock (same volume as the rice), bring to the boil, and keep at a hard boil for 2 minutes, then turn to very low and simmer, tightly covered, for 20 minutes. Turn off the heat, sprinkle with freshly ground white pepper and leave (covered) for 10 minutes. While the rice is standing, heat the oil in a frying pan, chop the almonds and hazelnuts coarsely in a grinder, add to the pan with the pine nuts and sauté lightly until golden.

Melt the butter in a small pan, dribble over the rice, then stir in the nuts and leave for another 2 minutes. Pile in a dome shape on a serving platter, smoothing the top, then sprinkle on the cumin seeds. Particularly good with grilled chicken, and also fish.

RICE WITH DATES

Riz bil Tamar

A dish popular everywhere, of Bedouin ancestry, and a good example of the Arab ingenuity with limited ingredients. In Baghdad pistachios were often substituted for the almonds, while for special occasions the cook in Damascus would add pine nuts too.

Serves 6–8
450 g (1 lb) long grain rice, volume measured
Maldon or sea salt
125 g (4 oz) unsalted butter
100 g (4 oz) blanched, sweet almonds
225 g (8 oz) fresh dates
freshly ground white pepper
To garnish finely chopped parsley (optional)

Wash the rice, rinsing in boiling water first, then under cold running water until quite clear. Drain thoroughly. Measure cold water to the volume of the rice, probably just under 600 ml (1 pint), and bring to the boil with a pinch of salt. Add the rice, return to the boil and then continue boiling hard for 2 minutes. Tightly cover the pan, turn down the heat and simmer slowly for 20 minutes.

Meanwhile, heat half the butter in a frying pan, add the almonds and fry gently for about 2 minutes until golden. Take the pan off the heat and remove the almonds with a slotted spoon. Stone the dates (an old book I have tells you to use a needle – I find a chopstick much quicker!) then stuff each date with an almond. Cut in half crossways with a sharp knife, then add the dates to the frying pan with 150 ml (¼ pint) water. Bring to simmering point, then gently simmer for about 15 minutes until the dates have absorbed most of the liquid. The rice should now be done, so turn off the heat and leave the pan a further 10 minutes. Melt the remaining butter, pour over the rice, and leave for 2–3 minutes. Stir the dates into the rice, season, pile on a serving dish and sprinkle with chopped parsley if wished – we did in Baghdad, but obviously in the desert this would be impossible.

PERSIAN RICE

Chelo

The attention to detail in all things, poetry, gardens, carpets, metalwork, and paintings – especially the miniatures – has largely contributed to the great finesse in Persian art. So too in her kitchen. Nothing is too simple, too humble, to be left to chance. This attitude is supremely demonstrated in the cooking of rice, from its long soaking to its ultimate steaming with butter and water, resulting in a delicious golden crust at the bottom of the pan. There is further perfectionism yet – in the serving of the rice. The crust, *tah dig* or *hakkakah* in Arabic, is ceremoniously offered to the guest of honour, while each person is given a small bowl of butter, an egg yolk in its half shell and a pinch of *sumac* to stir into the rice. This is considered to be 'plain rice' – to be served with kebabs or on its own. At other times it will be accompanied by the slowly simmered fruit and meat sauces, *khoresh*, of which there are hundreds. And for fish, especially fried, there is a further variation, with a

handful of fresh herbs – chives, tarragon, coriander, fresh fenugreek, parsley, dillweed – whatever is available, being added to the rice before it is steamed. This is often served at New Year, the 'greenness' signifying fecundity and happiness for the year to come.

Serves 6
450 g (1 lb) long grain rice
Maldon or sea salt
75 g (3 oz) unsalted butter
To serve (optional, see method and *Chelo Kebabs* –
    page 96)
1 egg yolk per person
150 g (6 oz) butter
small bowl of *sumac* (see page 158)

Rinse the rice two or three times in boiling water, then put in a large bowl well covered by cold water. Leave for 6 hours or overnight. Some old manuscripts state that salt, 'a good amount', should be tied in a muslin bag, and added at this stage. Most modern recipes add the salt (loose) to the boiling water. Either way the salt helps prevent the grains from sticking together, thus aiding a 'fluffy' rice. Interestingly, the ancient works claimed that loose salt (i.e. not in a bag) would release the starch from the rice, thus causing it to disintegrate and stick. Since solid rock salt would have been used in former times, perhaps the bag acted as a kind of filter to slowly release the salt into the water. Certainly I have tried this method (without the muslin) using all sorts of salt – rock (in large pieces and crystal), Maldon and free-running. There seemed little difference except that the latter produced a slightly more salt-tasting end result. However, when I used the local salt in Sri Lanka, which, unless kept in an airtight container (and even then sometimes), dissolves with great speed due to the humidity of the climate, the rice was somewhat sticky. As it also was, when I tried putting the salt into a muslin – a not altogether successful experiment. So the answer would seem to lie in the salt. For ease, and perfect rice, I now stick to adding the salt to the boiling water.

A short time before cooking, rinse in fresh cold water and drain. Bring a large pan of water to the boil, add 30 ml (2 tbsp) salt, then dribble in the rice. Boil hard until the rice is soft but not yet tender. Good *basmati* rice will take 8–10 minutes but I have found that some brands of long grain rice only take 4–5, so start checking after 4 minutes. When it cuts easily but still has a 'bite', drain and rinse in tepid water – this will remove any 'oversalting'. Shake the colander to remove any excess moisture.

Melt the butter in a small pan with 45 ml (3 tbsp) water, then pour half this mixture into the rice pan. Add the rice, then drizzle on the rest of the butter. Cover the pan with a clean tea towel, then put on the lid, tying the ends of the cloth over the lid so they don't burn, and let steam, over a low heat, for about 20 minutes. The tea towel absorbs the steam ensuring dry, fluffy rice, every grain perfectly whole and separate. (Such a simple technique – who, I wonder, first thought of it?) Carefully pile the rice on a warmed serving dish, leaving the crust until last. Then scrape that out, and arrange at the side of the platter. Serve the rice either as a dish on its own, or with kebabs, accompanied by butter, egg yolks (in the half shell) and *Sumac*. Or serve with *Khoresh Portagal* (page 31) in which case omit the butter etc.

RICE WITH SPINACH

Ispanaklı Pirinç

In Turkey, rice is often cooked with fresh vegetables – an idea I find particularly appealing. Spinach and tomatoes are my favourites, though aubergines and courgettes are often used too.

Serves 6
900 g (2 lb) fresh spinach
350 g (12 oz) long grain rice, volume measured
60 ml (4 tbsp) olive oil
2 onions, finely sliced
2–3 saffron strands
good pinch of ground cinnamon
Maldon or sea salt
freshly ground black pepper

Wash the spinach thoroughly, discarding any tough stalks and tattered leaves, then chop finely. Rinse the

rice in boiling water, soak for 5 minutes (in boiling water), then drain well. Heat the oil, add the onions and fry gently for about 5 minutes until softening. Remove with a slotted spoon, then add the spinach and cook quickly for 1–2 minutes. Arrange the onions on the bottom of a heatproof casserole, then spread the spinach over them. Pour the rice on top, flattening smooth.

Bring an equal quantity of water to the volume of rice to the boil, then pour over the saffron strands, and stir for a couple of minutes to start the colour running. Stir in the cinnamon, and a good seasoning of salt and pepper, then pour over the rice. Cook gently for about 20 minutes until all the water has been absorbed, then cover the pan and leave, with the heat turned off, for a further 5 minutes until the rice is fluffy.

TOMATO PILAV

Domatesli Pilav

Another dish from Turkey – delectable hot or cold, and pretty with its pale pink colouring. If you can buy fresh plum tomatoes, so much the better – their sweetness and full flavour is unsurpassed by any other variety.

Serves 6–8
45 ml (3 tbsp) olive oil
2 large onions, skinned and finely chopped
2–3 garlic cloves, skinned and crushed
30 ml (2 tbsp) pine nuts
900 g (2 lb) fresh tomatoes, preferably plum or beef steak, blanched, skinned and coarsely chopped
2½–5 ml (½–1 tsp) sugar (optional)
5 ml (1 tsp) dried mint
Maldon or sea salt
freshly ground black pepper
450 g (1 lb) long grain rice, volume measured

Heat the oil in a large pan, add the onions and fry gently until soft and nicely golden, about 15 minutes. Then add the garlic and pine nuts, pushing the onions slightly to the sides of the pan, and cook them for a minute or so. Put the tomatoes into the pan, season with 2½ ml (½ tsp) sugar unless using plum tomatoes, add the mint, salt and pepper. Fry, stirring and slightly beating the tomatoes with a wooden spoon, for 6–7 minutes, then cover with water. Bring to bubbling point, then gently stew the tomatoes for about 40 minutes until very soft and rich. You may need a little extra water, so check from time to time.

Rinse the rice in boiling water, then drain well. Add to the pan, stirring well in, then add about half its volume of water and bring to the boil. Cover and simmer for 20 minutes until the rice is tender, but check after 10 minutes to see if more water is needed – there will have been a certain amount of liquid from the tomatoes, so it is difficult to gauge exactly how much you'll need. Have the extra water simmering on the stove, so that you don't drop the temperature when you drizzle it in. When the rice is tender and delicately pink, it's ready. Traditionally served hot but also good, I think, cold.

RICE WITH LENTILS

Mujaddarah

A very old favourite this, familiarly named 'Esau's Mess' or 'Esau's Potage'. It appears in al-Baghdadi's book though meat was included then, left out now. The name literally means 'one having the smallpox' – as Professor Arberry aptly comments 'a grim jest indeed'. But don't let that put you off – it is delicious, much loved by poor and rich alike, and often served as a course on its own. Since it is so good cold, particularly with yogurt and cooling salads, I often include it on the *mezze* table. These are my preferred quantities, but each family has their own, some doubling the lentils to rice, or even vice versa. It's a question of personal taste – and what is in the storecupboard!

Serves 6
450 g (12 oz) large brown lentils, soaked overnight
3 large onions, skinned
45 ml (3 tbsp) olive oil
Maldon or sea salt

freshly ground black or white pepper
15 ml (1 tbsp) cumin seeds, crushed
2½ ml (½ tsp) ground cinnamon
225 g (8 oz) long grain rice

Drain the lentils and put in a large pan of water, covering to a depth of at least 5 cm (2 inches) and bring to the boil. Turn down the heat and simmer for 40 minutes to 1½ hours – this will vary enormously with country of origin and age. Check from time to time, topping up with more water as necessary .

Chop one of the onions very finely, slice the others in half circles and reserve. Heat 15 ml (1 tbsp) oil in a frying pan, add the chopped onion and sauté gently for 10–15 minutes until soft and lightly golden. When the lentils are almost tender, drain – if there is any liquid in the pan – then return to the pan with the onions, season well with salt and black or white pepper (I quite like a bit of both) then stir in the cumin and cinnamon. Measure the volume of the rice, then add it to the pan with the same amount of water and simmer for about 20 minutes until the rice and lentils are tender and the water has been absorbed (you may even need to add a little extra – check after 10 minutes).

While the rice is cooking, heat the remaining oil, add the sliced onions and cook, turning constantly, until they are very dark, almost, but not quite, burnt. Tip the lentil mixture on to a large shallow dish, strew with the onions and serve hot or cold.

BROWN LENTILS WITH VEGETABLES

Adis Samra Ma' Khudar

Another dish with many variations, the vegetables chosen being those particularly liked and/or locally available. In Baghdad we grew celery, courgettes, leeks, tomatoes, so this is how I know it. But equally you could use aubergines, sweet peppers, broad beans, potatoes, green beans or cauliflower – whatever looks best in the market that day.

Serves 6

225 g (8 oz) large brown or green lentils, soaked
    overnight
2–3 sticks celery, finely sliced
225 g (8 oz) leeks, trimmed and sliced (use as
    much of the green as you can)
225 g (8 oz) courgettes, topped, tailed and sliced
3–4 small tomatoes, blanched, skinned and sliced
Maldon or sea salt
freshly ground white pepper
5 ml (1 tsp) coriander seeds
5 ml (1 tsp) cumin seeds
30 ml (2 tbsp) olive oil
1 large onion, skinned and finely sliced
2–3 garlic cloves, skinned and finely chopped
30–45 ml (2–3 tbsp) finely chopped fresh
    coriander leaves or parsley
juice of 1½–2 lemons

Drain the lentils and bring to the boil in a large pan
with a good 600 ml (1 pint) water for 40 minutes–1½
hours, until the lentils are almost done. Add the
vegetables, salt and pepper. Grind the coriander and
cumin seeds in a spice grinder and stir in, then cook
for a further 10–20 minutes, until the vegetables are
just tender and nearly all the liquid is absorbed.

Heat the oil in a frying pan, add the onion and
cook fairly quickly until dark gold, add the garlic and
cook for another 1–2 minutes. Stir into the lentils
and vegetables mixing well in and let cook for 1–2
minutes, then pile into a serving dish. Scatter over
the coriander or parsley, sprinkle with lemon juice
and serve. Hot, warm or cold this is delicious.

EGYPTIAN
BROWN BEANS

Foul Medames

'The dish of the Pharaohs' my grandfather's cook
used to call this. And indeed it is very old, now
acclaimed as the Egyptian national dish, eaten by
everyone. At home, in expensive restaurants, bought
from street vendors – to be tucked into pittas.
Although originally a peasant dish, it has transcended
all boundaries, and its appearance on the table will
always be greeted with delight. The beans traditionally used are small, round and reddish brown, bigger
than a lentil, smaller than a chick pea. They can often
be found in Greek delicatessens, and I have used
'English Field Beans' from health shops very successfully. They may even be the same beast but bean
nomenclature is rather confusing and I have not
ascertained this for sure. In desperation, I have even
used dried haricot beans, which proved very good
though not quite so richly earthy.

Serves 6–10

900 g (2 lb) dried brown beans, soaked overnight
3–4 large garlic cloves, skinned and finely chopped
fresh parsley or coriander leaves, finely chopped
olive oil
lemon wedges
cumin seeds, crushed (optional)
paprika (optional)
Maldon or sea salt
6–10 *Hamine Eggs* (page 72)

Drain the beans and rinse in fresh water. Put into a
large pan, very well covered with cold water, bring to
the boil, then simmer for 1½– 2½ hours (this depends
on the beans used) until nicely tender but not mushy.

Arrange on the table little bowls with the garlic
and parsley, a jug of olive oil, plate of lemon wedges,
a small saucer each of cumin and paprika if used (in
many traditional recipes these are omitted, but this
was the way we always had it and I now miss them if
they're absent) and the salt. Naturally, there will be a
pepper mill – one for white and one for black is nice.
Shell the eggs and put on a plate.

When the beans are cooked, dish out into a large
bowl and let people help themselves. An egg is
usually put into the middle of the beans, then seasonings taken as wished, everything being slightly
mashed together to produce that inimitable amalgam
of flavours.

CHICK PEAS WITH SPINACH

Humus Ma' Ispanakh

A dish of Persian origin, now cooked all over the Middle East, sometimes with meatballs, sometimes without. There is a similar dish of lentils and spinach, also Persian, and traditionally said to cure the sick. I have given below the Turkish refinement of a yogurt topping with garlic, mint and paprika as it's particularly suitable for the *mezze* table. But you could equally well cook the Egyptian version, in which case fry some coriander seeds with the garlic and salt and stir in just before serving.

Serves 6

225 g (8 oz) chick peas, soaked overnight
450 g (1 lb) fresh spinach
30 ml (2 tbsp) olive oil
1 large onion, skinned and finely chopped
Maldon or sea salt
150 ml (¼ pint) natural yogurt
2 garlic cloves, skinned and crushed
freshly ground black pepper
5 ml (1 tsp) dried mint
paprika

Drain the chick peas and bring to the boil in a large pan of water, then simmer until soft. This will take from about 30 minutes to well over 1 hour, so check frequently. Wash the spinach, discarding tough stems and blemished leaves, then chop finely. Heat the oil in a large pan, add the onion and cook gently for about 15 minutes until soft. Add the spinach, and stew slowly for about 7–8 minutes. When the chick peas are quite tender, add them with 75 ml (5 tbsp) of their water to the spinach and onions, season lightly with salt and cook for another 5–10 minutes until the liquid is absorbed.

Beat the yogurt with the crushed garlic, a little salt, black pepper and the dried mint. Arrange the chick pea mixture on a large shallow serving dish, pour over the yogurt, then sprinkle with paprika – a zig-zag design is nice and in keeping with the dish's native habitat. Good hot – good cold.

BEANS WITH TOMATOES

Domatesli Fasulye

Another good Turkish marriage, popular elsewhere too. I have had it with both red kidney and haricot beans – the latter win on looks, their pale creaminess lightly tinged a rosy pink, but the former on a heightened nuttiness. Try both. The beans may also be cooked without the tomatoes, dressed with oil and lemon and left to cool before serving with raw onion and sliced fresh tomato.

Serves 6

350 g (12 oz) red kidney or haricot beans, soaked overnight
45 ml (3 tbsp) olive oil
2 large onions, skinned and finely chopped
2–3 garlic cloves, skinned and crushed
350 g (12 oz) fresh tomatoes, blanched, skinned and coarsely chopped
Maldon or sea salt
5 ml (1 tsp) paprika
1 bay leaf
pinch of cayenne pepper
30 ml (2 tbsp) finely chopped parsley
To garnish 15 ml (1 tbsp) finely chopped fresh basil

Drain the beans, rinse, then put into a large pan well covered with cold water. Bring to the boil, then boil vigorously for 10 minutes – this is *absolutely vital* if using red kidney beans in order to expel certain toxins they contain. Reduce the heat and simmer for 1½–3 hours, depending on age and the bean, so check with the package or shop when you buy them.

Heat the oil and fry the onions for about 10 minutes, then add the garlic and cook for another 2–3 minutes. Now put the tomatoes in, breaking them up slightly with a fork or wooden spoon, and cook for about 30 minutes until really pulpy. Add the salt, paprika, bay leaf, cayenne and parsley, then stir in the drained beans with about 120 ml (8 tbsp) of their cooking water and simmer for another 15–20 minutes until nicely soft. Turn on to a serving dish and sprinkle with the basil.

BREADS

Khubz

Take first a pair of loaves, of finest wheat,
The like of which on earth was never seen;
Then cut the crusts around, and lift them clean,
When naught remaineth but the supple dough,
Cover one round with fresh-cut slices, so!

IBN AL-RUMI[1]

Bread is not an afterthought in the Middle East. It is, of course, one of the staples of life, as elsewhere in the world. But it is also revered, thought of as a gift from Allah, especially in rural communities. I can remember our cook in Baghdad, muttering a 'grace' over the large flat rounds of dough before they were slapped on the walls of the oven. This, the most common Arab bread known as *khubz* in the Middle East, pitta to us (and the Greeks), is lightly leavened and comes out with a softly chewy crust, an absorbent inner surface, and a wonderful hollow in the middle – perfect for filling with *kibbeh*, *köfte*, pulses and salads of all sorts. These were baked every day at home by our cooks, but in Damascus I would often see children (mainly little girls, I noticed with some envy) running down the hill with a large flat basket, the dough just ready for cooking, covered by brightly coloured cloths, to the local bakery. Soon they were toiling up again, nibbling on warm pitta, the rest safely tucked in their wrappings to keep them hot on the journey home.

That is the most common bread but there are many others, in wonderful shapes and sizes and with an extraordinary posse of seasonings. Sesame seed is a favourite, scattered on tiny bracelets, or small sharp pointed 'sticks'; long flat plaits speckled with poppy seeds are another. Cheese and olives make a festive bread, while a medieval recipe calls for an encrustation of pistachio nuts, poppy seeds, saffron, salt, grated cheese and lots of pepper, sesame seeds,

ginger, cumin, the bitter rue and aromatic aniseed[2] – an aristocratic bread indeed. Even today a plain *khubz* dough will often be garnished before baking: a generous smearing of olive oil and *za'atar* or grated hard cheese transforming the *khubz* into *manakeesh*. Our cook in Damascus used to mix chopped raw onions with crushed coriander and cumin seed for the topping – dried mint too is favoured by the Syrians; while in Baghdad it was always fresh dill-weed, cumin and that cook's (and my) beloved cardamom. I'm not sure how traditional the latter is – but the flavour was excellent. And a Yemeni friend recently gave me her country's version: a dried red chilli and crushed fenugreek paste – thickly smeared on for her, thinly for me. But perfect in Sri Lanka, where 'chilli-hot' is loved, and the two ingredients commonly available. Fancy or plain, bread makes its appearance at every meal, to be used as an eating implement, wrapped round meat or vegetables, dipped into sauces and creamy salads – simply, to be enjoyed.

1. *Arab poet, murdered approximately* AD *896/283 Islamic calendar.*
2. *Kitab al Wusla el al Habibi; a medieval Arabic manuscript, circa 13th century, authors unknown, discussed and translated into French by Maxime Rodinson in his article 'Recherches sur les documents Arabes relatifs à la cuisine', published in* Revue des Études Islamiques, *1949.*

FLAT LEAVENED BREAD

Pitta (Khubz)

Not just bread, but a container, a scoop, a dipper, pitta is the all purpose bread for the *mezze* table. Flat, soft and easily hollowed into two, it is wonderful stuffed with *Falafel* (page 21) kebabs, salads of all sorts, *Foul Medames* (page 143), hot chick peas, almost anything. Equally good dipped into *Humus bi Tahina* (page 24), *Taramasalata* (page 24) or any of the creamy salads. Best of all, of course, with olive oil, and *dukkah* (pages 17–20).

Makes 8–10 pittas
450 g (1 lb) plain flour
2½ ml (½ tsp) salt
10 ml (2 tsp) Easy Blend yeast (if unavailable, see page 158)
30 ml (2 tbsp) olive oil

Sift the flour into a large bowl or food processor, sprinkle in the salt and the yeast and mix together. Dribble over the oil, then gradually pour in (with the motor running if using a processor) up to 300 ml (½ pint) lukewarm water. Take care with the last few spoonfuls of water, the dough should mix together but not be too sticky. Knead thoroughly for about 15 minutes (3–4 minutes in the machine – then the same again by hand) until the dough is very elastic and comes cleanly away from your fingers and the bowl.

Lightly brush a bowl with some oil, roll the ball in it – this helps prevent a crust forming while it's resting, then cover with a cloth and leave for 1–2 hours to rise. Knock back the risen dough a few times, then break off small pieces, about the size of a lemon. Roll, on a lightly floured board into a circle or oval, about ½ cm (¼ inch) thick. Don't roll too heavily or you can make it difficult to split them. Dust each round with a little flour on both sides, then put on a floured surface and cover with a completely floured cloth and leave to rise again for about 25 minutes. The complete flouring of the cloth

is extremely important. I once neglected the edges: disastrous – the *pittas* clung like limpets to the towel, utterly immovable! I had to scrape off what I could, reroll and start again. Not to be recommended.

Turn the oven on, to its hottest, at least 15–20 minutes before putting in the bread. Put a lightly oiled baking sheet in the oven for 4–5 minutes. Then place the risen pittas on the hot baking sheets, sprinkling them with a little cold water. (This keeps them soft but I must admit I – again – once forgot. The result was not a disaster but a gloriously puffed up bread, with a wonderful hollow inside. Perfect for instant eating, but a bit too crisp the next day, although a gentle warming up softened them slightly.) Bake for 5–9 minutes until they smell strongly yeasty. The first time you bake them you will obviously have to check after 5 minutes, but once you know how long your oven takes, cook them without opening the oven door. They should be pale in colour and soft, slightly swollen and hollow inside. Eat warm.

SESAME BREAD RINGS

Semit

On our first trip to Cairo, we arrived at night. It was too dark, and I was too sleepy, to see much but the next morning I was up with the sun. Flinging open my bedroom shutters, I looked down on the street below, already crowded with street vendors, busy vying with each other as to the goodness of their wares. Most intriguing was an extremely tall, intensely thin man on the corner, with two long poles over his shoulders, each one threaded with slim golden bracelets. Catching my eye, he moved across the road to stand directly under the window, calling up '*semit, semit*'. Five minutes later, there was one happy customer tucking into a breakfast of these crunchy sesame-seed encrusted rings. In Turkey, they are called *simit* or, confusingly, *çörek*, which, in the Arab countries, is a sweet bun with raisins.

Makes 8–12 rings

225 g (8 oz) plain flour

2½ ml (½ tsp) salt

5 ml (1 tsp) Easy Blend yeast (if unavailable, see
  page 158)

75 ml (3 fl oz) milk

15 ml (1 tbsp) butter

pinch of sugar

oil, for greasing

1 egg, beaten

45–60 ml (3–4 tbsp) sesame seeds

Sift the flour into a large bowl, or food processor. Sprinkle on the salt and the yeast and mix in. Bring the milk just to the boil, then stir in the butter. Take the pan off the heat, add the sugar and 50 ml (2 fl oz) tepid water. Stir, then gradually pour on to the flour, with the machine running if using a processor. Add a little more water if necessary to make a soft dough which leaves the sides of the bowl clean. Knead lightly, then leave to rest for 15 minutes, before kneading again, this time quite vigorously for 10–15 minutes by hand (3–4 minutes in a processor, then 2–3 minutes by hand), until the dough is nicely elastic and smooth.

Brush a large bowl with oil, roll the dough to oil all sides, then leave, covered, for 1½–2 hours until risen and doubled in size. Knock back the dough, then break into 8–12 even-sized pieces. I would suggest you make larger rings to start with, as they are less likely to close up when rising again. Lightly roll each piece between floured hands until you have a long thin sausage, then join the ends together to make a bracelet. Mix the egg with a couple of spoonfuls of cold water, and brush the top of each ring, then scatter fairly liberally with sesame seeds.

Oil a baking tray and arrange the rings on it, then leave to rise again – leaving plenty of room between each bracelet to allow for the spread. Thirty minutes in a warm, draught free place should be sufficient time. Bake in the oven at 220°C (425°F), mark 7, for 10 minutes, then lower the heat to 170°C (325°F), mark 3, for another 10–20 minutes until the bread is golden and sounds quite hollow when tapped on the bottom. Cool on a wire rack. Also good as rolls – give them an extra 5–10 minutes at the lower oven temperature to ensure the middle is cooked.

OLIVE AND CHEESE BREAD

Elioti

In Cyprus there is a marvellously hearty, rather dark bread full of black olives and cheese. A slice of this soon dispelled hunger pangs after a morning in the sea at Famagusta, which, in those days merely consisted of one hotel and one private house, at either end of that glorious sweep of bay. A tiny, very bent, darkly clad figure appearing from the direction of the hotel, signalled feeding time, and a little old lady would bring a large wicker tray full of these loaves, raw tomatoes and bunches of spring onions for those too lazy to return to the hotel for lunch. It is also a bread popular during Lent, when the very orthodox often leave out the cheese. I have also made it without the olives when needs must and it was excellent. Cypriot flour is brown-grey in colour, rather like buckwheat flour, but coarser so I mix it with stoneground wholewheat flour which I find gives the nearest likeness.

Makes one 550 g (1¼ lb) loaf

50 g (2 oz) buckwheat flour

175 g (6 oz) stoneground wholewheat flour

5 ml (1 tsp) Easy Blend yeast (if unavailable, see
  page 158)

Maldon or sea salt

15 ml (1 tbsp) olive oil

150 g (5 oz) black olives, stoned

75 g (3 oz) Feta or Hallumi cheese, grated

Mix the buckwheat and wholewheat flour with the yeast and a small pinch of salt, unless you omit the cheese in which case add 2½ ml (½ tsp) salt. Dribble over the oil, then gradually add 150–175 ml (5–6 fl oz) tepid water to make a stiff dough. If it seems a little dry, add a drop or two more water – the dough will be quite heavy and should be slightly sticky but not overwet. (This is one bread incidentally which does not make well in a processor.) Put the dough on a lightly floured board and knead hard until it feels softer, more elastic and smooth – this will take about 10–15 minutes. Oil another bowl, roll the dough in the oil, and cover with a cloth. Leave to rise in a warm place for 2–2½ hours.

Knock back the dough, then add the olives, chopped if they are very large, and the grated cheese. Knead quite thoroughly until they are well distributed throughout the dough, then shape into a flattish round and put on an oiled baking tray. Leave, covered, for a further 45 minutes to 1 hour until it has considerably expanded, then bake in the oven at 200°C (400°F), mark 6, for about 1 hour until nicely browned on top.

Remove from the baking sheet and cool on a wire rack. Eat within 4 hours if possible – to enjoy it at its peak. Otherwise warm it gently for 5–10 minutes. Very good with salad.

BLACK OLIVE BREAD

Zeytin Bittasi

Turkey has another version of olive bread, no cheese but refreshingly spiced with dried mint. It is much softer in texture, almost cake-like but slightly chewy. Excellent though with thick slices of sweet tomato and a sprinkling of oil and lemon.

Makes one 550 g (1¼ lb) loaf
2 eggs
150 ml (¼ pint) milk
225 g (8 oz) plain flour, sifted
5 ml (1 tsp) baking powder, sifted
good 5 ml (good 1 tsp) Maldon or sea salt
15 ml (1 tbsp) dried mint
45 ml (3 tbsp) olive oil
150 g (5 oz) black olives, stoned and chopped

Whisk the eggs with the milk and 30 ml (2 tbsp) tepid water, then gradually pour in the sifted flour and baking powder, beating quite thoroughly to avoid lumps (this can be made in the processor). Add the salt, then the mint and olive oil and whisk again. Fold in the chopped olives – the consistency should be that of a fairly thin cake mixture. Line a cake tin with bakewell paper or grease it very well, then pour in the mixture.

Bake at 180°C (350°F), mark 4, for 45 minutes, then brush the top with a little oil, raise the oven to 200°C (400°F), mark 6, and bake for a further 10–15 minutes until crisp and deep gold on top. A knife inserted should come out clean. Cool on a wire rack. Also excellent with sultanas – if unorthodox – instead of the olives. Best eaten within a few hours of making.

CORN BREAD

Dari Unu Ile Yapilmis Ekmek

The Turks also make a lovely golden corn bread. And, unlike many recipes for corn bread it's not too dry since it contains both yogurt and olive oil. Excellent with olives and the salty goat cheeses.

Makes one 700 g (1½ lb) loaf
125 g (4 oz) plain flour
10 ml (2 tsp) sugar
10 ml (2 tsp) baking powder
5 ml (1 tsp) salt
150 g (5 oz) corn meal
1 large egg
1 egg yolk
400 ml (14 fl oz) natural yogurt
45 ml (3 tbsp) olive oil

Sift the flour together with the sugar, baking powder and salt, then stir in the corn meal. Beat the egg into the egg yolk, then mix with the yogurt and olive oil. Pour the liquid, in a slow drizzle to begin with, into the flours, constantly stirring. Increase the speed as the mixture melds, then stir to make sure it's smooth. Don't over mix. Grease a loaf tin and pour in the batter, then bake in the oven at 210°C (425°F), mark 7, for 20–30 minutes until the top is golden and the bread firm. Leave for 5 minutes in the tin to cool, then transfer to a wire rack and cool for another 15–20 minutes. At this stage, I indulge in one lovely warm piece. Keeps well for 2–3 days if wrapped in foil and stored in a cool place.

DRINKS

Mashroubat

Cool drinks were brought to him and coffee flavoured with amber.
ALADDIN AND THE ENCHANTED LAMP[1]

The peoples of the Mediterranean in general and, I would say, the Arabs in particular, are of a very sociable disposition. Never will the unexpected caller, however fleeting his or her visit, be unwelcome. And their arrival will be heralded by the production first, of coffee, black, thick and strong; often too, by a cooling drink. Sherbets of wonderful hues, sweetly scented with rose or orange-flower water, creamy yogurt *ayran* or, in Iraq, buttermilk *shenina*, will be served in long tall glasses often encased in a silver fretted holder, and always on an ornately decorated tray. You cannot go shopping in Turkey without being offered a glass (small, waisted and heavily cut, on a small glass saucer to match) of mint tea. It is not polite to refuse – even if you say you are just looking, with no intention to buy, they don't mind, 'sit, sit', and little boys are despatched to the back (or next door) returning in an instant with the sweet-scented brew. Delightful, but shopping can take a while . . . House visiting is even more leisurely. A little something to eat, be it sweet or savoury, then enquiries as to everyone's health, pleasure at seeing the visitor, and a general exchange on life's affairs form a pleasant preamble before the guest may reveal the purpose of his visit. If there is one. Often the call may be merely social – keeping in touch with one's friends and family plays a large and important role in everyday life. The coffee pot empty, the news exchanged, the visitor will take his leave, moving on to his next port of call – perhaps another relative, a business appointment, a

message to be delivered. Whatever, a small cup of that steaming dark brew will not be long in appearing. Or it may be tea, particularly in Persia and Iraq, refreshingly made from dried limes (*numi Basra*) or coolingly spiced with mint. Bottles of spring water are a delicacy, especially in Turkey where special trips are often made to the favourite watering place, be it spring or well, and bottles brought home to be labelled, dated and treasured for special occasions. Water, of course, everywhere is a precious commodity, treated with a special reverence, considered a blessing of God and never wasted, nor refused to a beggar. I remember vividly a huge commotion outside our house one day in Baghdad, a large and vociferous crowd following a bedraggled bearded young man, who was being marched down the road between five policemen, one of them carrying a large galvanised metal bucket. Wide-eyed, I asked what was happening. Nanny's wretched mother gleefully told me he was a burglar and they were going to squash him in the bucket. Tearful, but totally believing, I turned to Ali, asking what had he stolen to deserve such a fate? He of course reassured me that the grisly punishment was a figment of 'Her' lurid imagination (we were utterly united in our loathing of that poor wretched female); but the youth had stolen the pail, so that his family had some means of fetching water from the river, too poor were they to replace their own, which had a hole in it. It is an incident I always remember when I see a tap wastefully running . . .

If water is precious, wine is rarer, especially in the stricter Islamic states, many of which are totally 'dry'. But of course, many centuries ago, much fine wine was made in the Middle East; Anatolia in Turkey particularly was noted for its wine some four thousand years before Christ. Turkey still makes some very respectable wines and so, bravely, does the Lebanon – even with battle tearing apart her vineyards. So superb have some of these been in recent years that they have walked off with top marks in blind tastings and gained coveted wine awards. *Retsina* is popular in Greece while Cyprus, of course, has her famous sweet dessert wine, *Commanderia*. Most potent of all is *arak*, *raki* to the Turks, *ouzo* to the Greeks, *zibib* to the Egyptians. Made from grape-must or the coco-palm, extra fierily from dates in Iraq, it is clear in the bottle, milky white with the addition of water. It has a flavour of aniseed, can be deceptively more-ish and should be treated with a healthy respect. You may yet need a small cup of black coffee.

1. From Tales from the 1001 Nights, *translated by N. J. Dawood, Penguin 1973.*

ROSE-WATER SHERBET

Sharbat Ma' Al Waad

A Persian favourite, also popular in Baghdad and Damascus. In both places our roses were spectacular, and the cook not only made rose-water but also his own colouring – how I'm not sure. I remember the pounding of mounds of deep red petals, boiling water poured over, but then what? I have never achieved the same effect. No matter, use a drop or two of food colouring, and float some petals in the glass. The effect is the same. Very pretty.

Makes about 1 litre (1¾ pints)
225 g (8 oz) caster sugar
juice of 1 lemon
50 ml (2 fl oz) rose-water
few drops of red food colouring
red rose petals

Dissolve the sugar with 300 ml (½ pint) water, stirring constantly. Add the lemon juice and the rose-water, then taste to see if more of either is needed. Cool, then chill. Dilute with about 450–600 ml (¾–1 pint) iced water, then stir in a few drops food colouring – just to lightly tinge pink. Add some ice cubes and strew on a few rose petals.

POMEGRANATE SHERBET

Abi Anar

A wonderfully exotic, deep purple drink, popular in Persia and also in Iraq. Regrettably, those glowing containers sitting on the café counters did not appeal to me as a child. Now, without a profusion of pomegranates to hand, I love its bitter-sweet flavour. It also makes a spectacular jelly. Try to buy plump-looking pomegranates – dry, wizened specimens will have no juice.

Makes about 1.1 litres (2 pints)
2–3 large pomegranates
175 g (6 oz) caster sugar, or more
5 ml (1 tsp) rose-water

Squeeze the pomegranates all over, pressing hard with the fingertips. You should feel the pips being crushed inside, and the fruit will become quite pulpy and soft to the touch. Holding the pomegranate inside a deep bowl, carefully make a slit in the skin with a very sharp knife (do take care, if the juice spurts out, it stains where it touches – badly). Squeeze gently to extract all the juice. Dissolve the sugar in 600 ml (1 pint) water. Add the pomegranate juice. Taste to see if you need more sugar – the sourness of this fruit is very variable, adding more if necessary. Pour into a jug and chill well. Add some ice cubes, sprinkle on the rose-flower water and serve with more iced water if wished.

PERSIAN SWEET-SOUR SYRUP

Sekanjebin

Another much loved, very refreshing concoction from Persia. The proportions vary considerably from person to person – I like it less sweet than many, so adjust the ingredients to suit. Grated cucumber is often added just before serving. I am a little ambivalent about that – but I do like crushed borage leaves, and pineapple mint for preference, although spearmint is the one traditionally used.

Makes 1 litre (1¾ pints)
450 g (1 lb) sugar
225 ml (8 fl oz) white wine, or cider, vinegar
juice of 2–3 lemons
12 fresh mint sprigs

Melt the sugar with about 600 ml (1 pint) water in a small pan, constantly stirring. Pour in the vinegar and lemon juice (start with 2 lemons, and add more at the end if you like) and simmer gently for 10–15 minutes, to drive off the vinegar fumes. Add 6–8 mint sprigs after 5 minutes. Take off the heat, cool, then chill for 1–2 hours. Discard the mint, and serve, diluted to taste, with a jug of iced water and fresh mint sprigs in each glass.

FRESH LEMONADE

Limoun Taza

Like English schools, we had a short mid-morning break, but unlike our faraway compatriots, we were given tall glasses of ice-cold fresh lemonade – much better than lukewarm milk. It was one of the things that I missed most when I started school in England. At home we also used to make it with fresh limes – a rather wicked extravagance in Britain, but delightful.

Makes about 1.1 litres (2 pints)
12 large lemons
about 180 ml (12 tbsp) caster sugar
4–6 sprigs lemon balm, verbena, or mint

Grate the zest finely of 2–3 lemons, then squeeze all the lemons. Dissolve the sugar in the lemon juice over a gentle heat, start with a little less to begin with, adding more if wished. As soon as the sugar has dissolved take off the heat and pour into a jug. Stir in the herbs and chill for at least 1 hour, then dilute with about 600 ml (1 pint) iced water or to taste. Never fails.

YOGURT DRINK

Ayran

Known as *ayran* in the Lebanon and Turkey, simply as *laban* in Iraq and Syria, and *abdag* in Persia, this is a great favourite everywhere – sold on street corners, in cafés small and large, or served to unexpected callers to refresh and cool them after their hot and tiring journey – however short that may have been!

Makes 1.1 litres (2 pints)
600 ml (1 pint) natural yogurt
Maldon or sea salt
45–60 ml (3–4 tbsp) fresh mint, chopped and lightly crushed or 15–45 ml (1–3 tbsp) dried mint

Whisk the yogurt in a large jug, then pour in 600 ml (1 pint) water, constantly beating. The Turks add considerably more water, their preferred proportions being one to four, but I like it more yogurty – taste and see. Add a pinch of salt, then whisk in the mint – you can make the whole thing in a blender if you wish, for a smooth, frothy effect. Chill for 1 hour, at least, then add some ice cubes to the jug and serve in long tall glasses. Also nice, very un-Arab but I think they would approve the prettiness, is to sprinkle on a few borage flowers. Those specks of intense madonna blue are cooling in themselves.

BUTTERMILK DRINK

Shenina

Afternoons in Baghdad were joyous. Down to the club for swimming, where the pool was huge. Strictly forbidden for children of course but since I swam on the bottom I could usually get a few minutes in before I was spotted and banned to the 'kiddies' pool, of which I was extremely contemptuous. However, another little friend and I then discovered the 'canals' which ran around the periphery of the club, about a yard deep and twice as wide. These fed the pools with fresh water and were wonderful for clandestine swimming. Moreover at one point they passed the back door of the kitchens, where we befriended a young Arab girl. It quickly became a regular port of call, for a gossip and a glass of this delicious drink. A similar drink is made in Persia using yogurt, called *mast*.

Makes about 1.1 litres (2 pints)
600 ml (1 pint) buttermilk
pinch of salt
450–600 ml (¾–1 pint) soda water
freshly ground allspice

Whisk the buttermilk with a good pinch of salt, then chill for 1–2 hours. Add chilled soda water to taste, a few ice cubes and a goodly sprinkling of allspice.

MINTED TEA

Shai Ma' Na'na

This is, to my mind, still one of the best 'coolers' for a blazing day, and a favourite Baghdad drink. The Moroccans have a similar drink made with green tea but usually drunk hot – also good.

Makes 1.1 litres (2 pints)
30 ml (2 tbsp) Earl Grey, or any good Indian tea
75–100 g (3–4 oz) caster sugar
small bunch of fresh mint

Rinse the teapot with a little boiling water (unless it's silver) then add the tea and pour in about 600 ml (1 pint) boiling water. Stir in the sugar, add the mint (reserving a few sprigs) and top up with another 600 ml (1 pint) boiling water. Infuse for about 8–9 minutes, then pour into a jug and cool. Chill for 1 hour, then serve in tall glasses with a sprig of fresh mint in each.

ARAB COFFEE

Kahveh

The making, and drinking, of coffee is surrounded by ritual everywhere in the Middle East. Introduced to the Arabian peninsula via the Yemen, probably from across the water from ancient Abyssinia where the plant flourishes in the wild, it was widely drunk by the dervishes to induce a trance-like state, no doubt also helping to keep them awake during their marathon prayer recitals – all day, and sometimes all night as well. The (coffee) habit soon spread throughout Arabia although it didn't reach Turkey until some 700 years later, about 1550, when, legend has it, a merchant from Aleppo in Syria introduced it to the court of Suleiman the Magnificent. Despite the hostility of very orthodox Muslims who felt that coffee had detrimental effects, it was greeted with delight and soon became established.

The preparation of the coffee is pure art, and treated with much reverence. The beans are first freshly roasted and very finely pulverised. In the desert, huge brass pestles and mortars are used. The noise of heavy pounding early in the morning is the Bedouin equivalent of our alarm clock, while in Iraq I never failed to awaken to the crunching and whirring of the large, beautifully decorated brass grinder, strategically situated in the courtyard below, right underneath my balcony. The smell of those coffee beans still haunts me to this day.

The beans crushed, the water is boiled in a small, long-handled copper, brass or enamelled pan with a pointed lip for easy pouring. These are called *tanaqa* and come in various sizes, making from one to five cups, never more, and the cups are tiny – similar to a *demi-tasse*. With or without handles, they are often also highly painted or else fit into small fretwork metal containers which will match the tray – again heavy with decoration, often inlaid with a contrasting metal – silver, copper or brass – spelling out a quotation from the Koran. The water bubbling, the coffee is sprinkled over, a cardamom pod or crushed clove added, and it then has to 'froth' three or four times, before it is ready to be served. Important guests first, then the eldest members of the family.

Makes 5 small cups
60 ml (4 tbsp) Turkish or espresso coffee
1 cardamom pod, husk removed and seeds ground
(optional)
2 cloves, ground (optional)

Bring 300 ml (½ pint) water just to boiling point in a small pan (if you want to make Arab or Turkish coffee regularly, it's worth investing in the special pot – specialist kitchen shops often stock them). Take off the heat, sprinkle on the coffee and spices, if using, lightly stir once, then return to the stove and simmer gently until the coffee begins to froth. Lift up high above the heat, let it subside, then heat again until it foams once more. Stir. Return to the heat for one more frothing, then take off and let it stand for 1 minute to let some of the grounds sink. Pour into small cups, giving each person some of the froth (*weysh*) – a slight shake of the pot should make it pour easily. Do not stir the coffee once it is in the cups. This is a delicately spiced but very strong brew – traditionally the Arabs added no sugar to their coffee, although many now do, making it very sweet indeed.

TURKISH COFFEE

Türk Kahvasi

Coffee houses are as popular today in Turkey as when they made their first appearance 400 years ago. Many happy hours are spent therein, discussing the world, the family, the local gossip, and playing *tric-trac* – the fast, and lethal, Arab version of backgammon. Always invariably accompanied by steaming hot cups of coffee. The Turks and Greeks, on the whole like sugar in their brew, and as the sugar is cooked with the coffee, you are always asked which stage of sweetness you prefer, *murrah* (unsweetened, although often even this has a little added – the premise being one does not actually want it bitter), *mazbout* (medium sweet), or *zukkar ziada* (extremely sweet). I use a medium sweet recipe but you can always add more sugar if you wish. A favourite occupation in both these countries begins once the coffee is finished: the reading of the grounds. You will often see the saucer being firmly held over the empty cup, swung round three times high in the air, then quickly inverted. After a minute or two, the cup is upturned and the fortunes read. Often, with unnerving accuracy.

Makes 5 small cups
a good 25 ml (5 heaped tsp) Turkish or espresso
coffee
25 ml (5 tsp) sugar
orange-flower water (optional)

Bring just over 300 ml (½ pint) water to the boil, sprinkle over the coffee, then sprinkle the sugar on top. Do not stir. Bring it to foaming point, take it off the heat until the froth subsides, then return again to the boil until frothing once more. Take off the heat, give the pot a sharp knock against the side of the stove, then boil once more. As it foams this time, stir the coffee and sugar quickly, twice, then pour a little froth into each cup and top up with coffee. Sprinkle with a drop of orange-flower water if wished – use a pipette, because I do mean drop. The perfect pick-me-up when the party is over.

GLOSSARY

The Arab may be vague about quantities and timing but ingredients are another matter. Substitution is no problem but freshness is essential and great care is taken in choosing particular foods for a particular recipe. If the aubergines in the market are not the right shape for stuffing – why then something else can be stuffed. Or the aubergines made into a different dish. It is, I suppose, a continuity of that flexible state of mind, but it is an attitude shared by all great chefs – the menu is decided upon after seeing the day's produce. There are, however, certain ingredients vital to the Middle Eastern kitchen. These are of course, easily available to the cook in the Middle East, who may even buy his spices freshly ground every day from the tiny stalls in the *souk*. In the West, this is impossible but whole spices will keep perfectly well for 2–3 months. Provided they are kept in the dark (spice racks on view may look attractive but the flavours are not improved) and freshly ground just before using, they will retain their impact. A coffee grinder reserved for spices is therefore a good idea, and I have also amassed over the years a collection of pepper mills, one for allspice, one for white pepper, another for black, and so on. I would miss my little gathering of 'men', some elegantly tall, some short and squat, some painted, others plain wood of varying hues, gravely conferring in the centre of the dining table. That is part of the fun of the kitchen – it's not all just hard work: one has occasionally to indulge in the odd 'necessary' extravagance . . .

Allspice (*Pimenta dioica/P. officinalis*) The only spice in the Arab kitchen not grown in the area. Native to Central America and the West Indies and commonly known either as Jamaica Pepper (most of the world's supply came – and still comes – from that island) or allspice, from its hints of cloves, cinnamon and nutmeg. Thus often used instead of the 'four spice' mixture – cinnamon, cloves, ginger and nutmeg. In Iraq frequently combined with fresh ginger and a touch of fenugreek. Resembles a large peppercorn, and a 'must' for a mill of its own.

Burghul Also called bulgar wheat, *bourgouri* or *pougouri* and often described as cracked wheat. Cracked by boiling, then dried and crushed; check that health food shop cracked wheat is cooked, otherwise buy whole wheat, wash it (pick out small gravel etc) then boil in a large pan until it begins to open. Dry in a low oven, then grind coarsely for *pilau*, finely for *tabbuleh* and *kibbeh*.

Butter More prevalent as a cooking fat in the Middle East nowadays than formerly, when a slowly melted lamb or sheep's tail was the favoured medium (*alya*). Clarified butter is now often used instead: melt slowly in a heavy-based pan, then pour through a fine sieve or muslin, leaving the white sediment behind. Will keep well 3–4 weeks in the refrigerator. If using ordinary butter, always buy unsalted – the burning point is higher.

Cardamom (*Elettaria cardamomum*) Native to South India and Sri Lanka, the world's biggest buyer being the Middle East. Very aromatic and expensive relation to ginger. Comes in a large seed pod, white to pale green or brown. Even larger pods, dark brown in colour and often covered with tiny hairs, are sold as black cardamom. Inferior in flavour and scent but much cheaper, and better – at a pinch – than ground cardamom which is often adulterated. Break open the pods and lightly crush the seeds inside. Often added to coffee.

Chervil (*Anthriscus cerefolium*) A herb native to the Middle East, similar to a feathery parsley in appearance, with a hint of parsley and aniseed in its flavour. Very popular in the Arab kitchen. Now often available fresh, in packs, from major supermarkets. But also easily grown in the West as a summer annual. Much cheaper, and fresher. Wilts quickly so cut just before using if possible. Substitute parsley, preferably flat-leaved, if you must.

Cinnamon (*Cinnamomum zeylanicum*) Native to Sri Lanka and parts of South India; highly prized since early times and the cause of many a war. One of the most important Middle Eastern flavourings, particularly with lamb. Looks like a rolled up piece of dried bark, which is exactly what it is. Buy it in whole 'quills' if possible and grind pieces in a spice grinder: the antiseptic oils – a natural food preservative – are quickly lost once the bark is ground. For sprinkling as a garnish buy the ground spice (unless you possess, and are adept with, an oriental grinding stone) – almost impossible to mechanically reproduce that fine powder. But, buy in small quantities and replenish frequently.

Coriander (*Coriandrum sativum*) Native to Southern Europe, and another highly used spice since early times, both seeds and leaves playing an important role. Seeds, slightly reminiscent of oranges (and a natural meat preservative) are dry roasted, then crushed. In Egypt, fried with garlic and salt, it forms one of the main spice mixes to garnish chick peas, spinach, meatballs. Leaves (also known as Chinese parsley – much used all over Asia) resemble flat-leaved parsley but are easily distinguished by the characteristic aroma produced on slight crushing. An important component in salads, cooking and as a garnish. Can be bought fresh from supermarkets and Indian groceries – also easily grown from the seed bought as a spice. Sow in spring – giving some protection from late frosts, and start cutting when a few inches high. Flavour almost impossible to describe but once tasted always recognised.

Cumin (*Cuminum cyminum*) Very distinctive flavour and smell, softened by dry roasting before crushing. Asian in origin but grown around Mediterranean for over two thousand years. Often confused with caraway, to which it is closely related though quite different in taste. Vital to the Middle Eastern kitchen and easily available – don't attempt substitutes.

Dill (*Anethum graveolens*) Another Asian native naturalised in the Middle East centuries ago. Used both for the feathery leaves (known as dillweed) and seeds – the latter similar in flavour to caraway but more assertive. An easily grown annual, similar in appearance to the perennial fennel but smaller and lacking the taste of anise. Home-dried dill keeps quite well, certainly better than the commercial but expose to as little light as possible. Seeds sold in Sri Lanka under this name are in fact fenugreek – dill itself being unknown, despite being grown in many parts of neighbouring India.

Fenugreek (*Trigonella foenum-graecum*) European and Asian native; very assertive in taste, can be bitter if over-roasted – don't let the seeds turn red if home-roasting. Usually bought ready ground as difficult to reduce to a fine powder in a grinder. Nonetheless, I prefer to roast for 10 minutes in a medium oven, and grind as fine as I can. And then use the merest pinch. The pre-ground never fails to remind of cheap curry powders. Much used in Iraq with fresh ginger and ground cinnamon.

Feta A cheese made from goat and/or sheep's milk. The curds are ripened in their own salted whey. Made in Greece and Turkey (a 'must' in their everyday salads), and extensively used all over the Middle East, both raw and in cooking.

Fila pastry (the Egyptian spelling – also *filo*, *fillo*, and *phyllo*) Paper-thin sheets of pastry, made from a flour and water dough, stretched until almost translucent. It can be bought ready-made in Greek bakers and better supermarkets. Used for small pastries and large pies throughout the area.

Hallumi, Hellim *Hallumi* to the Greeks, *Hellim* to the Turks, in fact a Cypriot sheep/goat's cheese. Hard, salt, and long-keeping – betraying its Bedouin origins. Used in the Lebanon to make grilled kebabs (hence known as kebab cheese) but much more expensive than Feta.

Kasseri A Greek sheep's cheese, the curds being cut and stirred then heated and pressed into shape. Rubbery when young, harder and more salt on maturing. Mild, keeps well.

Kephalotyri Greek, made in the same way as *Kasseri* though goat's milk also used. Hard, akin to Parmesan, and good for grating. Named after the Greek hats – 'kephalo' – and hence often pressed into a skull shape, giving its other name of 'head cheese'.

Lemons (*Citrus limon*) The Middle Eastern variety tend to be small, green-yellow in colour, often wrinkled and very juicy. Almost always used in place of vinegar in salad dressings, which are much sharper than the French equivalent – though the heaviness and sole use of olive oil offsets this. Also dried, pickled and preserved in brine, and often then added to stews and sauces.

Limes (*Citrus aurantifolia*) Particularly used in Persia, often replacing lemons. Also form a special spice when dried, known as *numi Basra*, either ground to a powder or added whole to stews. Can be bought from Pakistani groceries. Smaller than those normally seen in the West and, confusingly, usually yellow when ripe.

Marjoram (*Origanum majorana*) Sweeter than its wild cousin, oregano, hence its popular name – sweet marjoram – though also sometimes known as knotted marjoram. Loses its flavour if overcooked, so add just a few minutes before serving. An easily grown perennial, though often classed in England as a half-hardy annual. But I rarely was without, except in the bleakest of East Anglian winters. Then pot marjoram – always lurking in the background – took over. Hotter, and not so sweet, but hardier. Marjoram is not a herb to be without – in the Arab, or any other kitchen.

Merguez Hot, spicy sausage found all over Africa, particularly popular in Tunisia and Algeria. Made from goat or mutton, and highly flavoured with the spice mix *Harissa*.

Mint (*Mentha spicata*) The common or garden spearmint is the one most usually used in the Middle East: dries wonderfully, keeping its flavour and aroma. Very dominant in the Arab kitchen, huge quantities gathered, then dried in the sun before going into the cooking pot or salads. Also used fresh for salads, tea and added to yogurt. Deliciously easy to grow but inclined to be thuggish when happy – in a damp, shady spot. In fact, has a better flavour when in full sun, so water hard if need be. Bring a few roots indoors in a shallow seed tray in the autumn for a fresh winter supply, albeit much reduced.

Oils Olive oil is the preferred cooking medium throughout the region, although the ancient cookery books talk of sesame oil, still used by the Copts today. Obtained from the seeds by cold pressing, fine quality sesame oil is almost odourless and tasteless. Rarely found outside the area; the Chinese sesame oil, and the gingelly oil of Southern Indian cooking, are far stronger and somewhat overpowering for the Western palate if used alone. If the flavour of sesame is desired, add a few drops only, towards the end of cooking. Olive oils now come in a huge variety of purity, and prices, and it is worth experimenting to find the one(s) you especially favour. For a lighter flavour, oils may be mixed – either two olives, or even half olive and half sunflower or corn oil. For dishes to be served cold, oil of whatever sort is a must since butter will unpleasantly congeal. Buy olive oil in cans, or store in a dark, cool place – light is not conducive to its keeping qualities.

Okra *Bamia* to the Arabs, *bamies* to the Greeks, ladies' fingers in England, these small pointed triangular pods should always be bought very fresh, pale and softly green. Never cut the tops off the pods as this will release the glutinous juices – except for stews when used as a thickening agent for the sauce. A delicious vegetable and now more widely available.

Orange-flower water Distilled from the newly opened flowers and sprinkled not only on sweet pastries but often on coffee, and lamb dishes. Available from good delicatessens and chemists.

Oregano (*Origanum vulgare*) I have found there is a certain amount of confusion as regards oregano, rigani and marjoram. In fact all are close relations, this being the powerfully flavoured wild marjoram so prolific in Greece. Rarely available fresh in England, though it will grow perfectly respectably given a chalky soil and sunshine. The flavour however will seldom be as pungent as in Southern Mediterranean plants, constant dry heat being its greatest requisite. Dries extremely well though, keeping its aroma – though not for ever. As with all dried herbs and spices, buy small quantities – often.

Parsley (*Petroselinum crispum*) Probably the most common herb of the area (and indeed half the world –

coming a close second to fresh coriander in the South Asian and American kitchens). The flat-leaved variety is the Middle Eastern norm, easier of cultivation and, say the Arabs, stronger in flavour though personally, I find the curly leaved plant more peppery. Both kinds freeze well – dip the heads in boiling water for a second then cut off the stalks (keep for soups, etc) and freeze the leaves flat before packing loosely in a box.

Pine nuts Small, slim white seeds from the Mediterranean Stone Pine (*Pinus pinea* – other varieties are used in other parts of the world; most pine kernels being edible albeit some are too small, or too reeking of turpentine, to be worthwhile). Much favoured in the Middle East since ancient times, particularly by the Syrians and Lebanese. Used for sauces, stuffings, with meat, rice and garnishes. Sweetly nutty, they keep well in an airtight jar in a cool, dry place, even the refrigerator if you have to (I do) but alas, are never cheap. No substitute, utterly indispensable, and worth every penny spent.

Pistachio (*Pistacia vera*) Turkey's favourite nut but much loved and grown elsewhere. Pale green, once shelled and skinned, used not only in meat and fish dishes, but also to make a delicate ice cream. Again expensive but nothing can really replace them.

Pomegranate (*Punica granatum*) Known, grown and much appreciated in the Middle East for thousands of years. King Solomon sang of them, the wandering Jews recalled them with longing, the Romans imported them from Carthage. Exact origin uncertain, but probably Western Asia – certainly Afghanistan grows some of the finest today. Flavours range from the inedibly acidic to the cloyingly sweet – the best being a perfect amalgam of both. The colour – transparent to a magnificent deep purple/red – is, unhelpfully, no clue as to fineness, or not, of taste. However avoid hard, wizened-looking fruits – they will be as dry as they look. Still extensively used in the Arab kitchen, especially by the Persians, for cooking, drinks, and to be eaten raw. The seeds, dried, are a favourite garnish.

Pulses The dried edible seeds of legumes, peas, beans and lentils. Widely used throughout the Middle East, for stews and purées; also roasted and eaten like nuts. Traditionally all had to be soaked overnight but many varieties bought nowadays need much less soaking, if at all, though chick peas, small hard and round, and dried haricot beans usually still do. Most will keep well in an airtight container but haricot beans must be used within a year – after that, no amount of cooking will render them anything other than bullet-like. Red kidney beans must always be boiled hard for at least 10 minutes to eliminate the toxins. Apart from chick peas, which may be cooked *ad infinitum* without spoiling, check all other varieties after say 30–40 minutes of cooking, unless you are going to purée them. For once soft, they will disintegrate quickly.

Rigani (*Origanum dictamnus, vulgare*, and others) A mix of dried leaves and flower buds, usually of the very potent *O. dictamnus* or the wild marjoram though in Greece other types often used as well. Inclusion of the flowers is the constant, giving the pungent aroma and flavour so typical of Greek kebabs. Sometimes available from Greek delicatessens otherwise substitute oregano.

Rose-water Essence of roses: very ancient, sweet and heavily scented. Used on salads and meat dishes, as well as sherbets. Buy it from chemists, making sure it's pure – the perfume often has added chemicals.

Saffron (*Crocus sativus*) The orange stigma of the mauve autumn-flowering crocus. Has always been rare and expensive. Not surprising, since it takes 70,000 hand-picked blooms, the 3 stigmas per flower also to be carefully removed by hand, then dried, to produce only one pound (450 g) saffron. Native to Asia and parts of Southern Europe, the best comes today from Spain, Mexico and Kashmir though England was an important producer: Saffron Walden changed its name mid-fourteenth century in honour of the spice grown on its surrounding hills. Used in the Middle East to colour rice, chicken and fish dishes. Always buy it in strands – powders will almost certainly be adulterated. Thankfully, a couple of strands go a long way – don't be tempted to overdo it: too much will give a bitter flavour, too deep a colour. Lightly primrose yellow in tint, and a sweet honey scent is the effect wanted. Turmeric is often used to imitate the colouring (in Sri Lanka, sold under the name of saffron): coarser in hue and taste.

Sesame seeds (*Sesamum indicum*) Grown widely in the Orient since early times though probably born in Africa. A strong-growing, frost-hating annual, valued for its seeds which are small, flat and oval. White when raw, roasting produces the nutty flavour and aroma so popular in the Middle Eastern kitchen. Crushed they produce the paste known as *tahina*, vital to many Arab dishes. See also Oils.

Sumac (*Rhus coriaria*) An edible member of the large Rhus family, with hairy fruits, deep red to purple in colour when ripe. Uncooked and crushed, the powder is sprinkled on salads and meats to give a lightly sour, lemony flavour. Lemon is the nearest substitute – indeed the Romans used *sumac* before that fruit made its appearance on the scene. Much favoured in Lebanon, where the berries are gathered in the mountains, dried, then crushed and soaked in warm water for about 20 minutes. The resultant liquid is used, the berries discarded. The drink is refreshing and the local remedy for those suffering from 'Beirut belly'. Although it can be home grown, better to leave to the experts: many members of the tribe are poisonous – and any smooth berried variety will almost certainly be so.

Tahina A thin paste made from crushed sesame seeds which forms the basis for many cream salads and sauces, besides giving its distinctive flavour to *humus* (page 24), the purée of chick peas popular every-where. Can be bought in jars from ethnic grocery stores or health shops, and keeps well. Before using always stir in the thin liquid which rises to the top.

Turmeric (*Curcuma longa*) Sometimes called 'poor man's saffron' since the merest pinch will colour a dish bright yellow. A relative of ginger, and like that spice, a root, although always bought ground. A nice, lightly bitter flavour with a hint of hotness, but don't fall into it. Always sold as 'saffron' in Sri Lanka.

Vine leaves (*Vitus vinifera*) Leaves from the grape vine used particularly in Turkey and Greece, stuffed with meat, rice, onion and nut fillings. Also much used wrapped around fish to give a distinctively smoky flavour. Can be bought in packets in brine and will keep well unopened. Fresh leaves freeze well after 2 minutes' blanching.

Yeast Easy Blend yeast has wonderfully simplified baking. Mix into the dry ingredients and then add the liquid. If unobtainable, use 13 g (½ oz) of fresh yeast or 7 g (¼ oz) of dried to 450 g (1 lb) of flour. Unlike Easy Blend yeast, you need to prove dried and fresh yeast before adding to the flour.

Yogurt One of the staples of the Middle Eastern kitchen, made almost every day in almost every home. Used for salads, stews, drinks, dressings, cheeses. Greek yogurt is usually pasteurised and much thicker – good for cooking but not for making your own.

INDEX